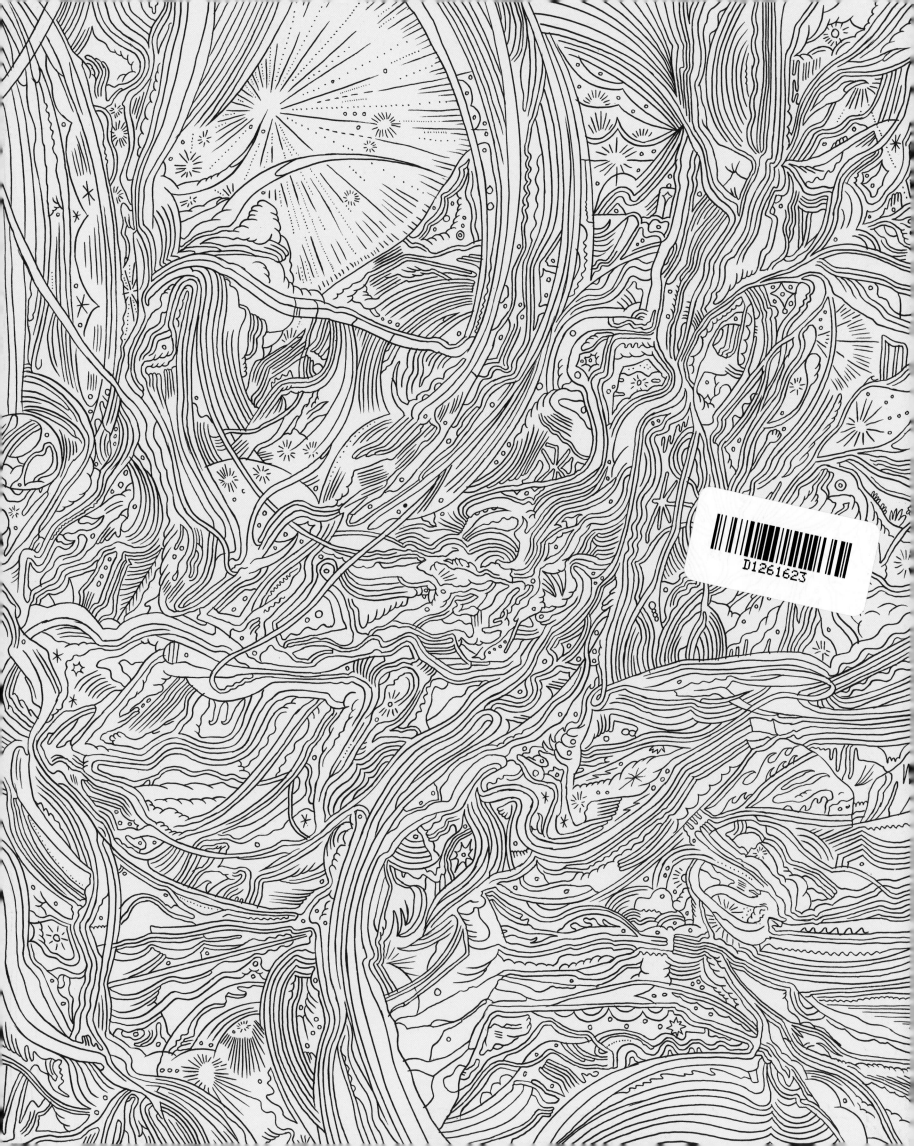

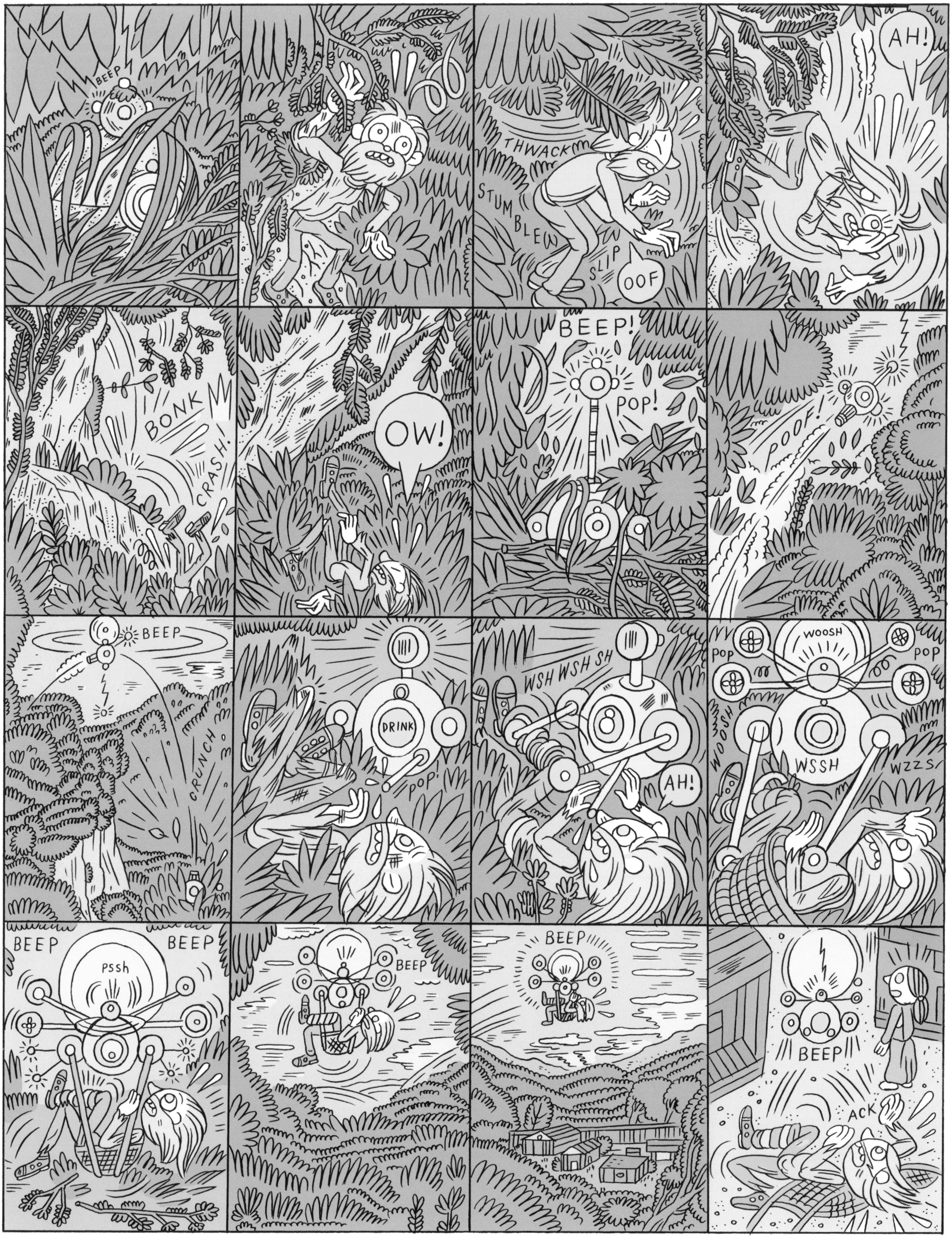
BEEP
THWACK
STUMBLE
SLIP
OOF
AH!
BONK
CRASH
OW!
BEEP!
POP!
POOF!
BEEP
CRUNCH
DRINK
POP!
WSH WSH SH
AH!
WOOSH
POP
POP
WOOSH
WSSH
WZZS
BEEP
BEEP
PSSH
BEEP
BEEP
BEEP
ACK

IN THE ALLEGORY OF THE FOUR HORSEMEN ~ ACCORDING TO THE MYSTERIES OF PHILOSOPHY ~ IS SET FORTH THE CONDITIONS OF HUMANS DURING THE STAGES OF THEIR EXISTENCE. IN THE FIRST & SPIRITUAL STATE, THEY ARE CROWNED. AS THEY DESCEND INTO THE REALM OF EXPERIENCE, THEY CARRY THE SWORD. REACHING PHYSICAL EXPRESSION – WHICH IS THEIR LEAST SPIRITUAL STATE – THEY CARRY THE SCALES, AND BY THE "PHILISOPHIC DEATH" ARE RELEASED AGAIN INTO THE HIGHER SPHERES. THE HORSEMEN OF THE APOCALYPSE MAY BE INTERPERED TO REPRESENT THE SOLAR ENERGY RIDING UPON THE FOUR ELEMENTS, WHICH SERVE AS THE MEDIA FOR ITS EXPRESSION.

~ MANLY P. HALL ~ FROM THE SECRET TEACHINGS OF ALL AGES ~ p. CLXXXVIII

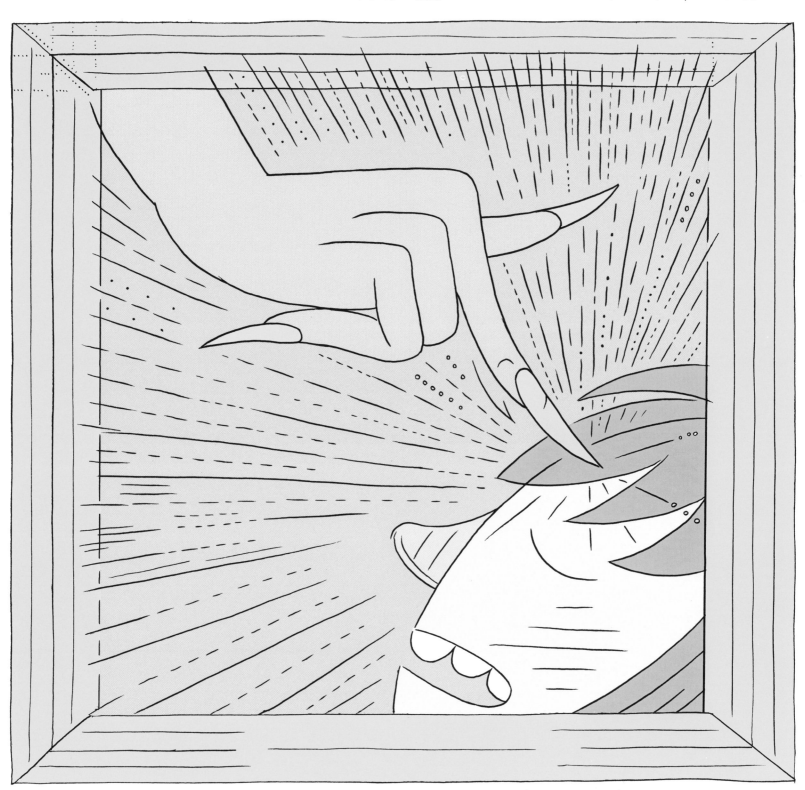

FANTAGRAPHICS BOOKS INC.

7653 LAKE CITY WAY SEATTLE, WA 98115 USA FANTAGRAPHICS.COM

EDITOR AND ASSOCIATE PUBLISHER: ERIC REYNOLDS DESIGNED BY: RON REGÉ, JR. PUBLISHED BY GARY GROTH

FIRST PRINTING: FEBRUARY 2022   PRINTED IN CHINA   ISBN: 978-1-68396-511-4   LOC#: 2021944269

HALCYON HERMENEUTICS

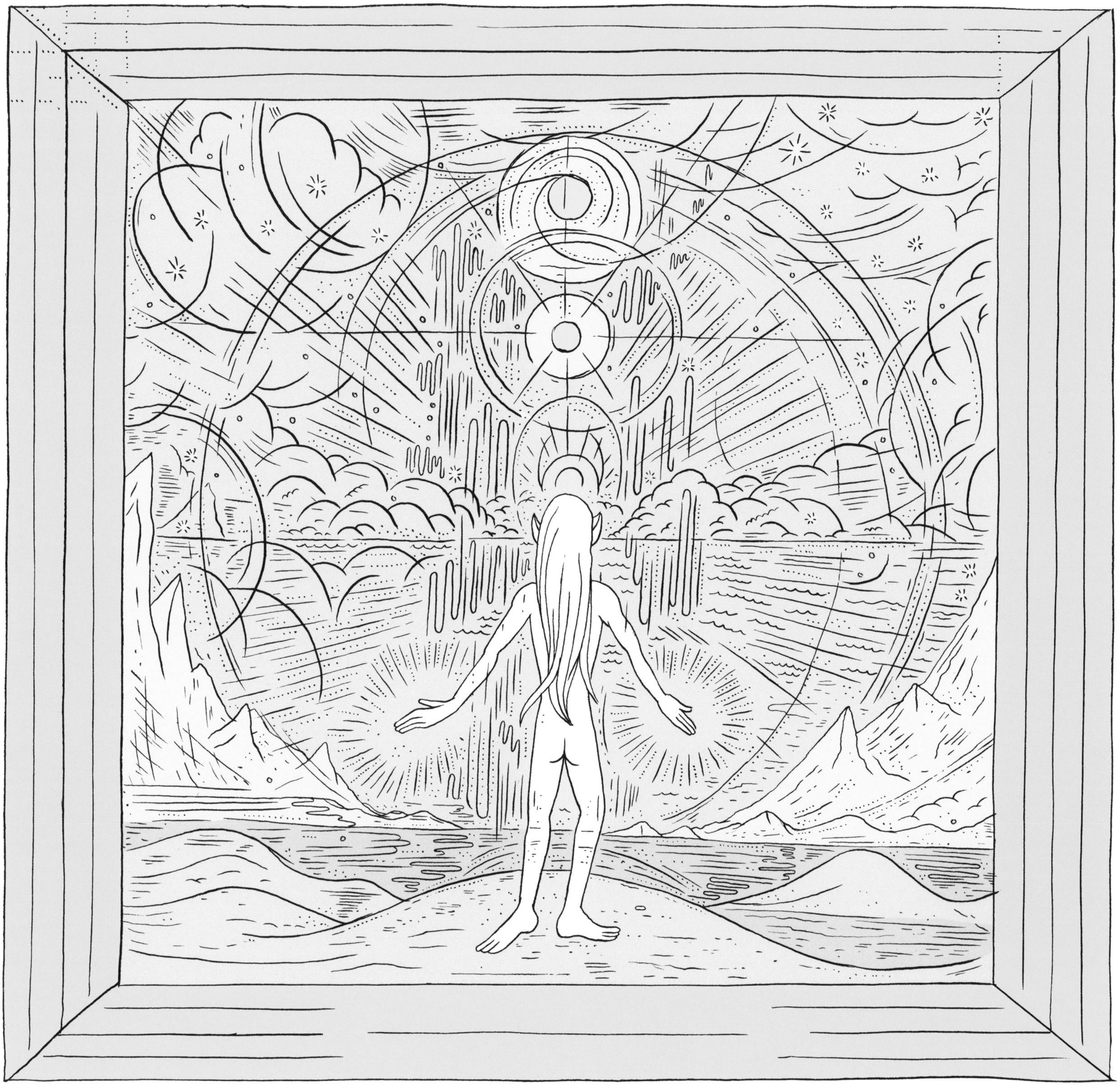

OR "THE NEW CARTOON UTOPIA"

CHANNELED & TRANSCRIBED

~ BY RON REGÉ, JR. ~

AT THE INTERSECTION OF SCOTT AND ECHO PARK AVENUES, LOS ANGELES

~ 02019 & 02020 ~

"PREVIOUSLY"

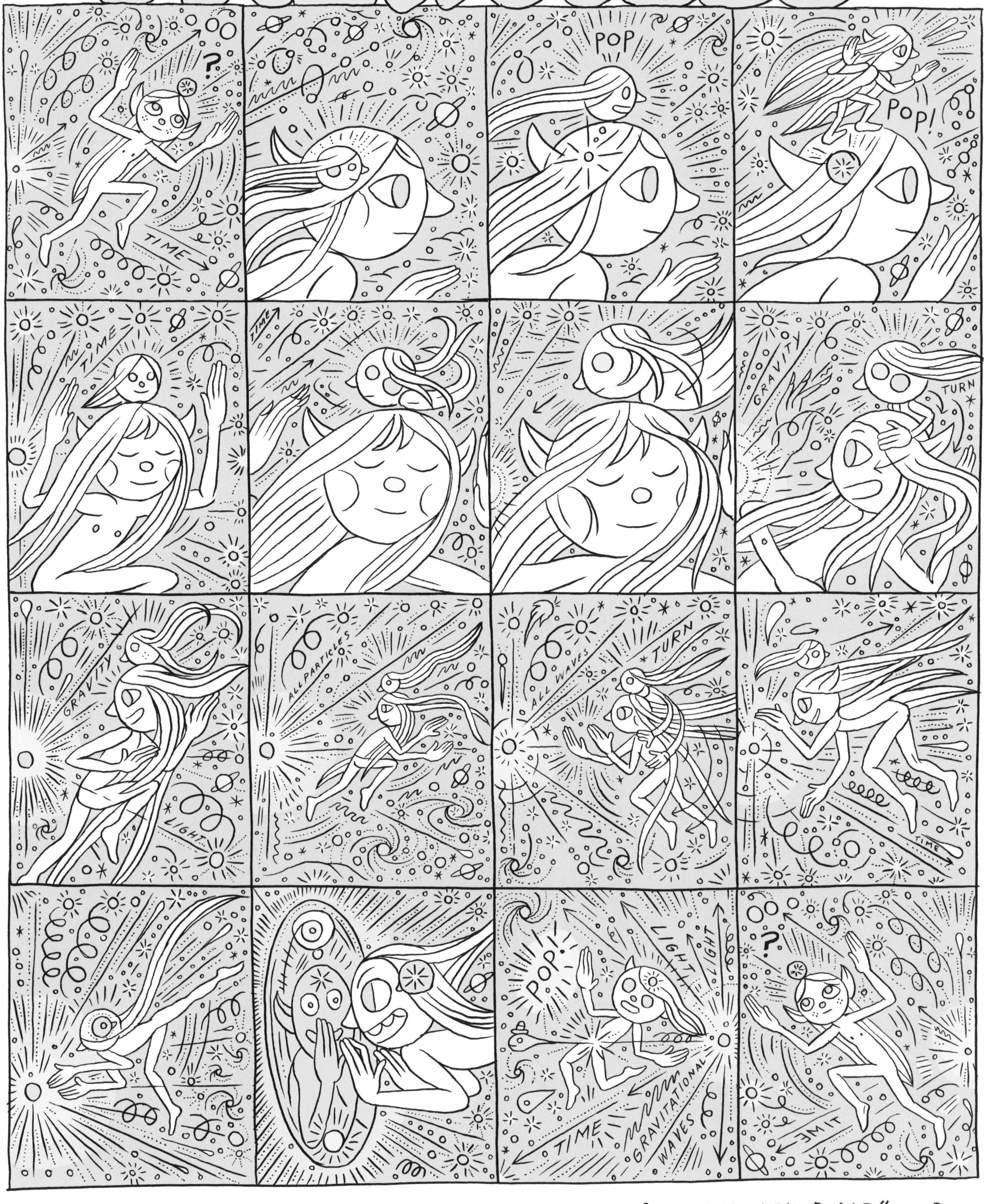
?
TIME
POP
POP!
TIME
TIME
GRAVITY
TURN
GRAVITY
LIGHT
ALL PARTICLES
ALL WAVES
TURN
TIME
POP!
LIGHT
LIGHT
TIME
GRAVITATIONAL
WAVES
?
TIME

← REPEAT INFINITELY ~ " — YOU WERE NEVER BORN & YOU WILL NEVER DIE " — →

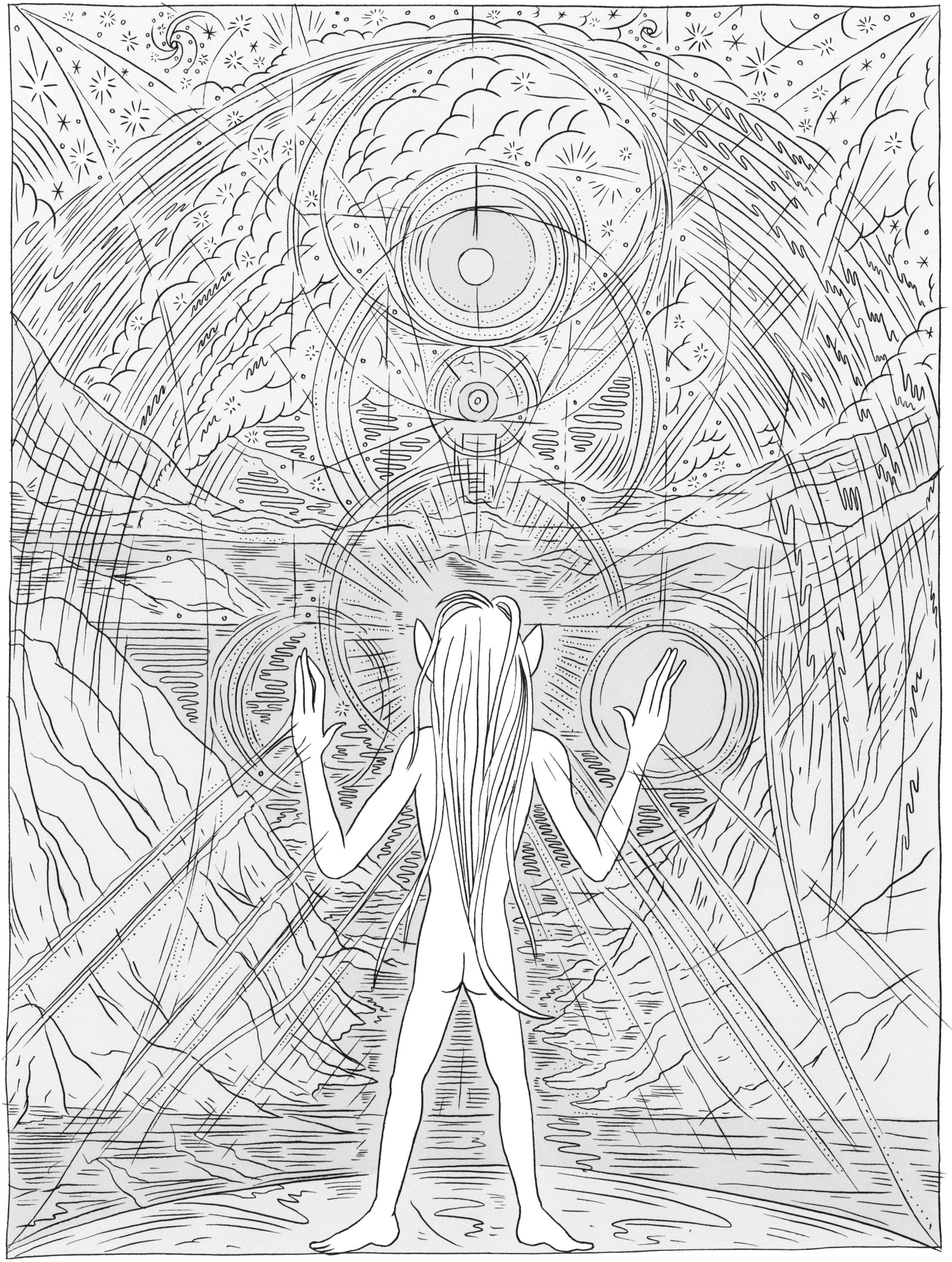

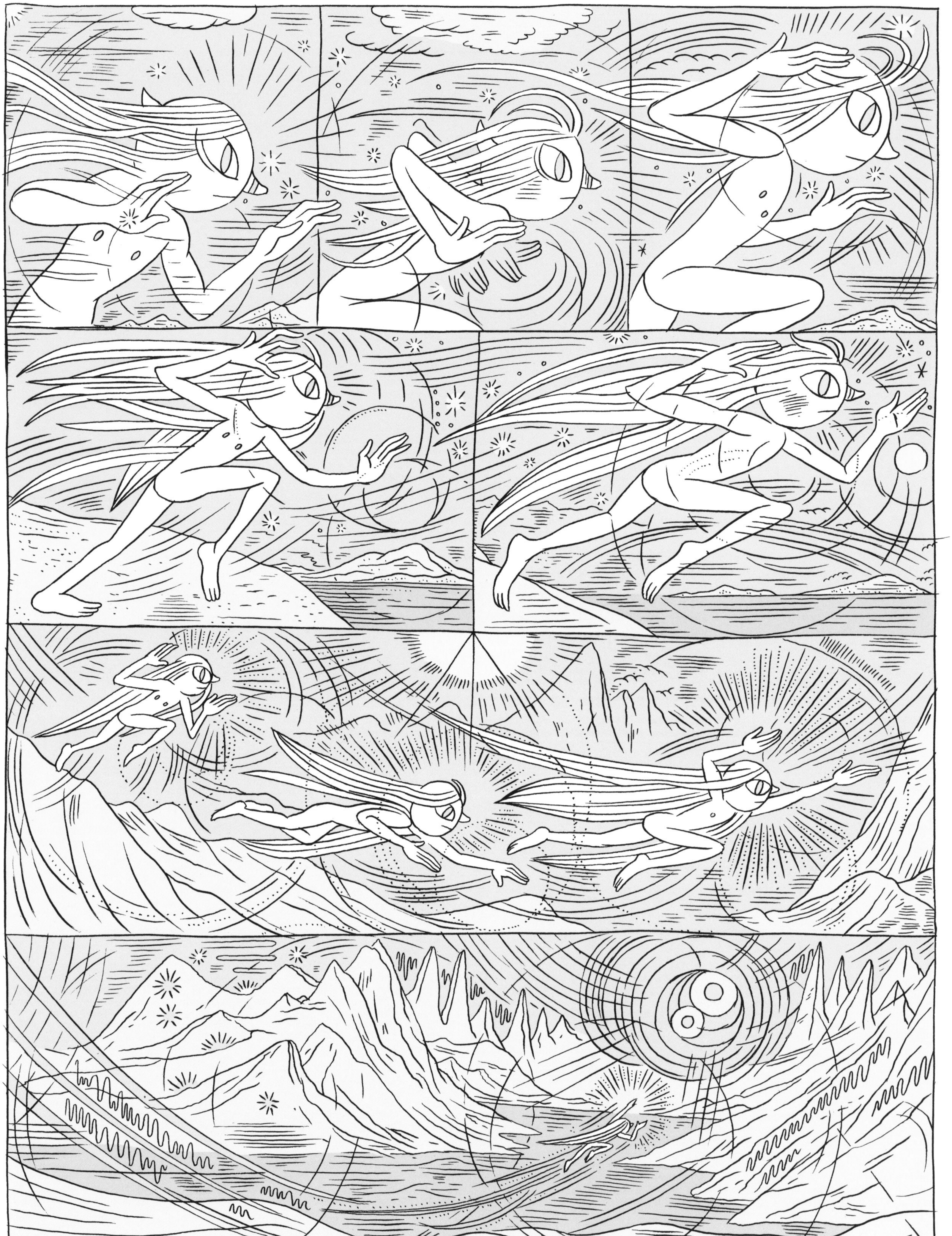

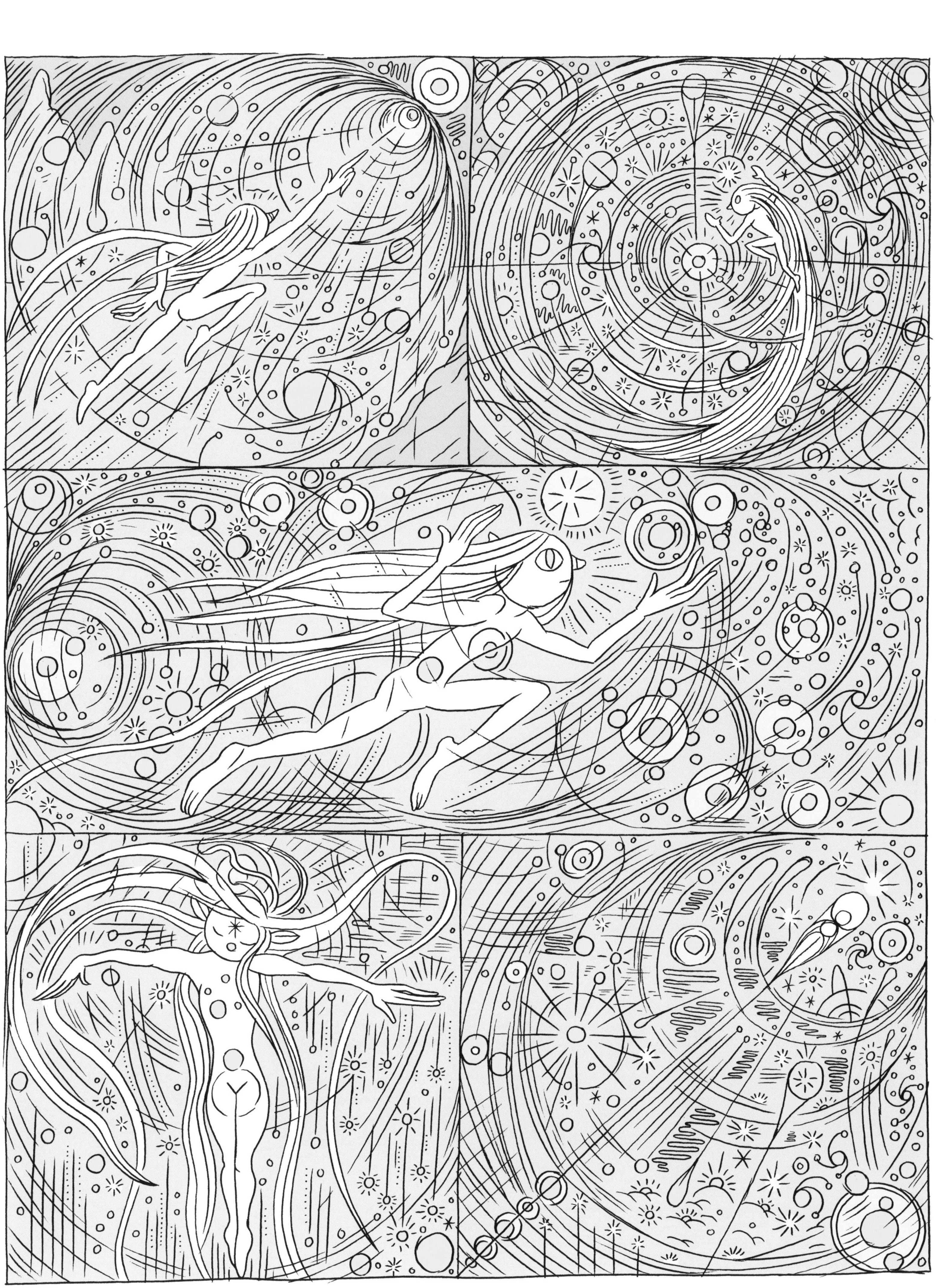

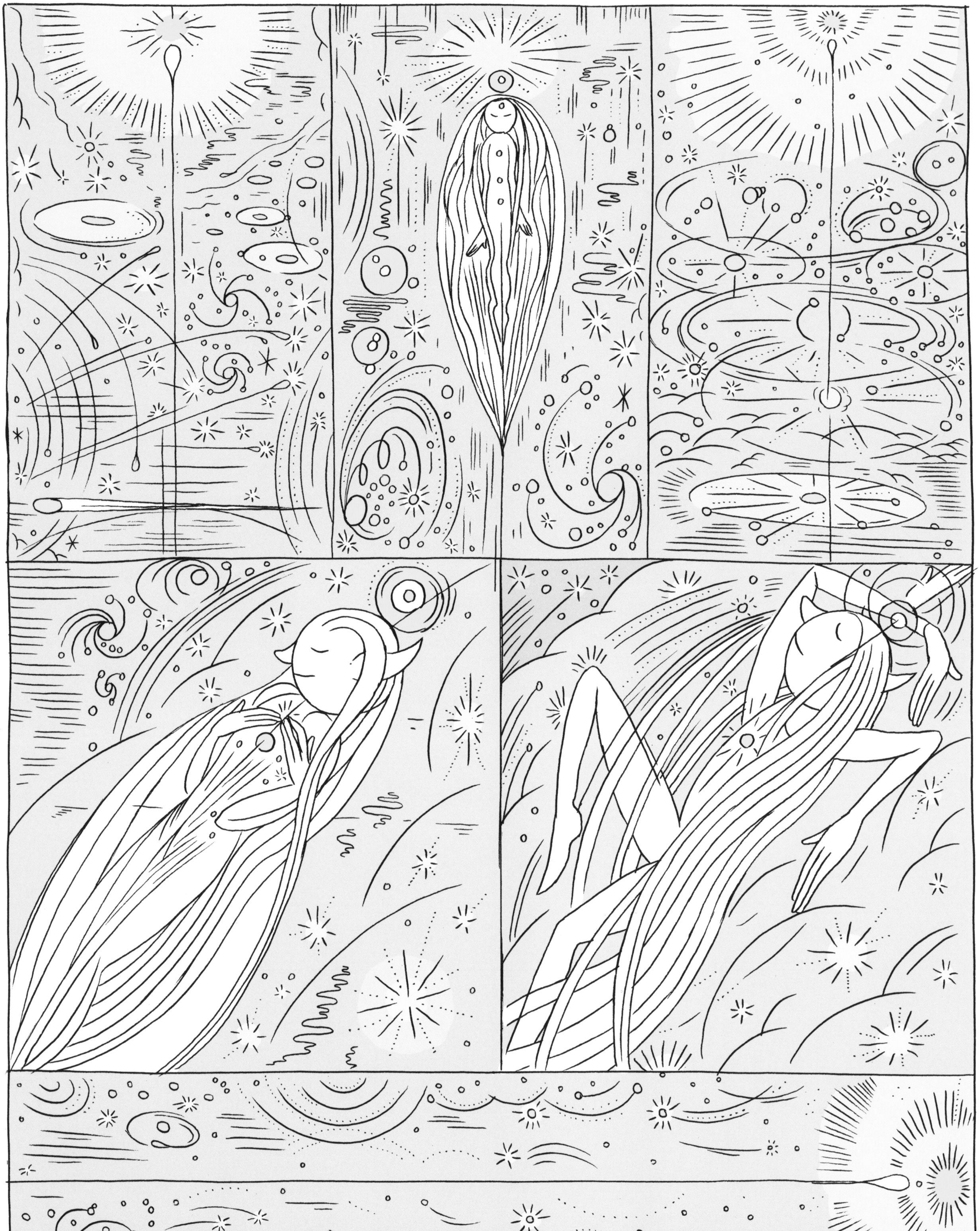

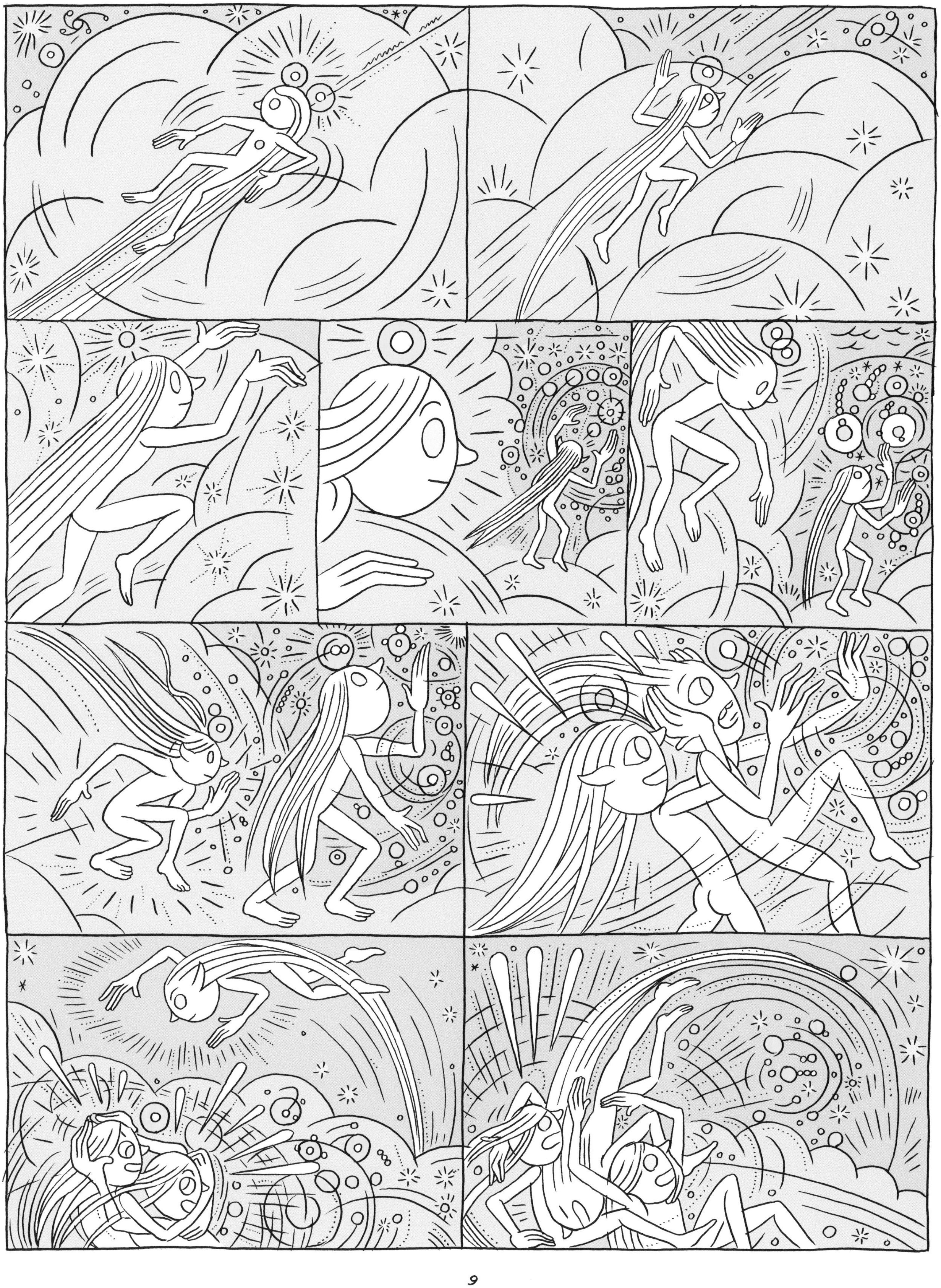

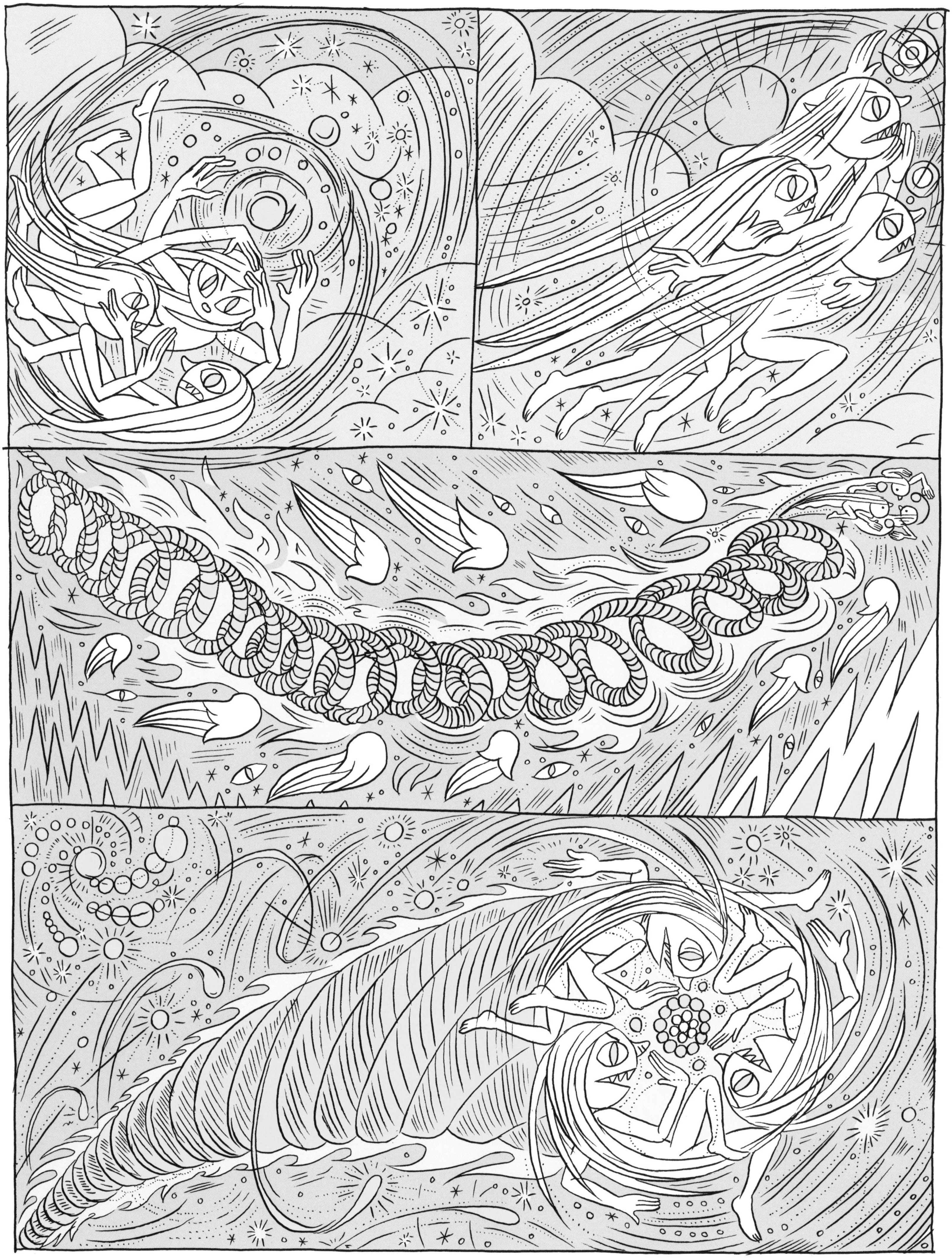

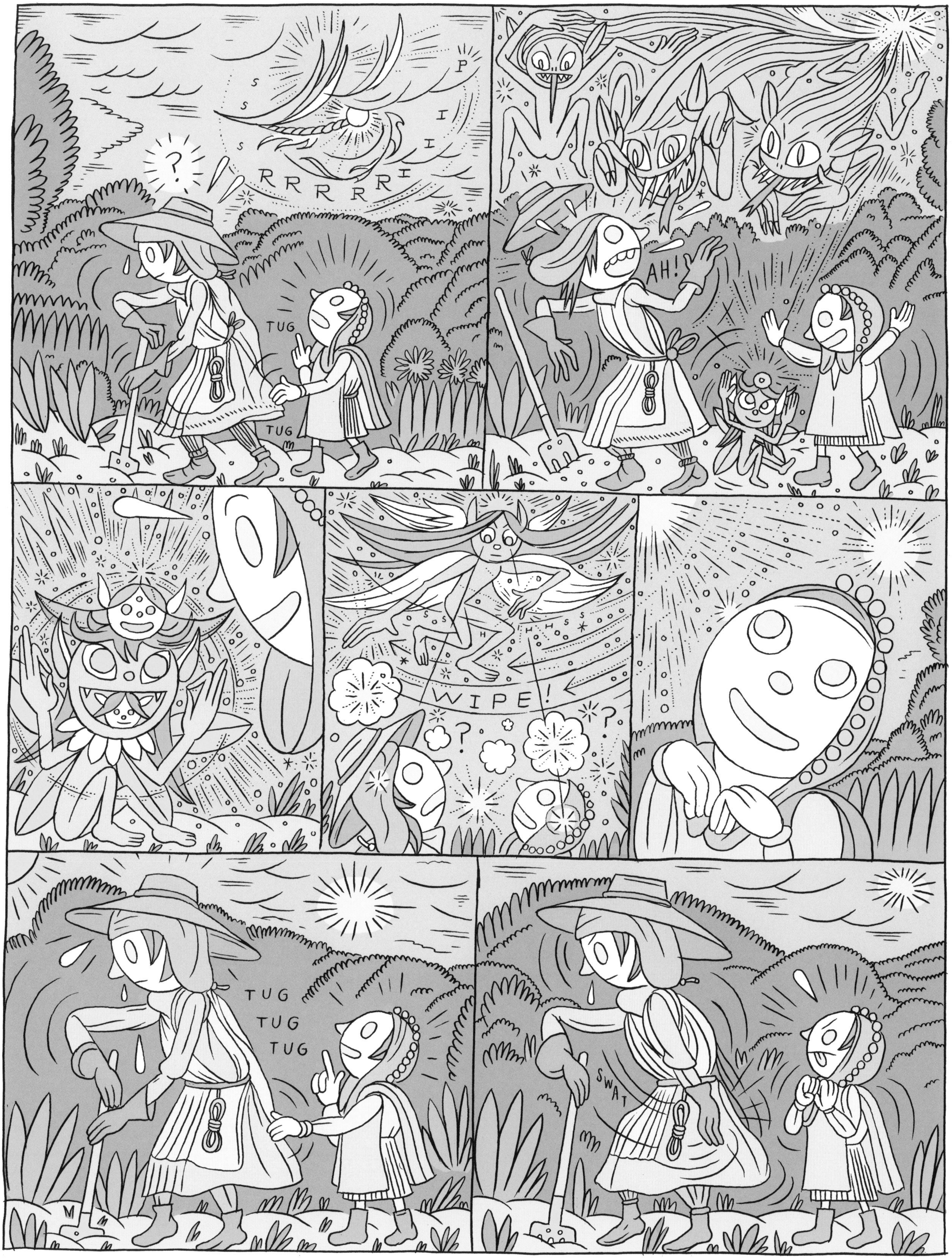
?
S S I
RRRRRRI P
TUG
TUG
AH!
SSS H HHSS
WIPE!
?
?
TUG
TUG
TUG
SWAT

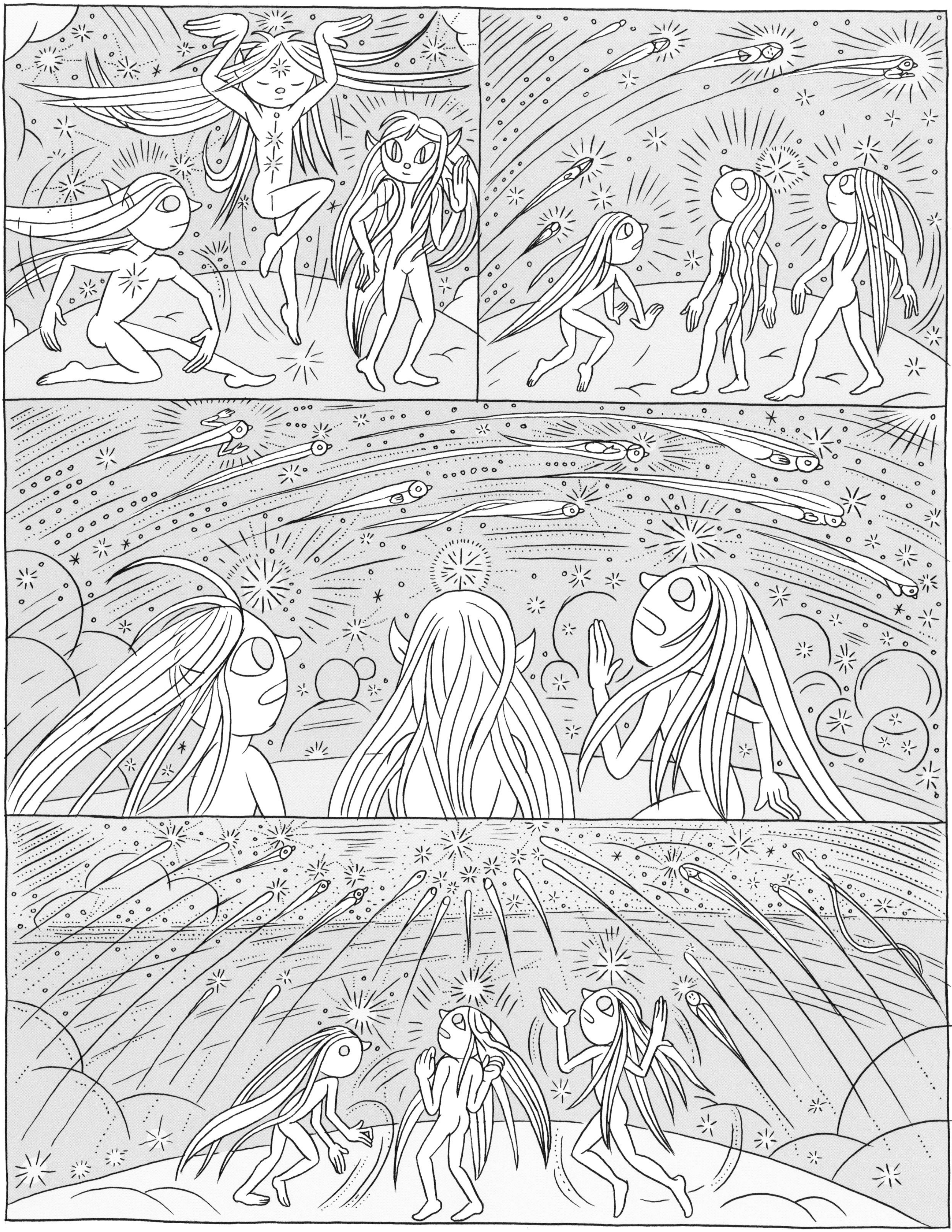

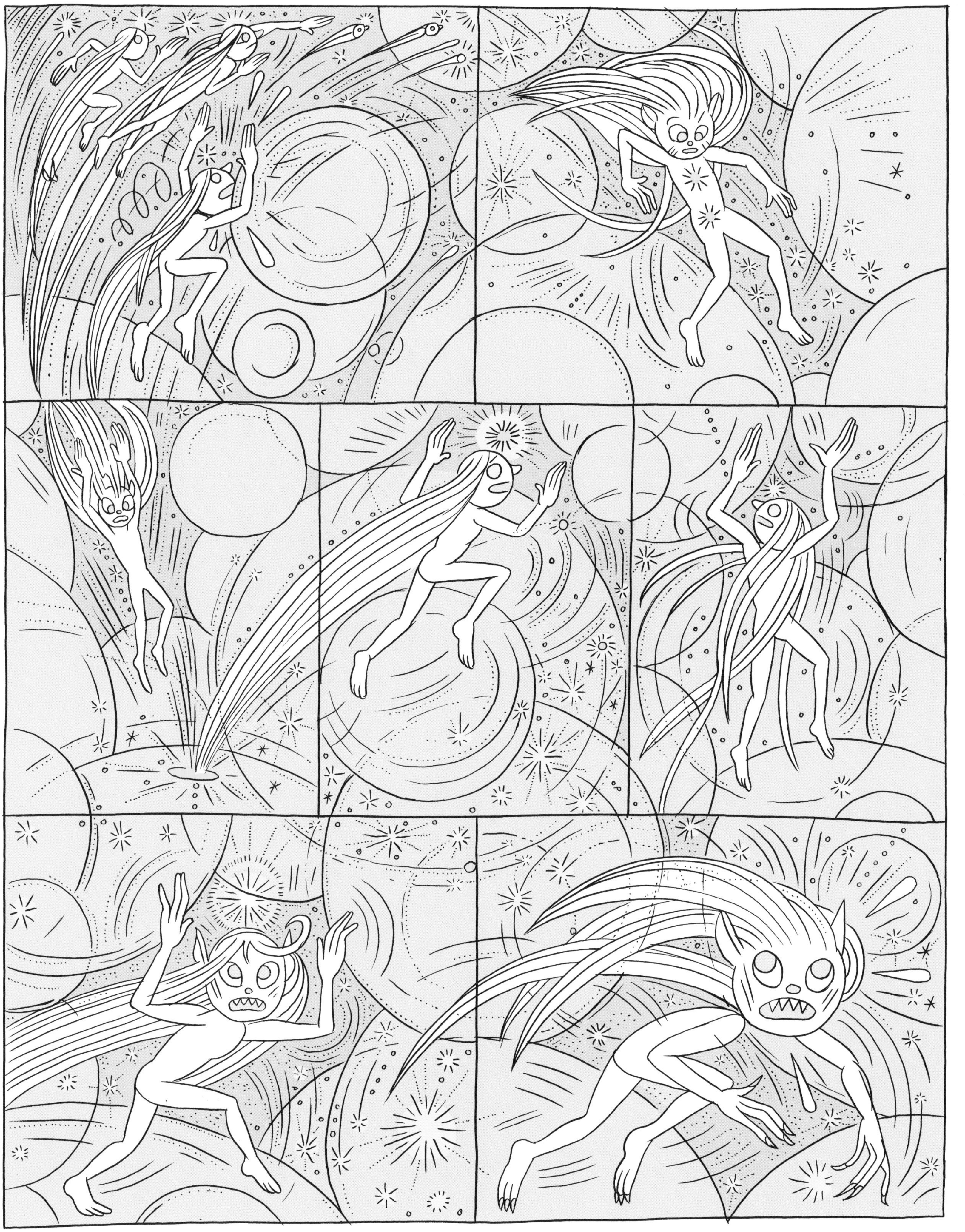

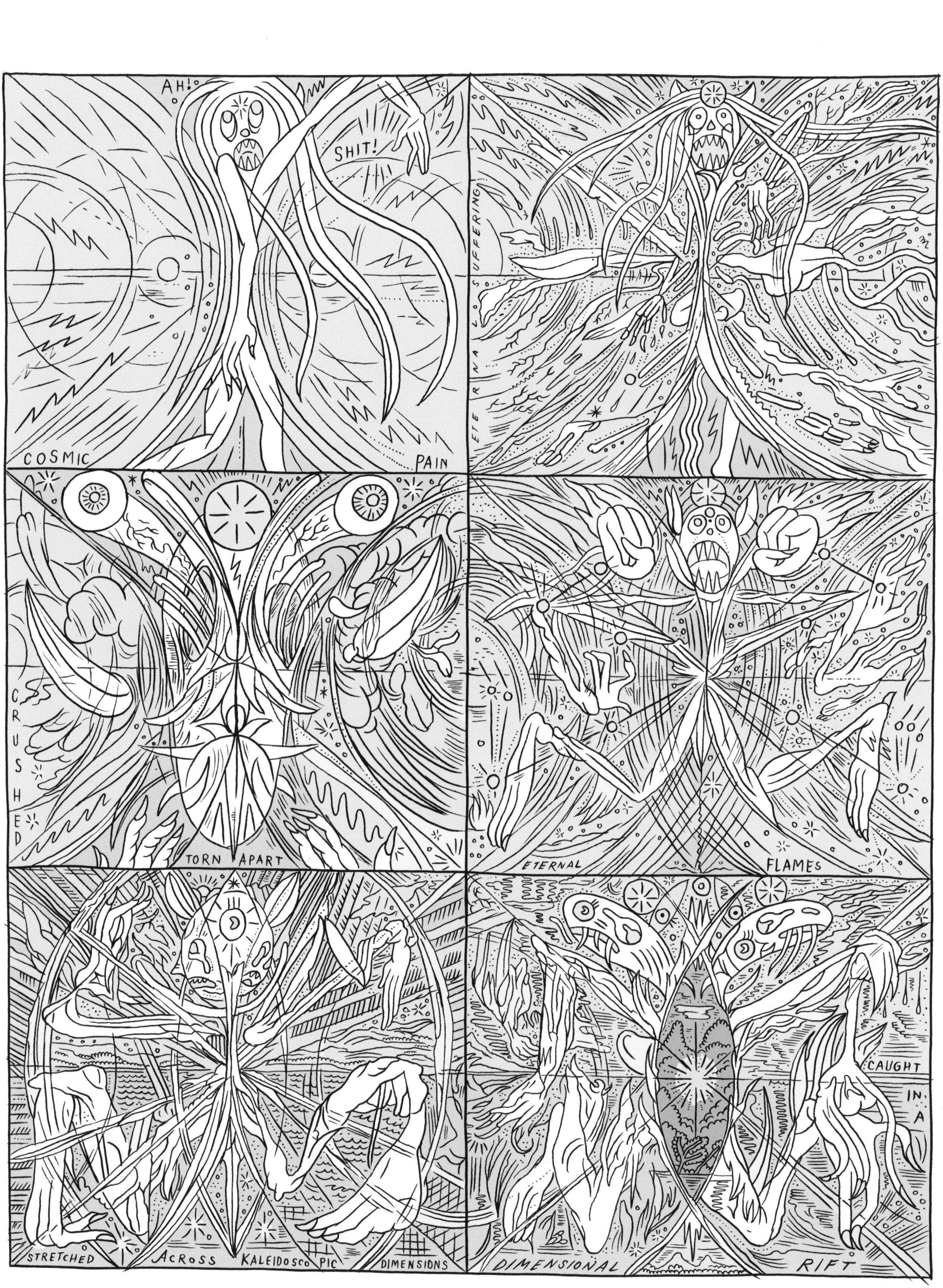
AH!
SHIT!
COSMIC
PAIN
ETERNAL SUFFERING
CRUSHED
TORN APART
ETERNAL
FLAMES
STRETCHED
ACROSS
KALEIDOSCOPIC
DIMENSIONS
CAUGHT
IN A
DIMENSIONAL
RIFT

THE DREAM * BEGINS HERE

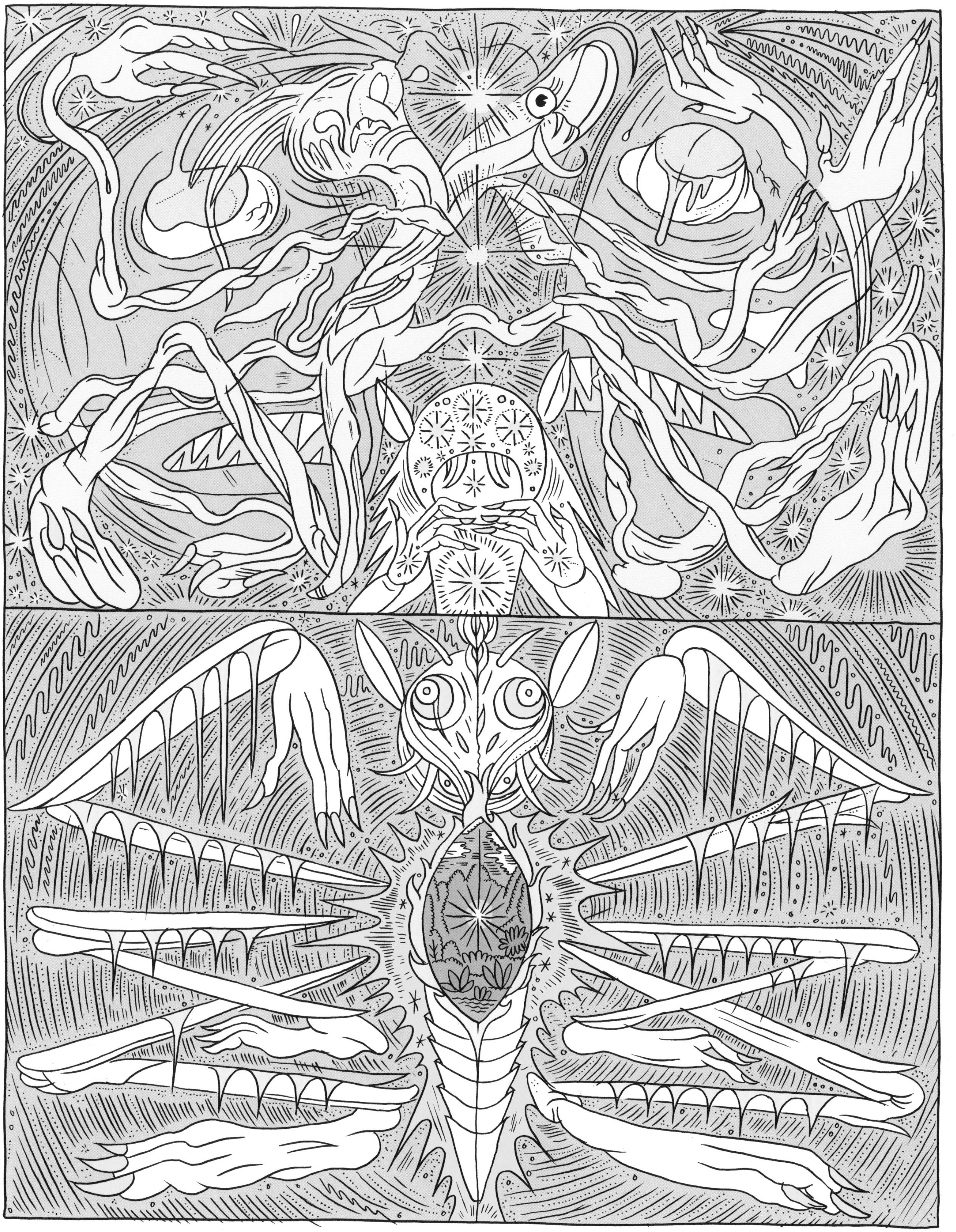

LATE ONE EVENING, AFTER A MEAL OF FORAGED VEGETABLES AND MOLDY BREAD.

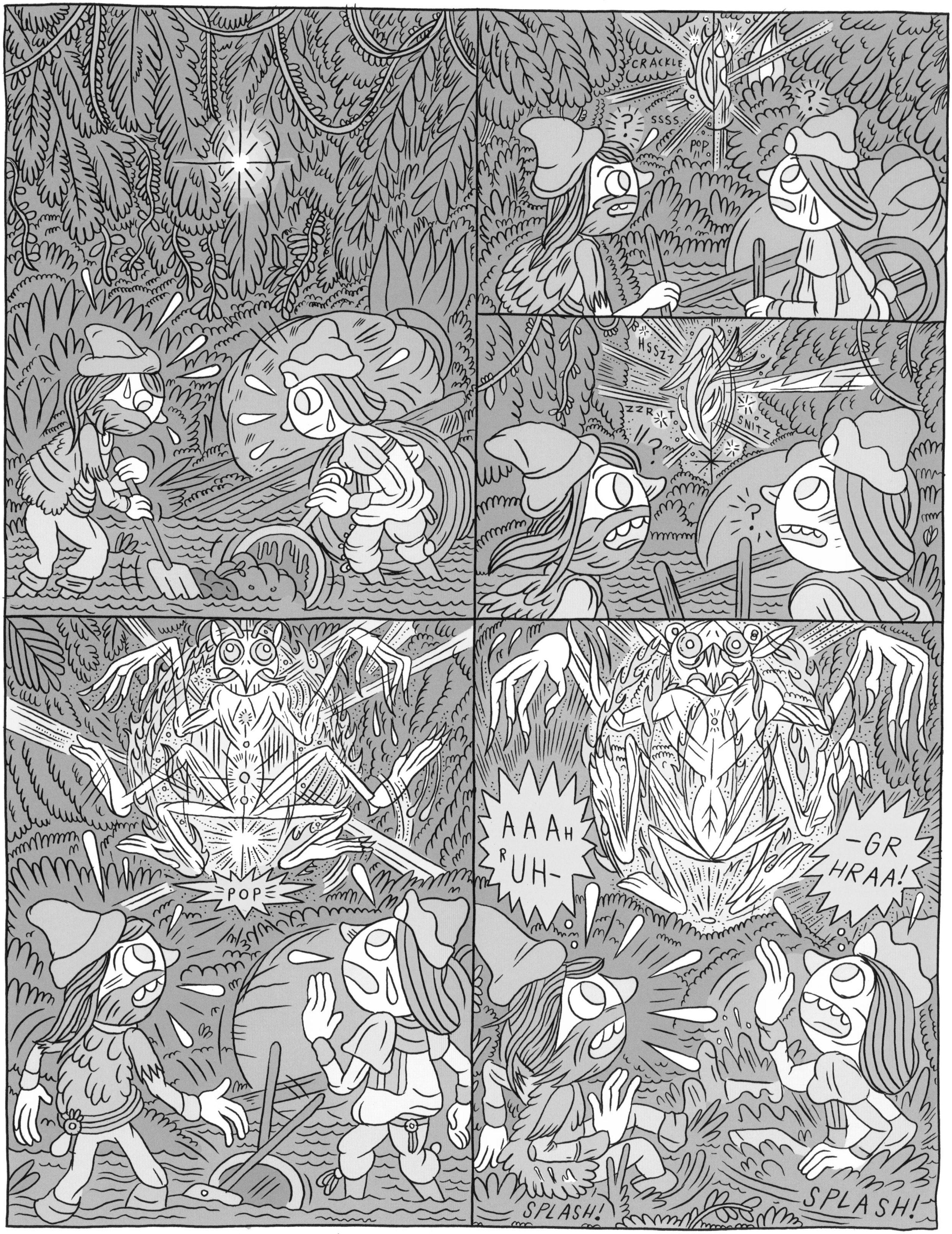

CRACKLE
?
SSSS
POP
?
HSSZZ
ZZR T
SNITZ
?
?
POP
AAAH RUH-
-GR HRAA!
SPLASH!
SPLASH!

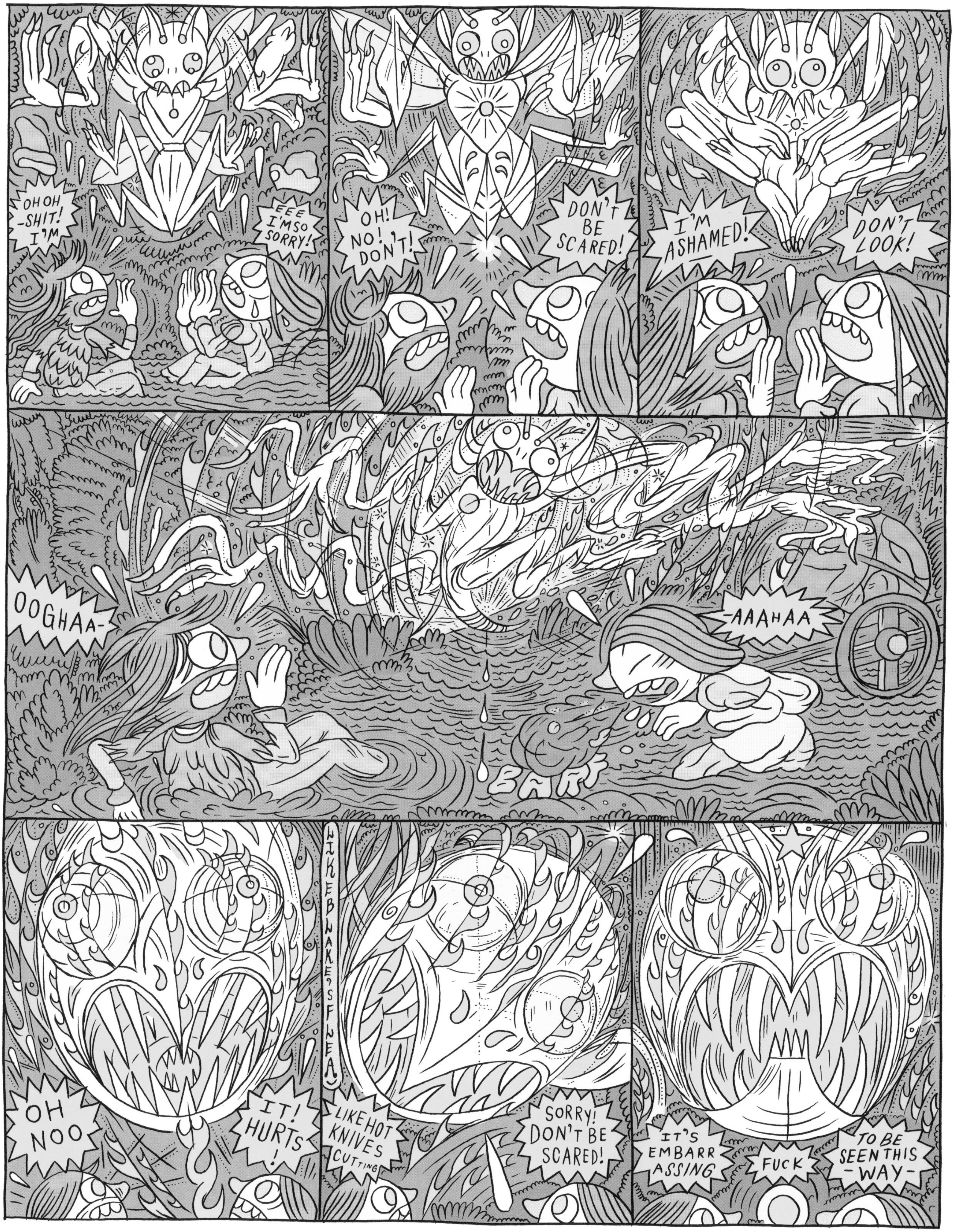
OH OH -SHIT! I'M
EEE I'M SO SORRY!
OH! NO! DON'T!
DON'T BE SCARED!
I'M ASHAMED!
DON'T LOOK!
OOGHAA-
-AAAHAA
BARF
OH NOO
IT! HURTS!
LIKE HOT KNIVES CUTTING
SORRY! DON'T BE SCARED!
IT'S EMBARR ASSING
FUCK
TO BE SEEN THIS -WAY-

WE NEVER SPOKE OF IT AGAIN ~ WE NEVER TOLD ANYONE WHAT WE SAW THAT NIGHT.

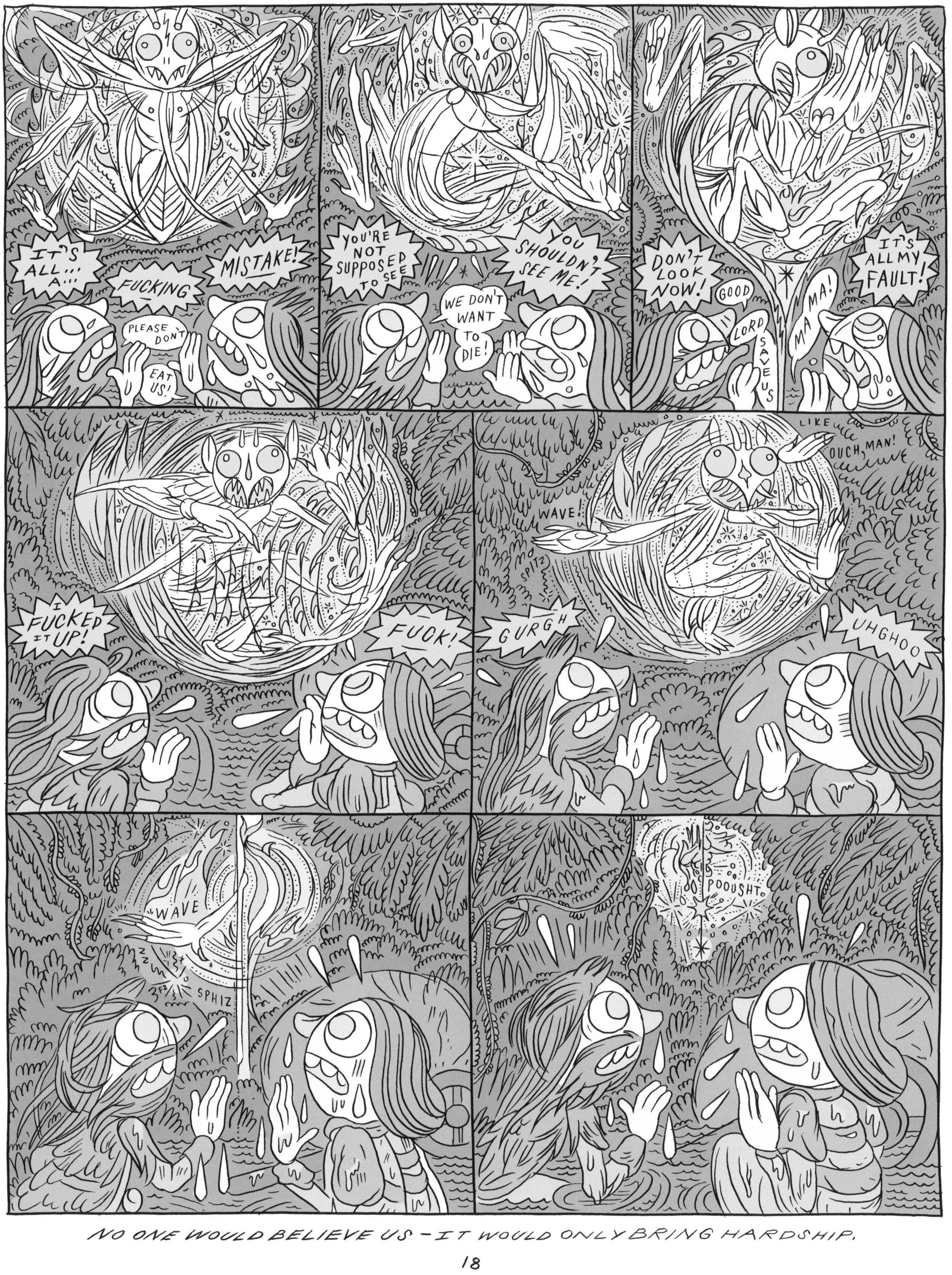
IT'S ALL... A...
FUCKING
MISTAKE!
PLEASE DON'T
EAT US!
YOU'RE NOT SUPPOSED TO SEE
YOU SHOULDN'T SEE ME!
WE DON'T WANT TO DIE!
DON'T LOOK NOW!
IT'S ALL MY FAULT!
GOOD LORD SAVE US
MA MA!
I FUCKED IT UP!
FUCK!
LIKE OUCH, MAN!
WAVE!
SPITZ
GURGH
UHGHOO
WAVE
SPHIZ
POOUSHT

NO ONE WOULD BELIEVE US - IT WOULD ONLY BRING HARDSHIP.

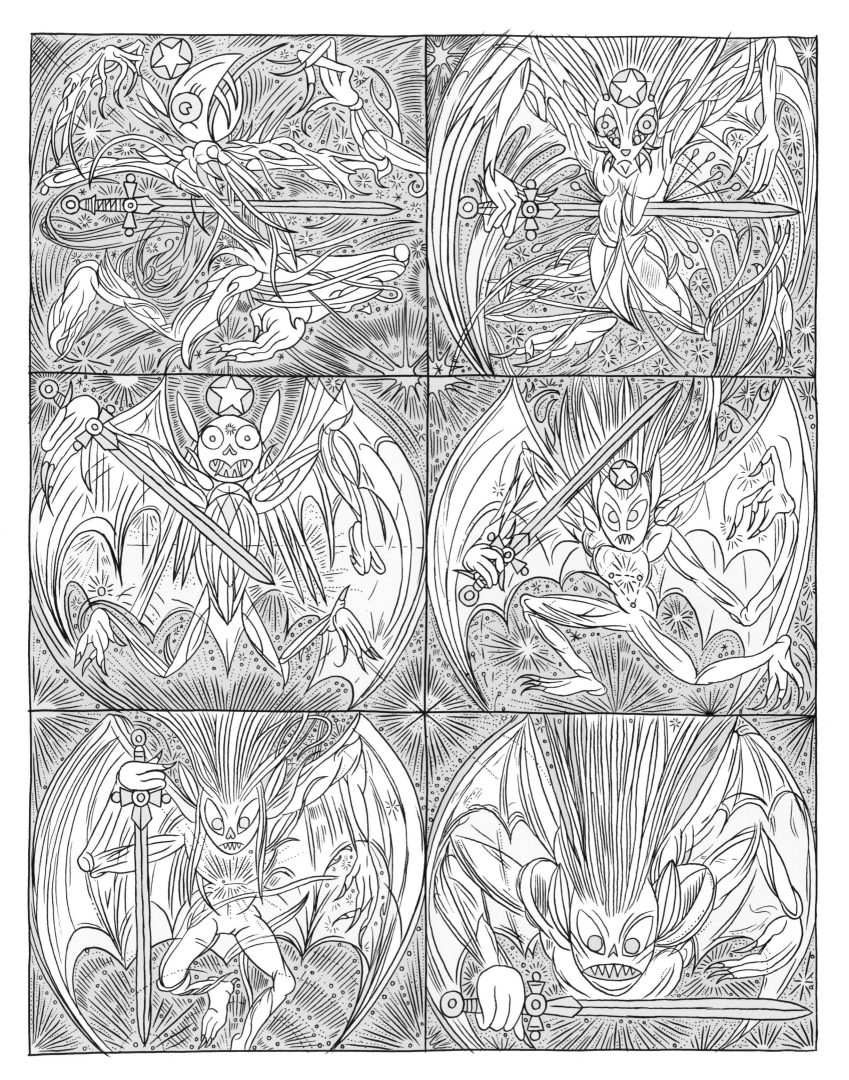

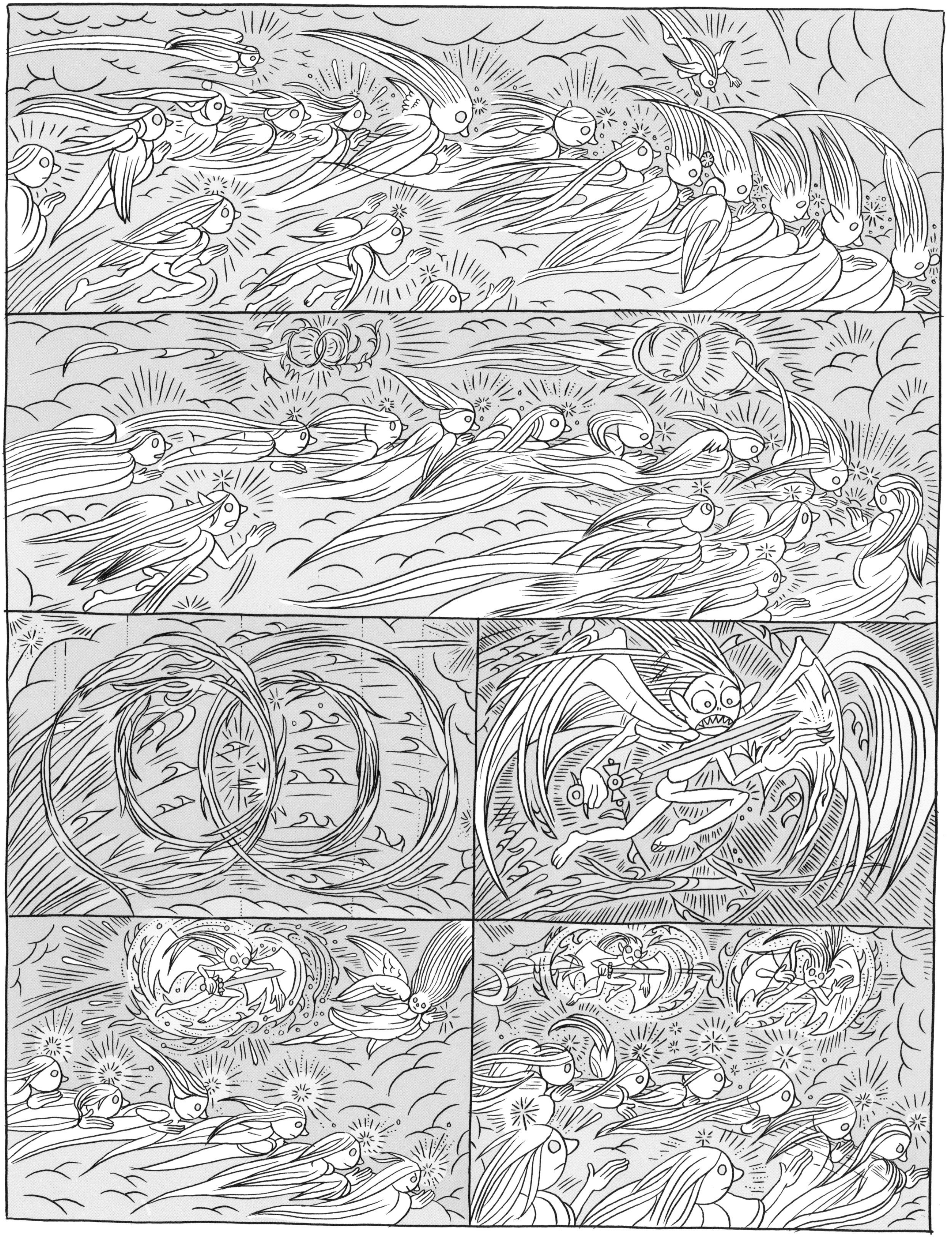

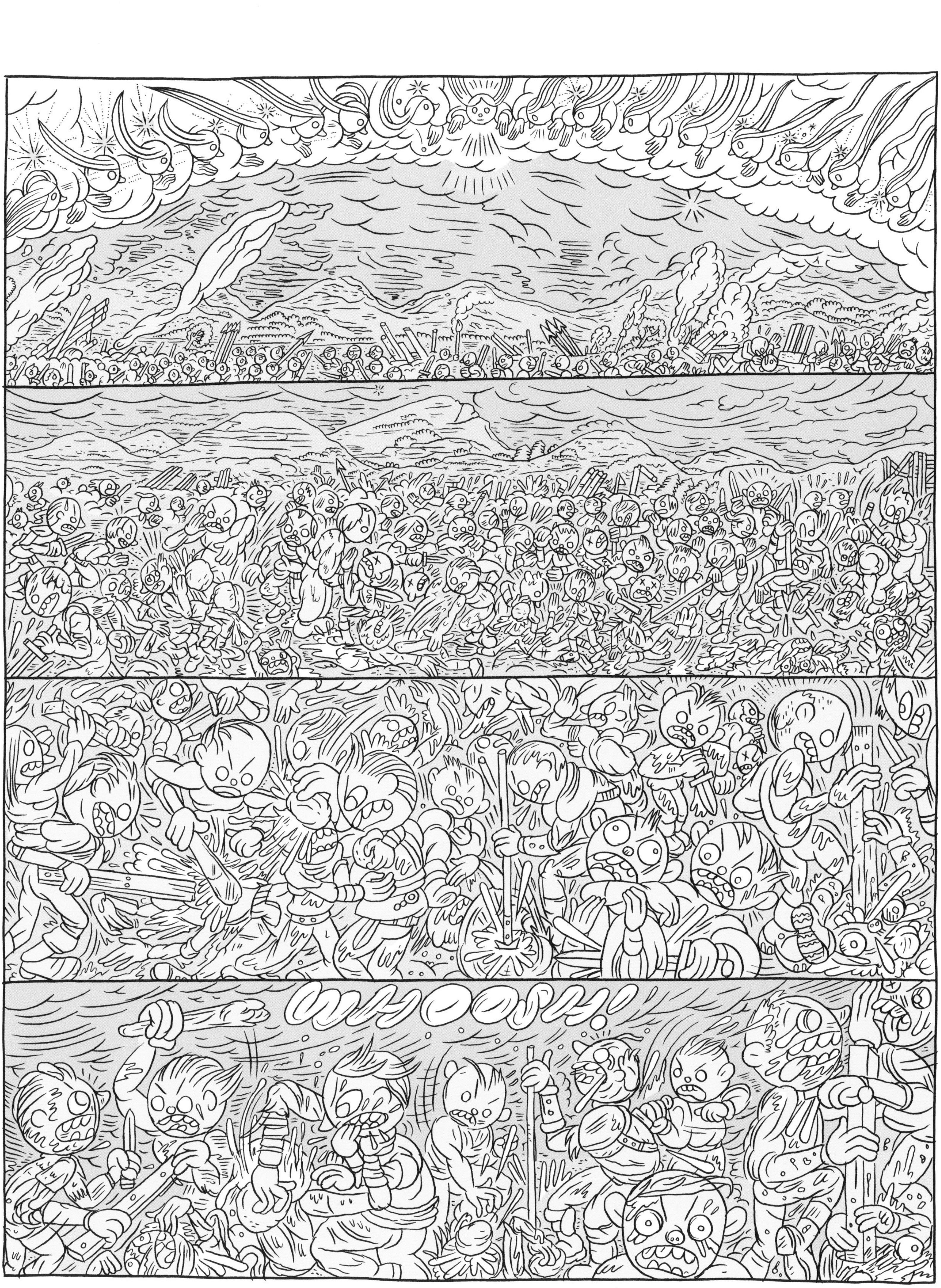
WHOOSH!

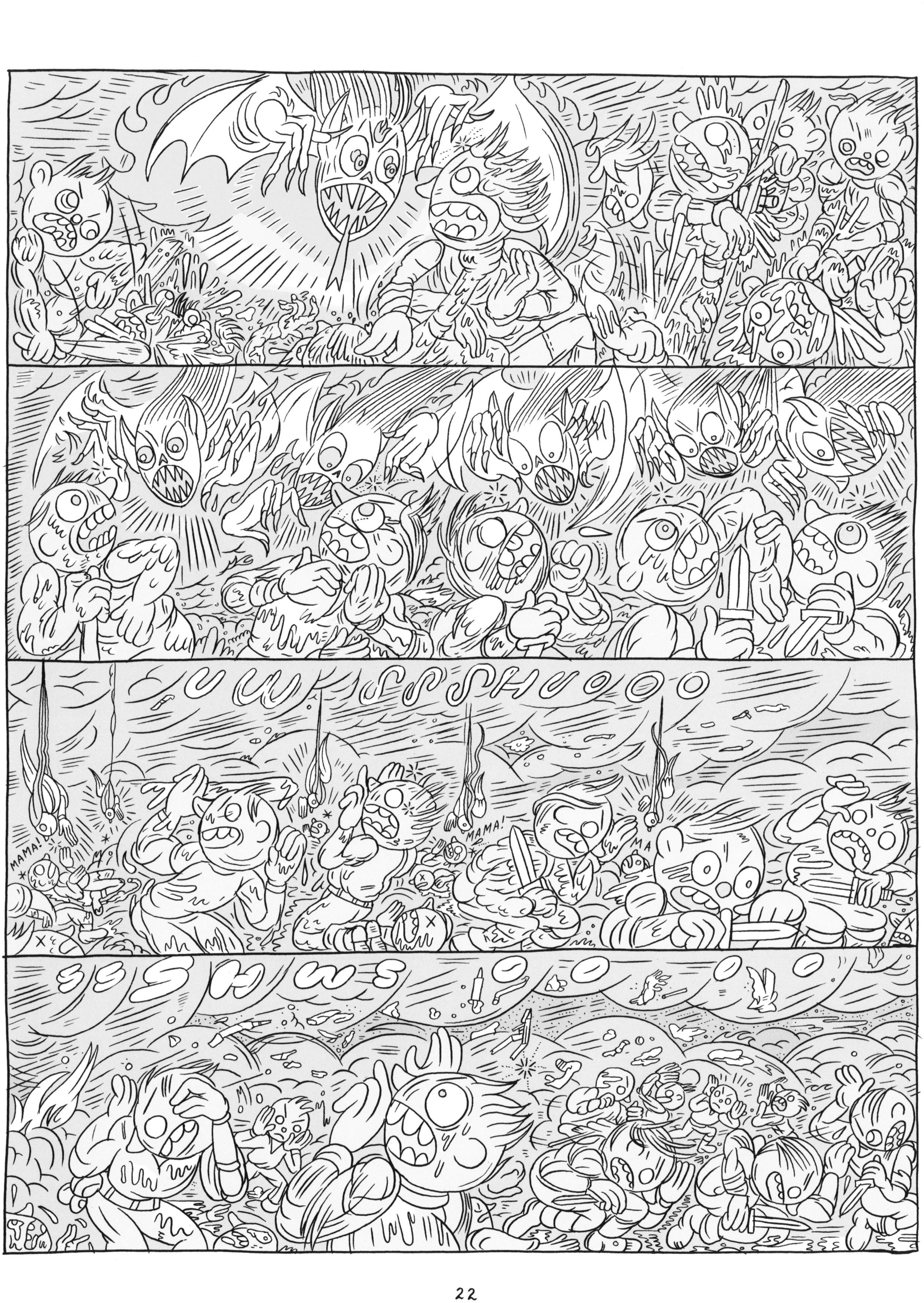
UUWSSSHUOOO
MAMA!
MAMA!
MA
SSSHWSOOOO

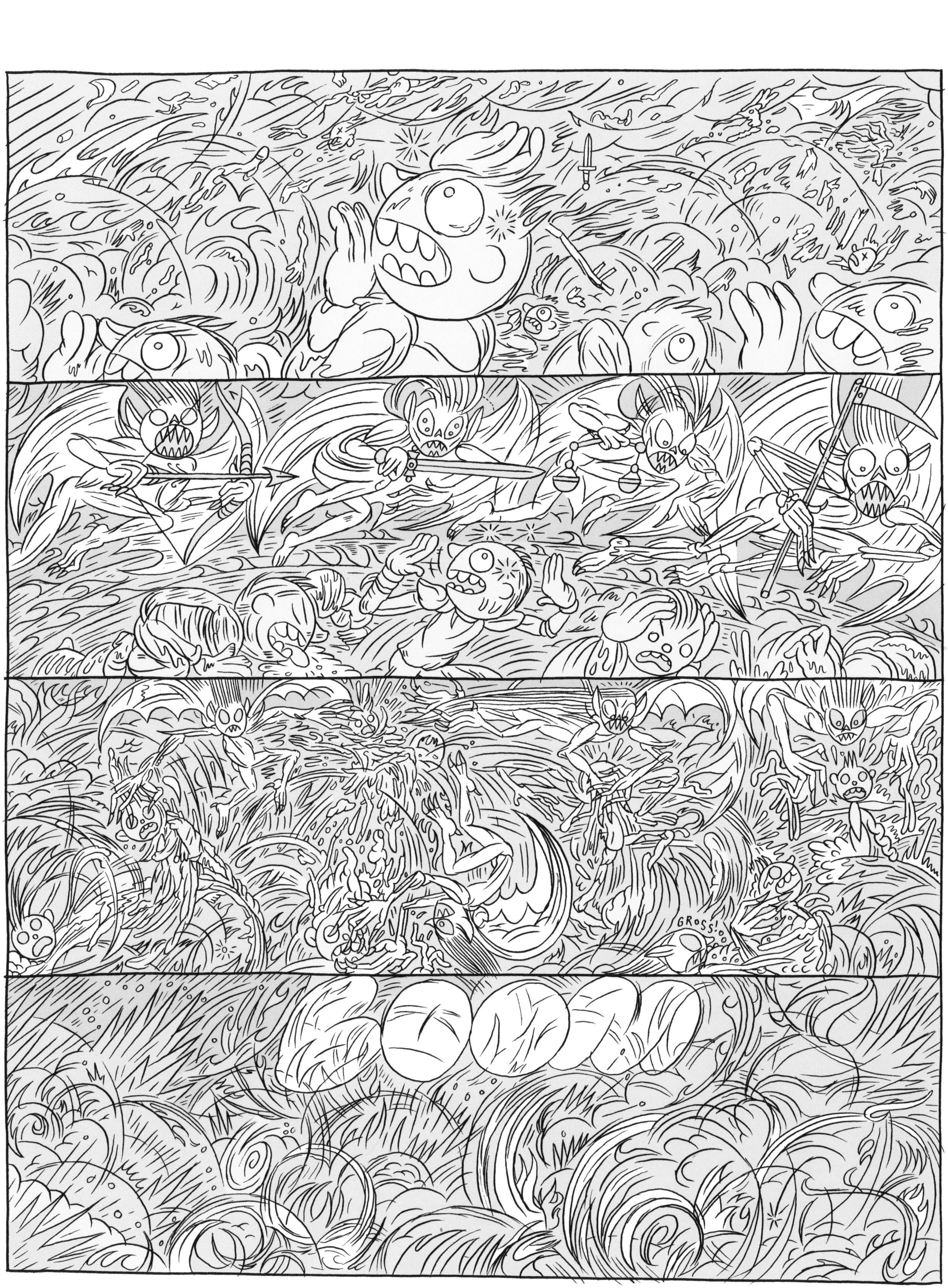
GROSS!

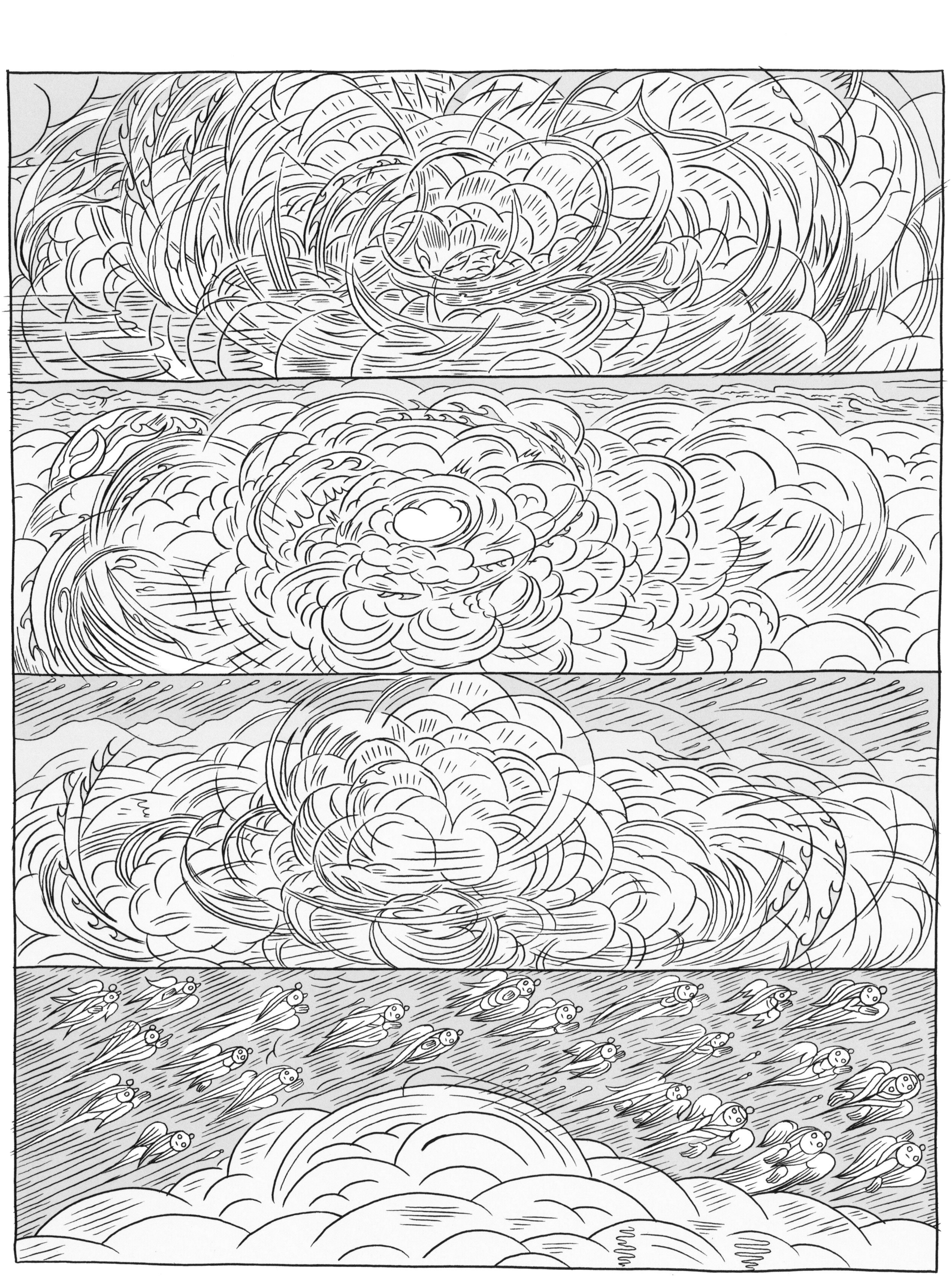

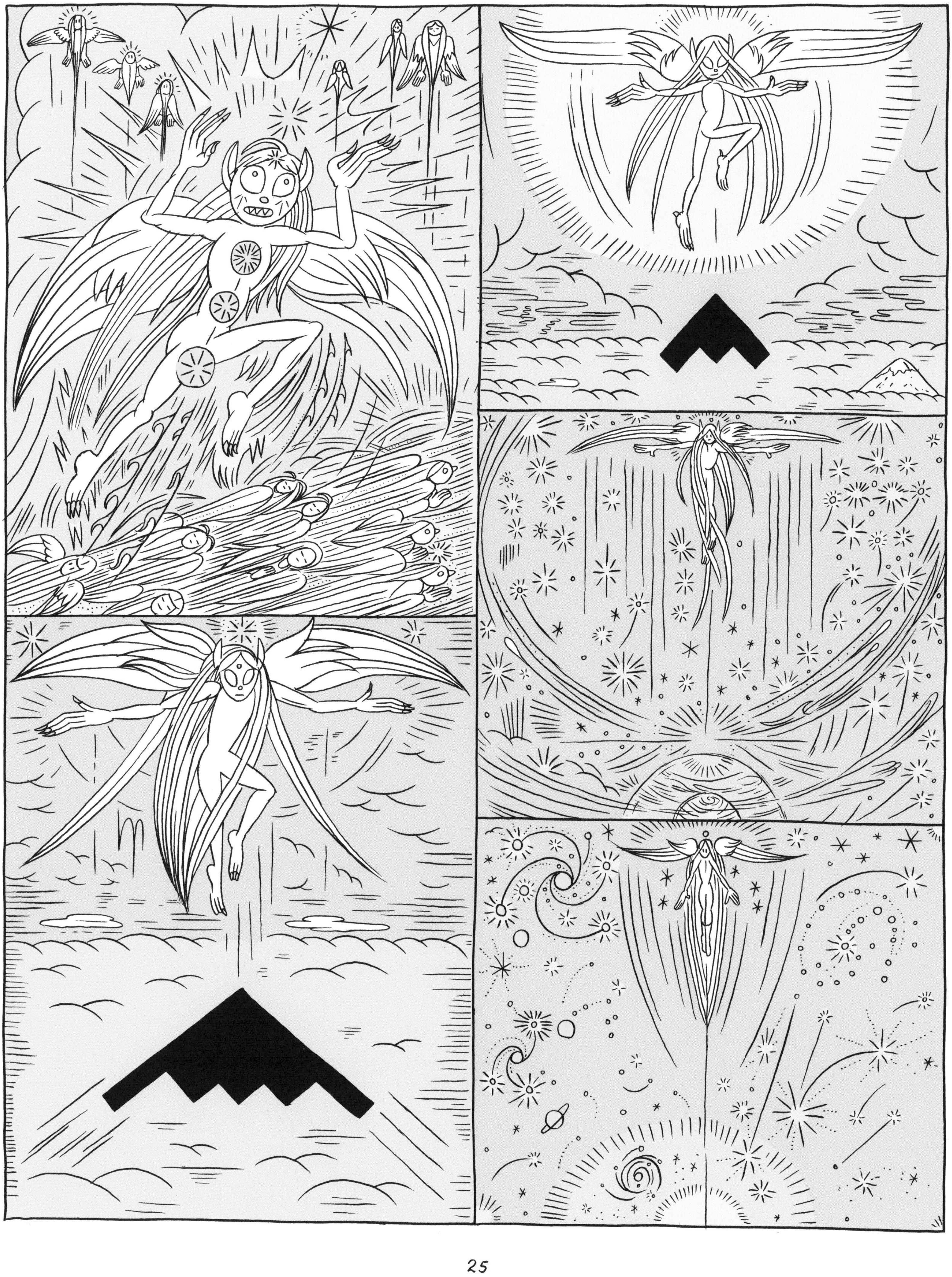

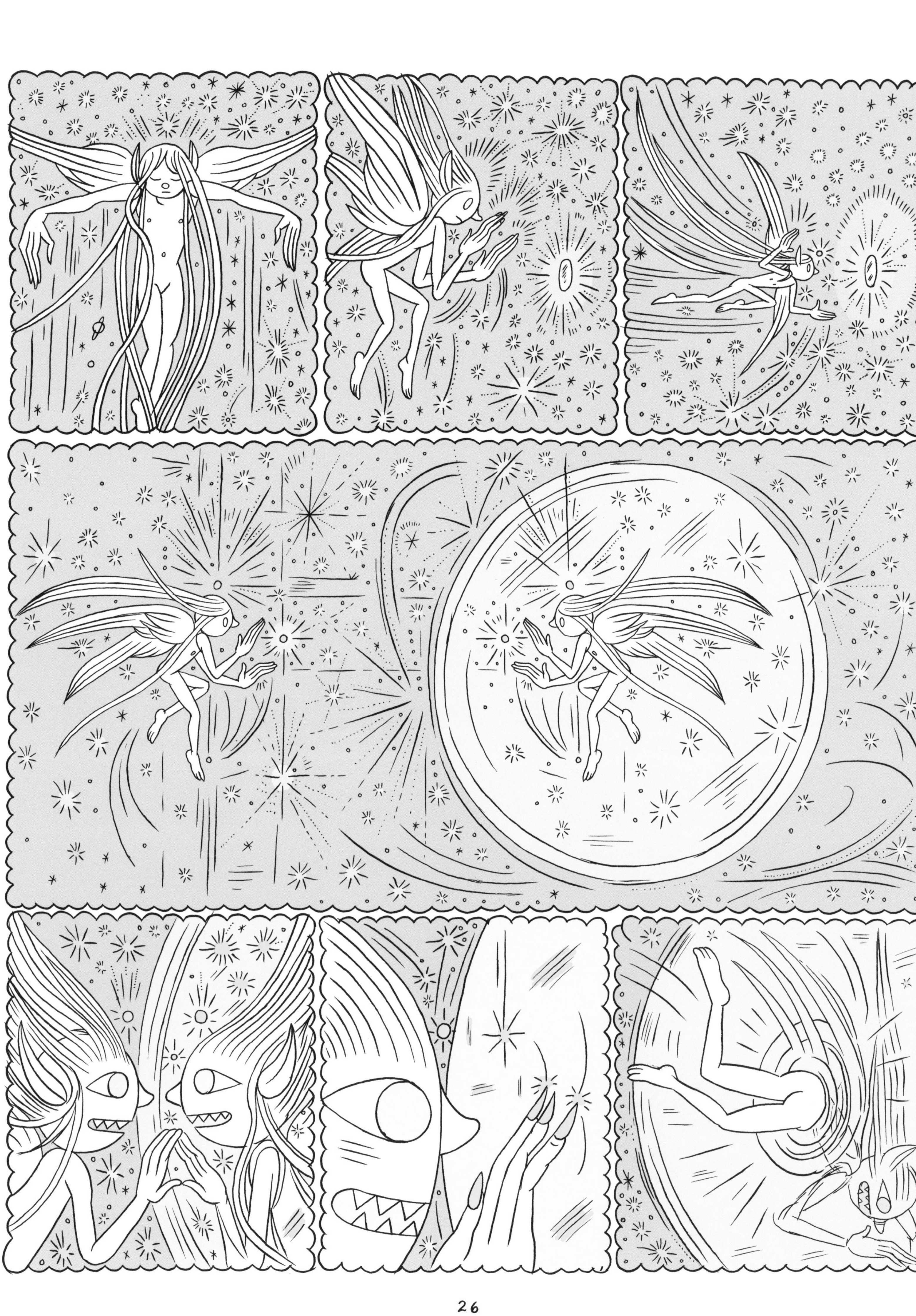

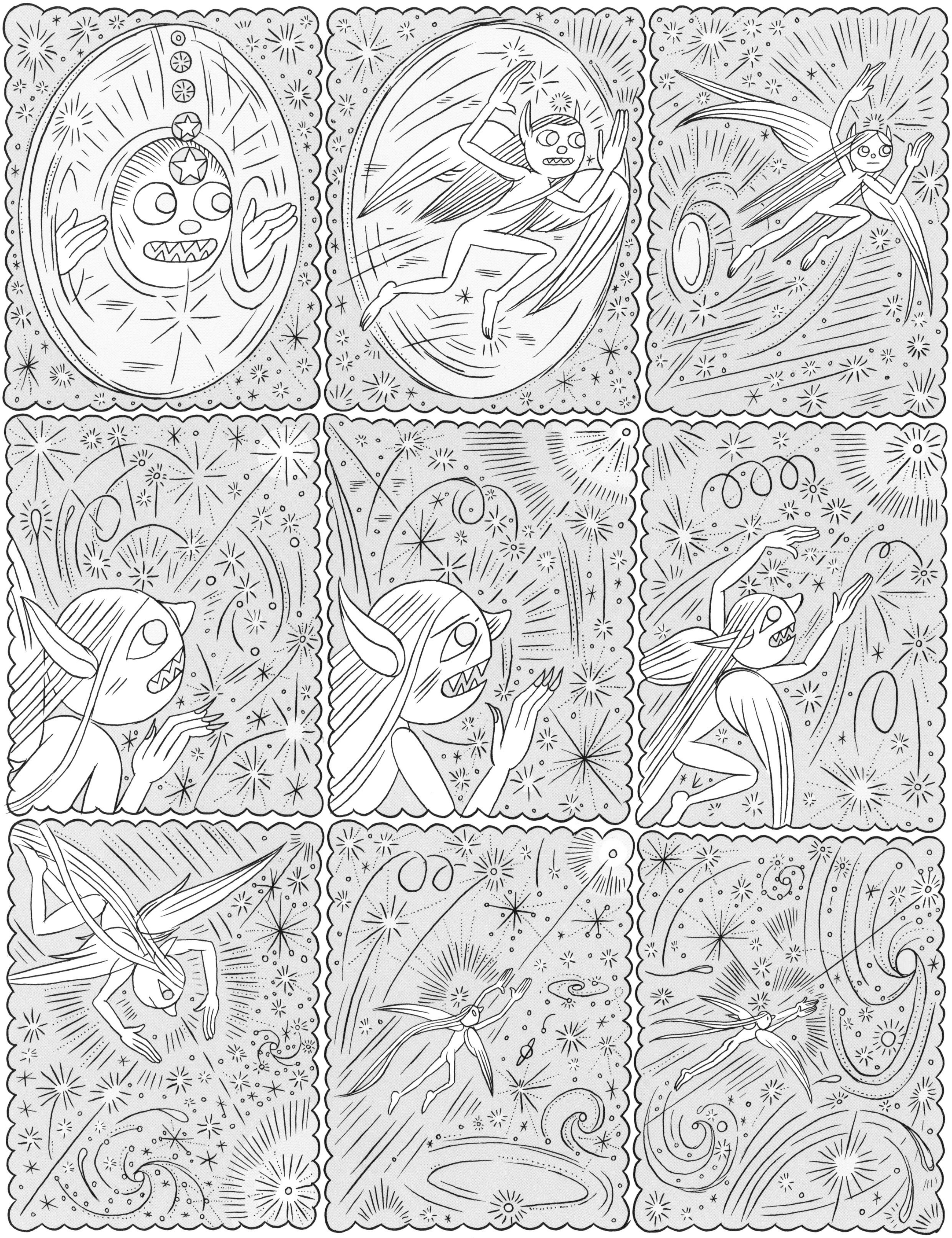

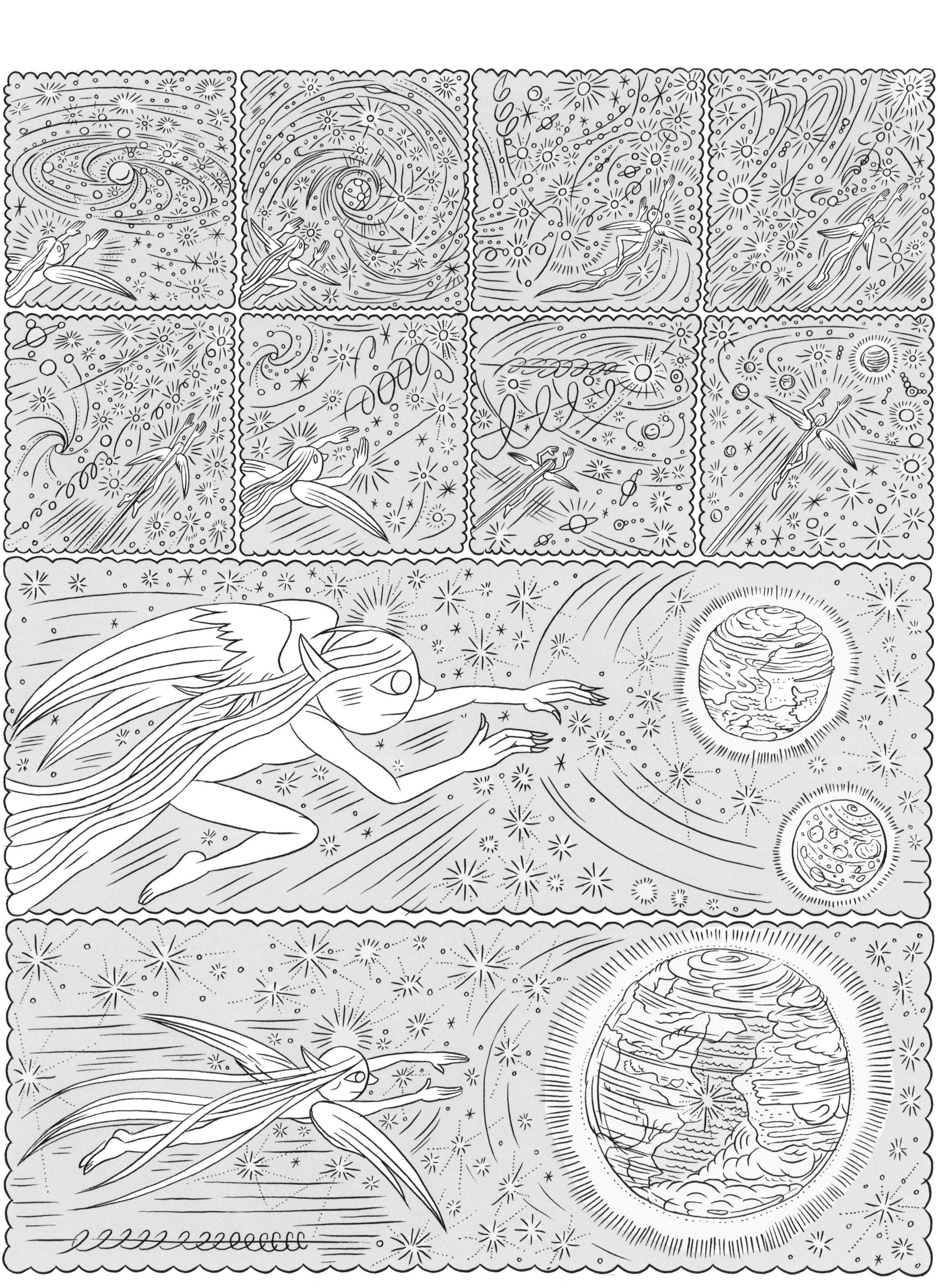

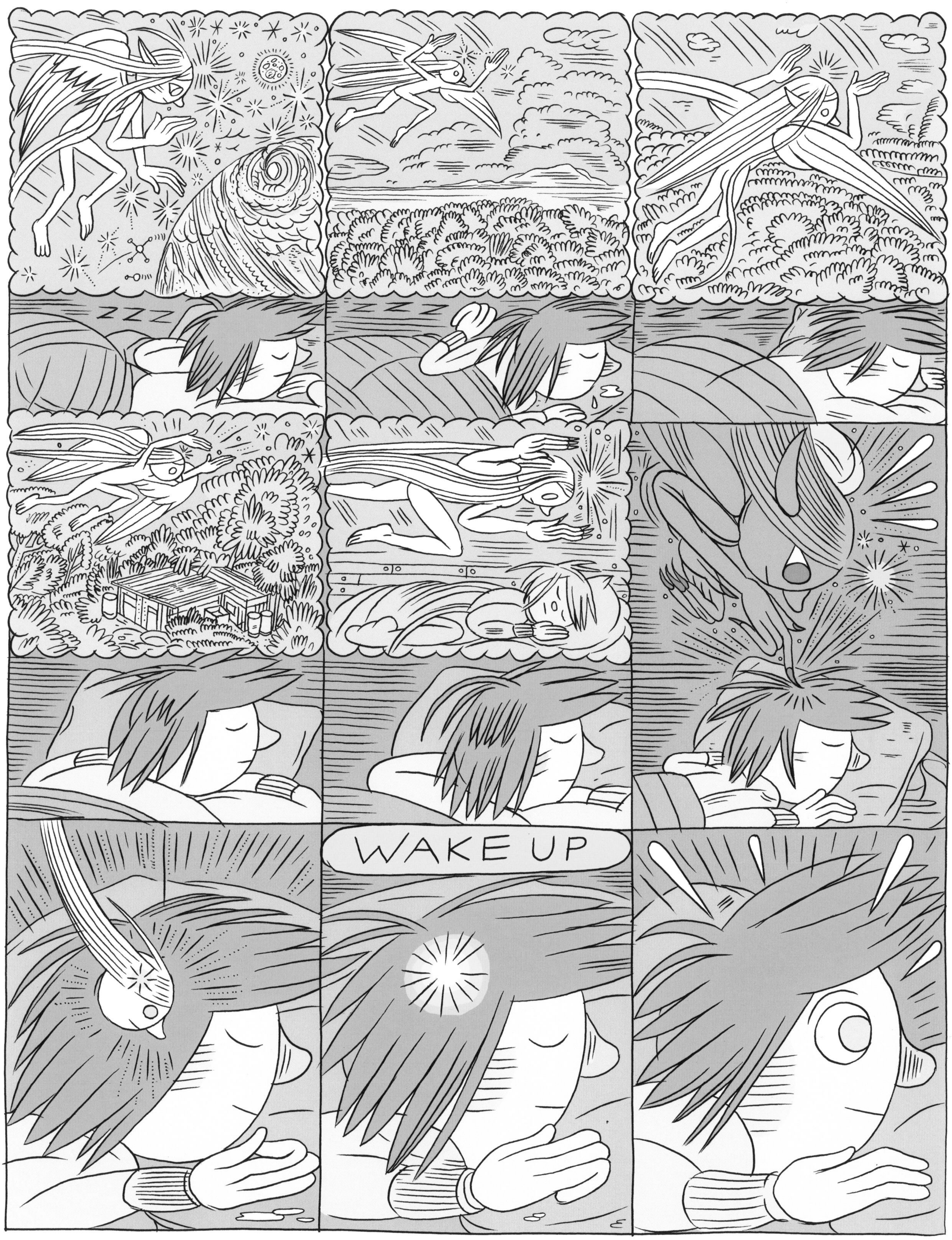
ZZZ
ZZZ
WAKE UP

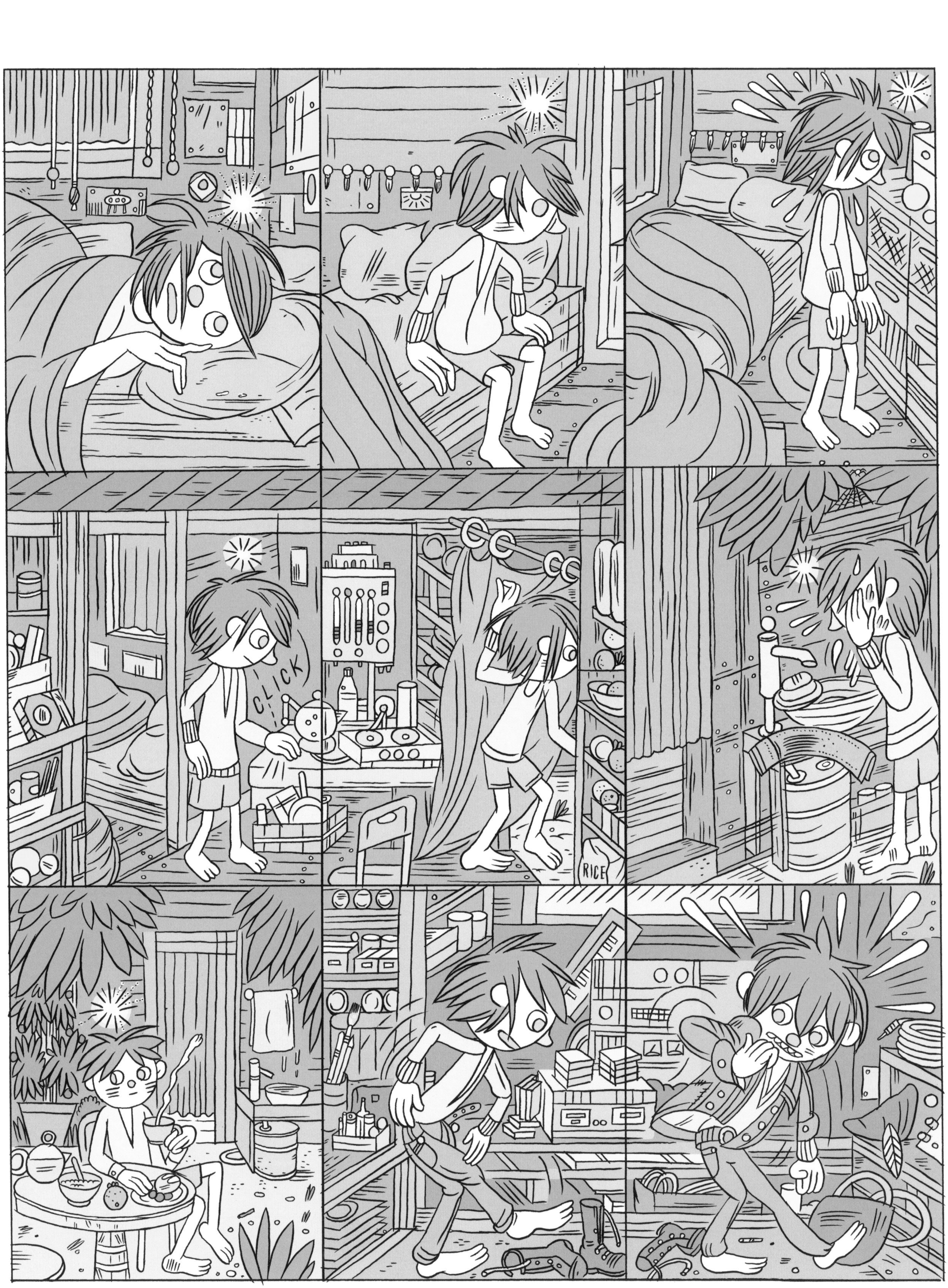
CLICK
RICE

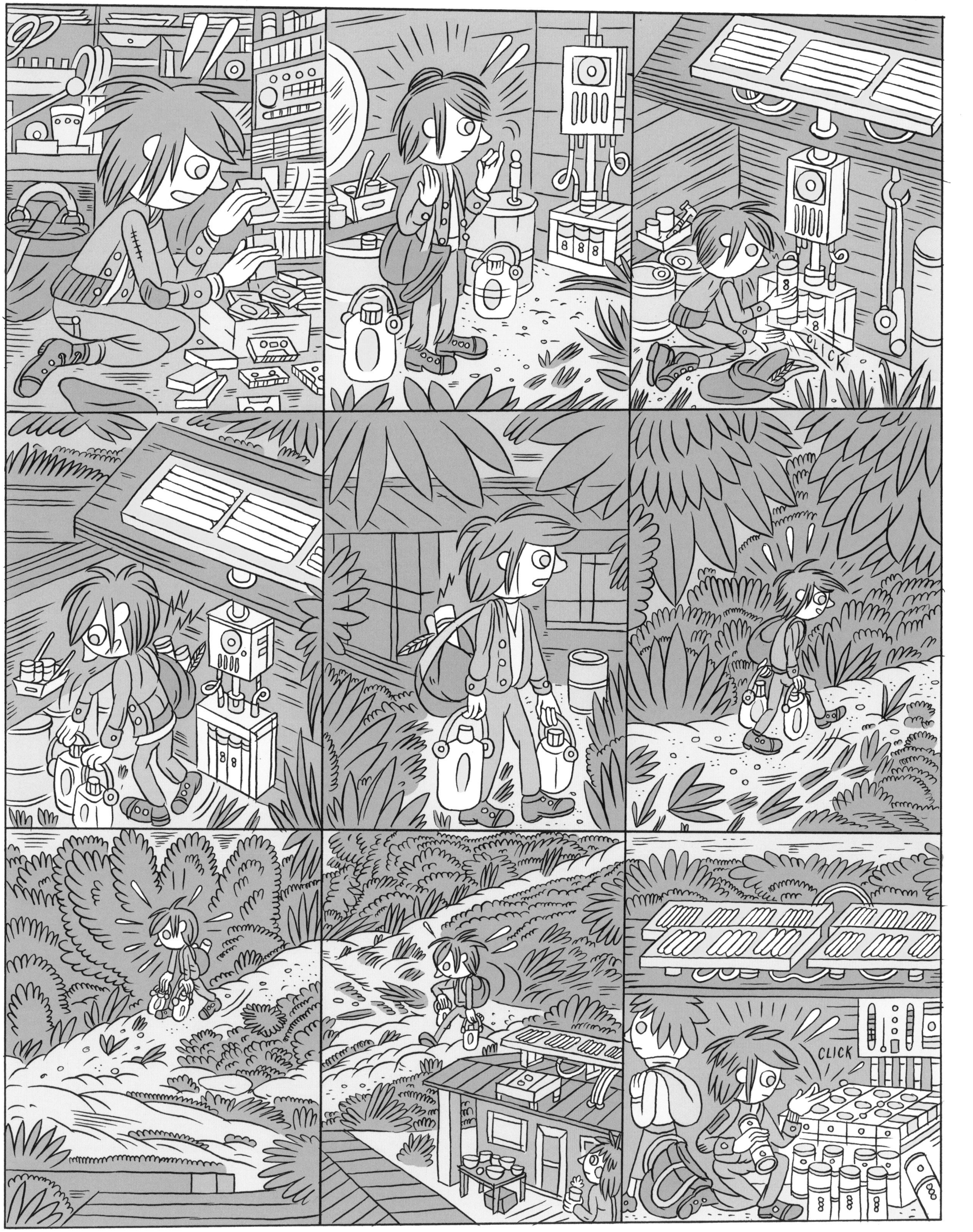
CLICK
CLICK

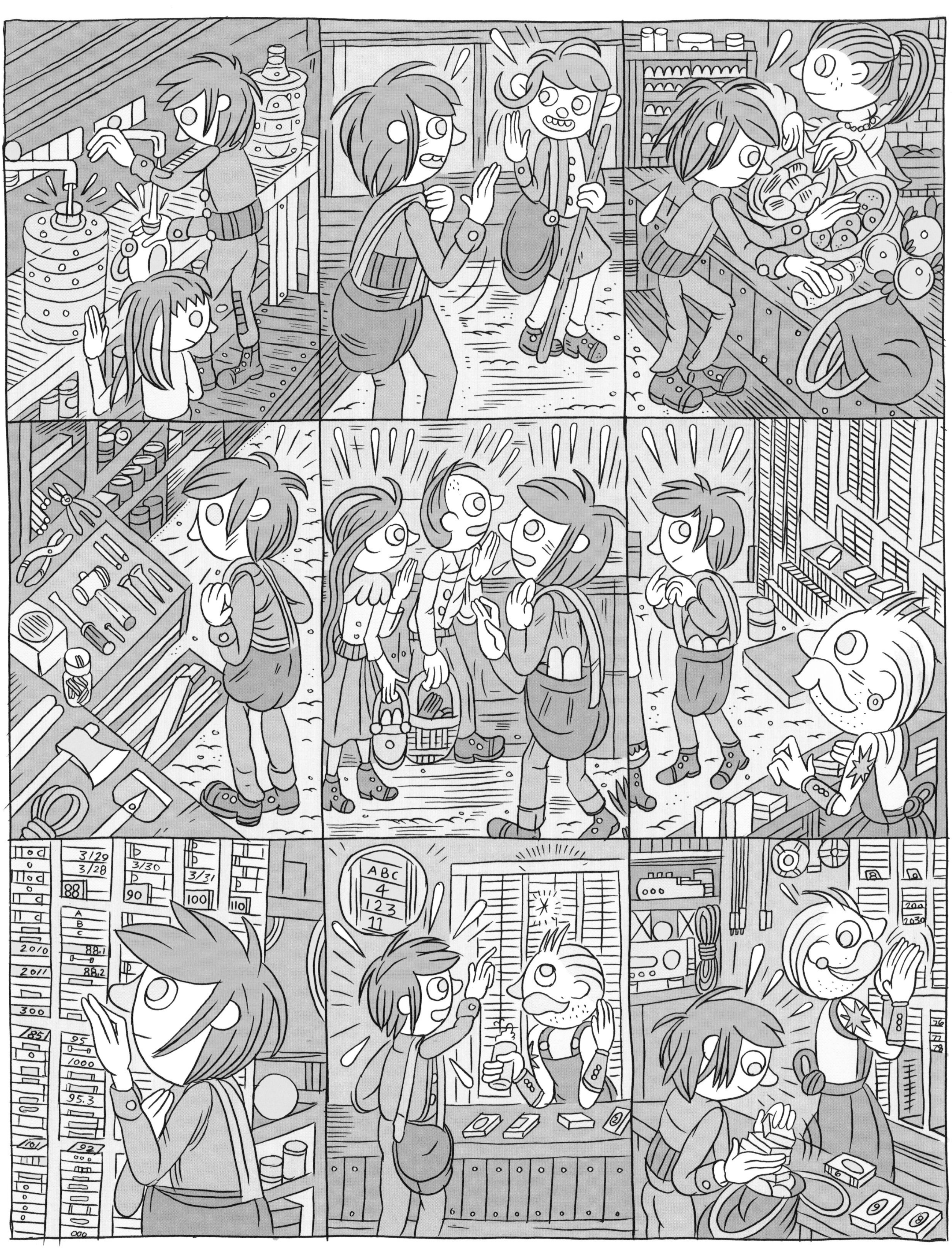
3/29
3/28
3/30
3/31
88
90
100
110
2010
2011
88.1
88.2
300
85
95
1000
95.3
101
92
ABC
4
123
11

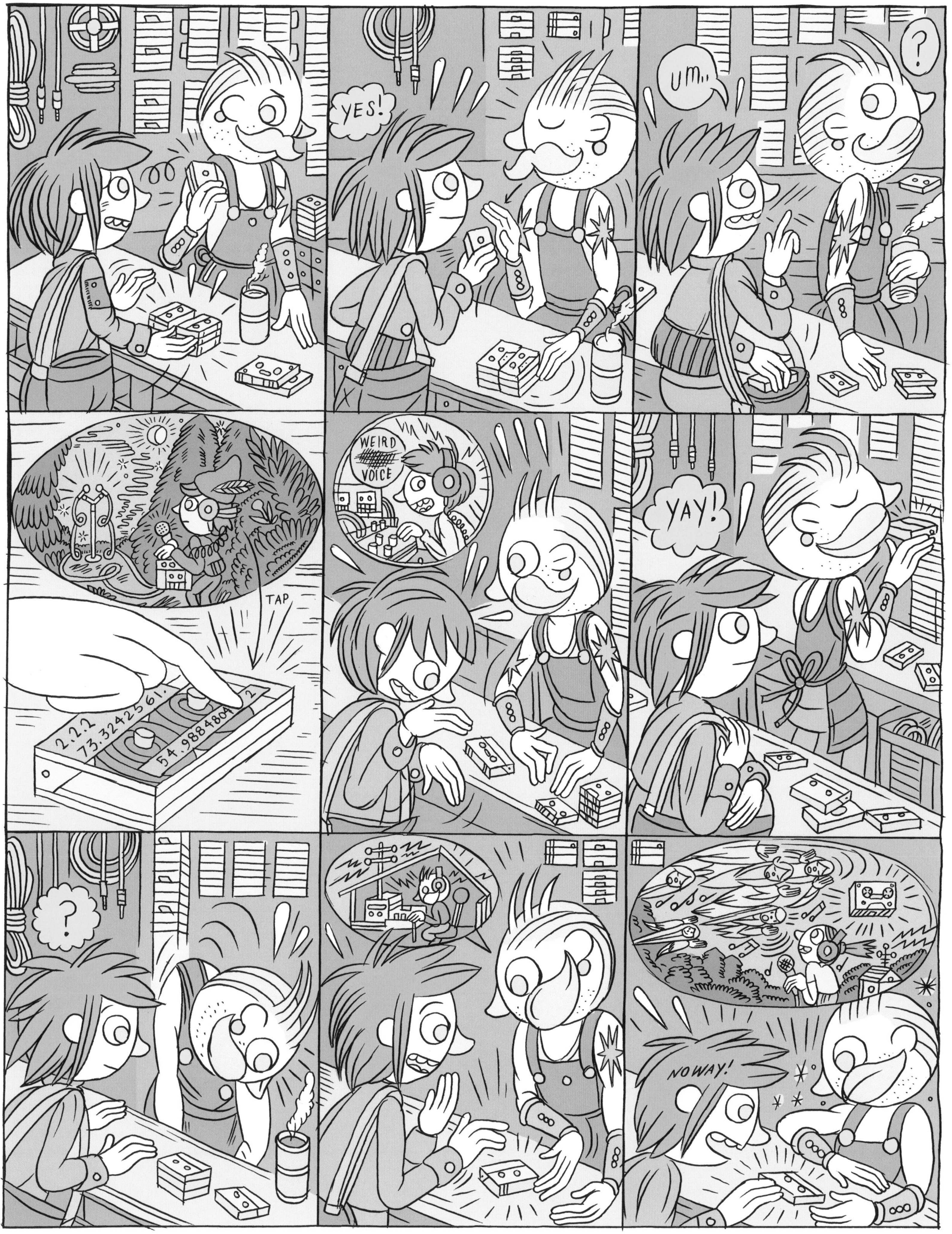
YES!
UM..
?
WEIRD
VOICE
TAP
2.2.2
73.3242561.
54.9884804
2
YAY!
?
NOWAY!

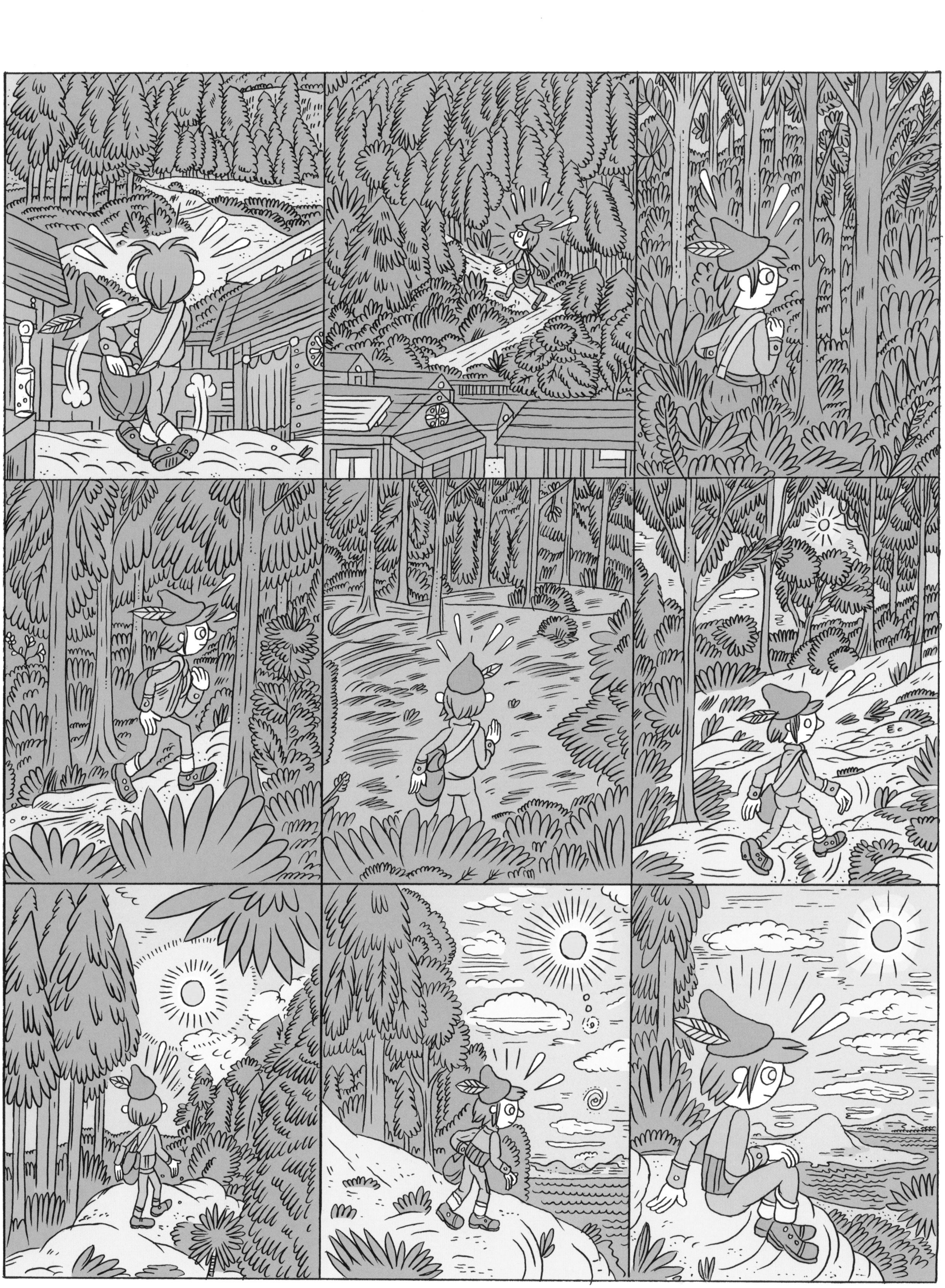

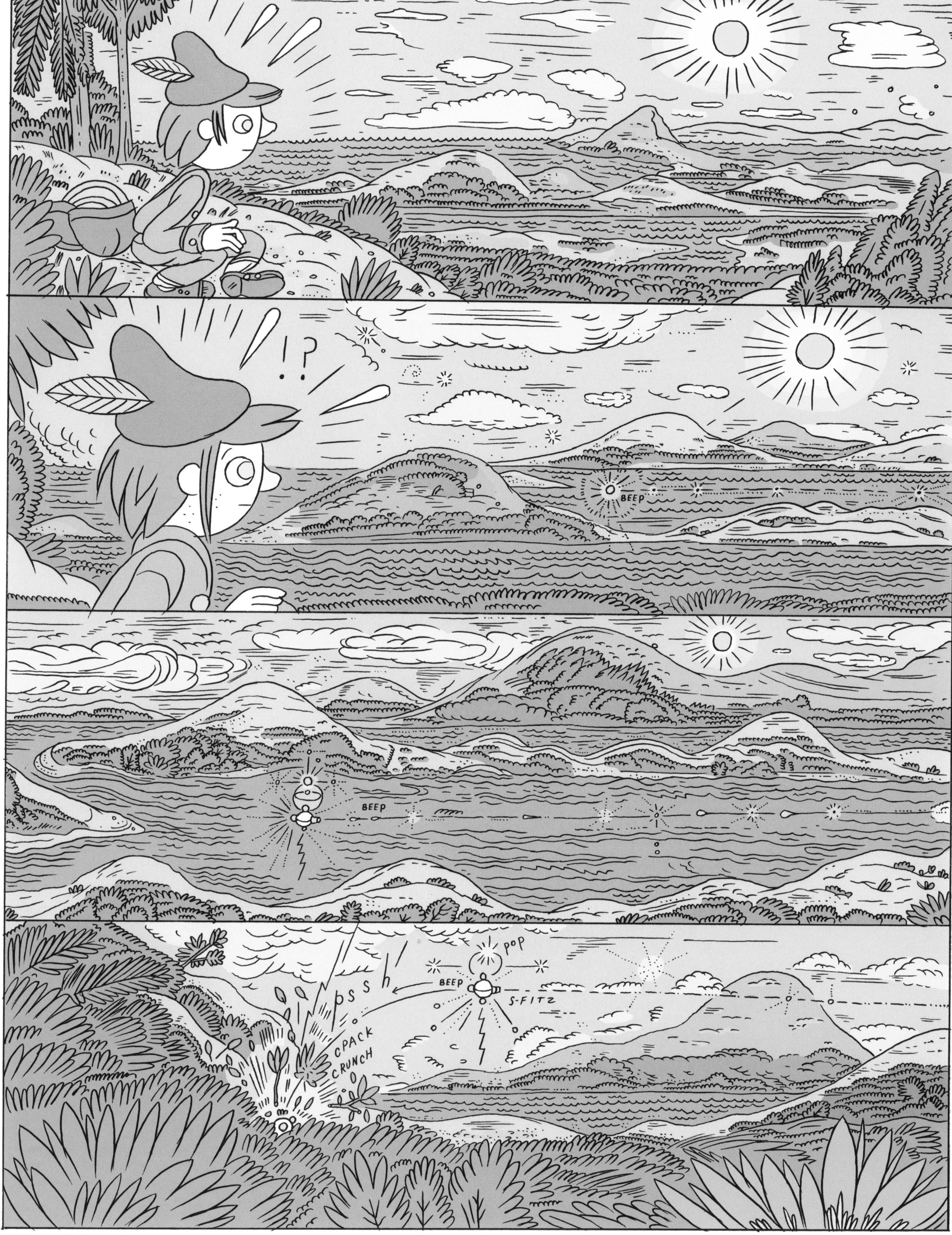
!?
BEEP
BEEP
pop
BEEP
pssh
S-FITZ
CRACK
CRUNCH

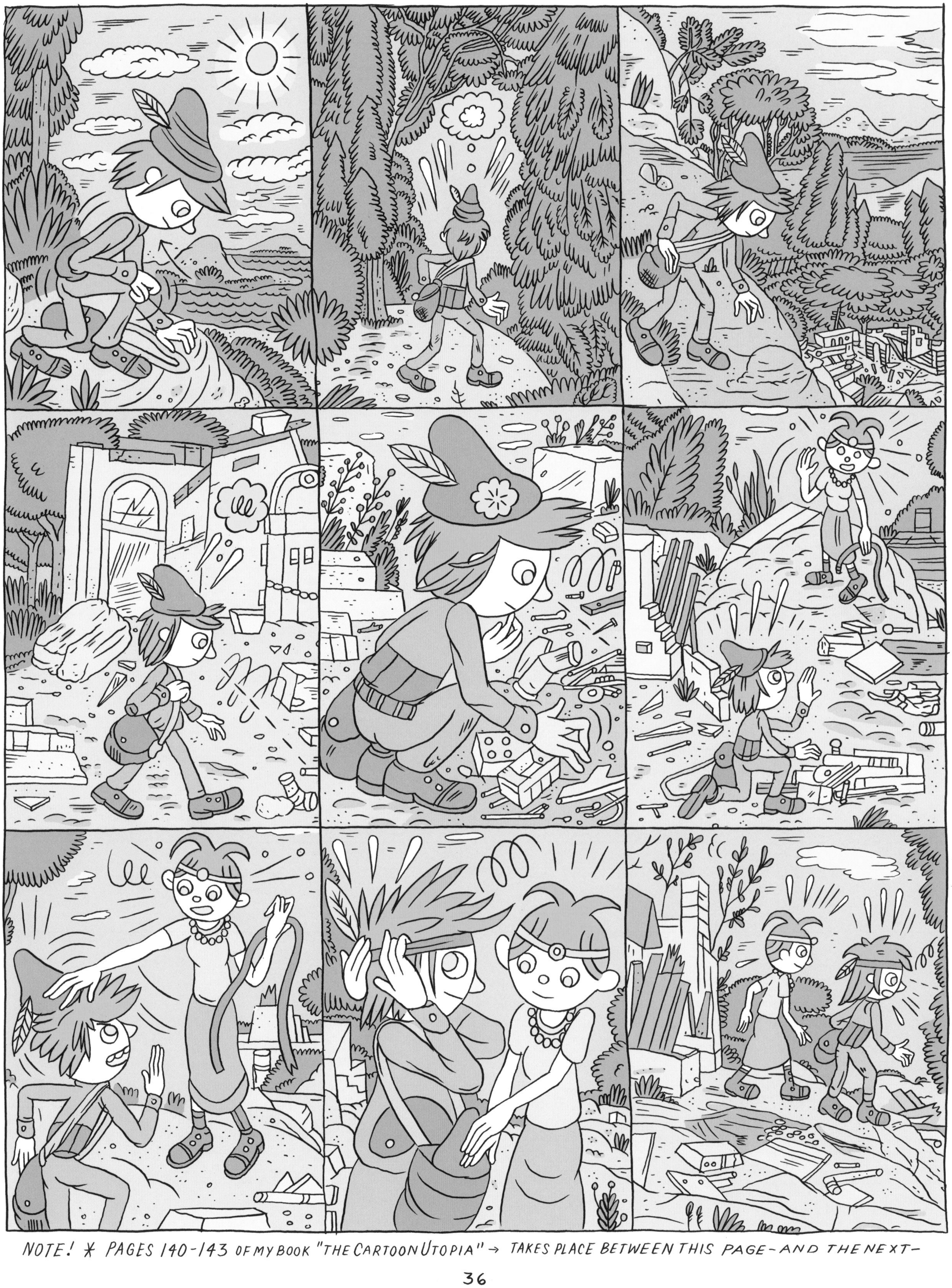

NOTE! * PAGES 140-143 OF MY BOOK "THE CARTOON UTOPIA" → TAKES PLACE BETWEEN THIS PAGE - AND THE NEXT -

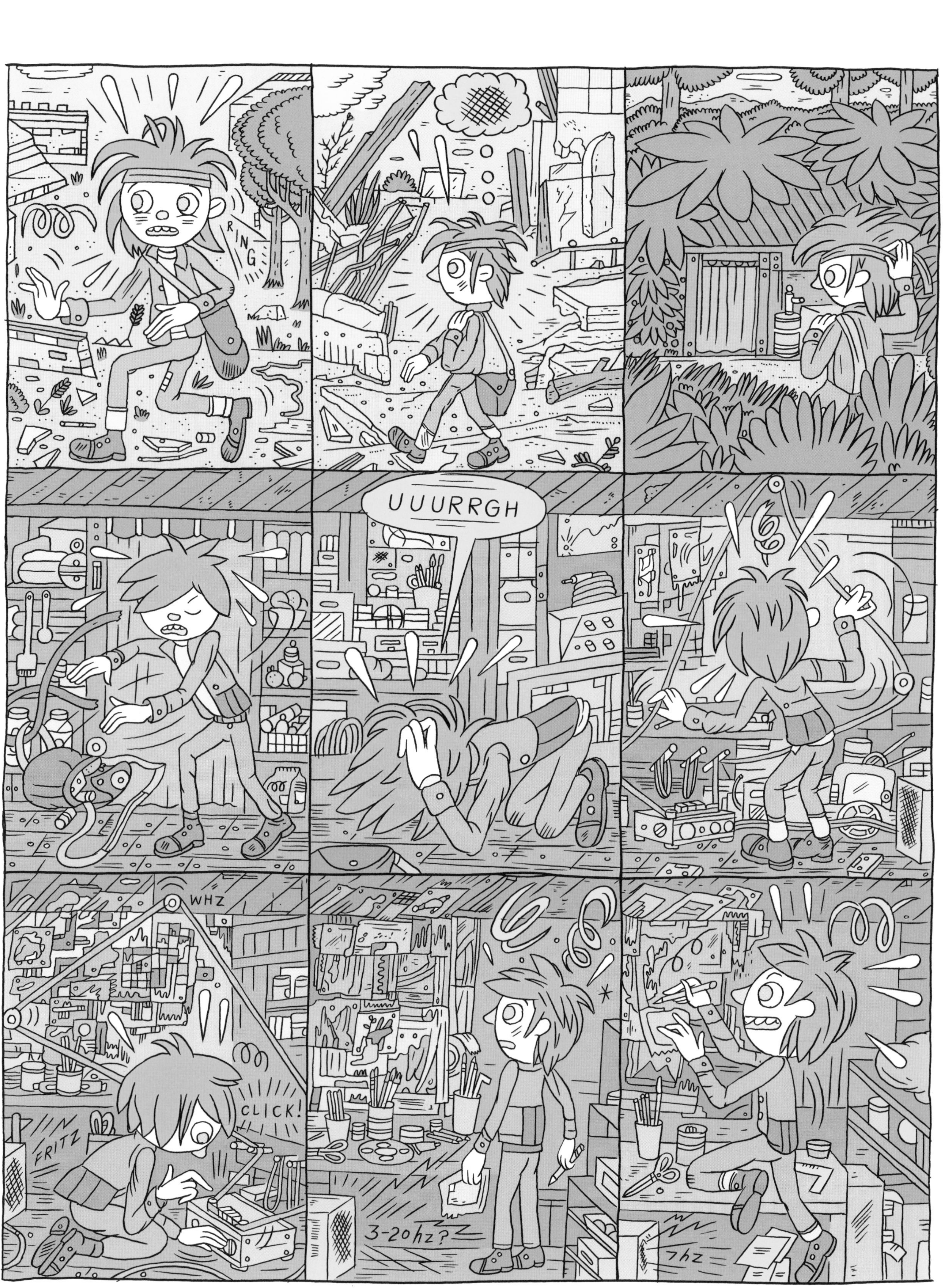
RING
UUURRGH
WHZ
CLICK!
FRITZ
3-20hz?
7hz

THE WISE OLD UTOPIAN DREAMS + DOZES ABOARD THE AUTONOMOUS SOLAR BLIMP

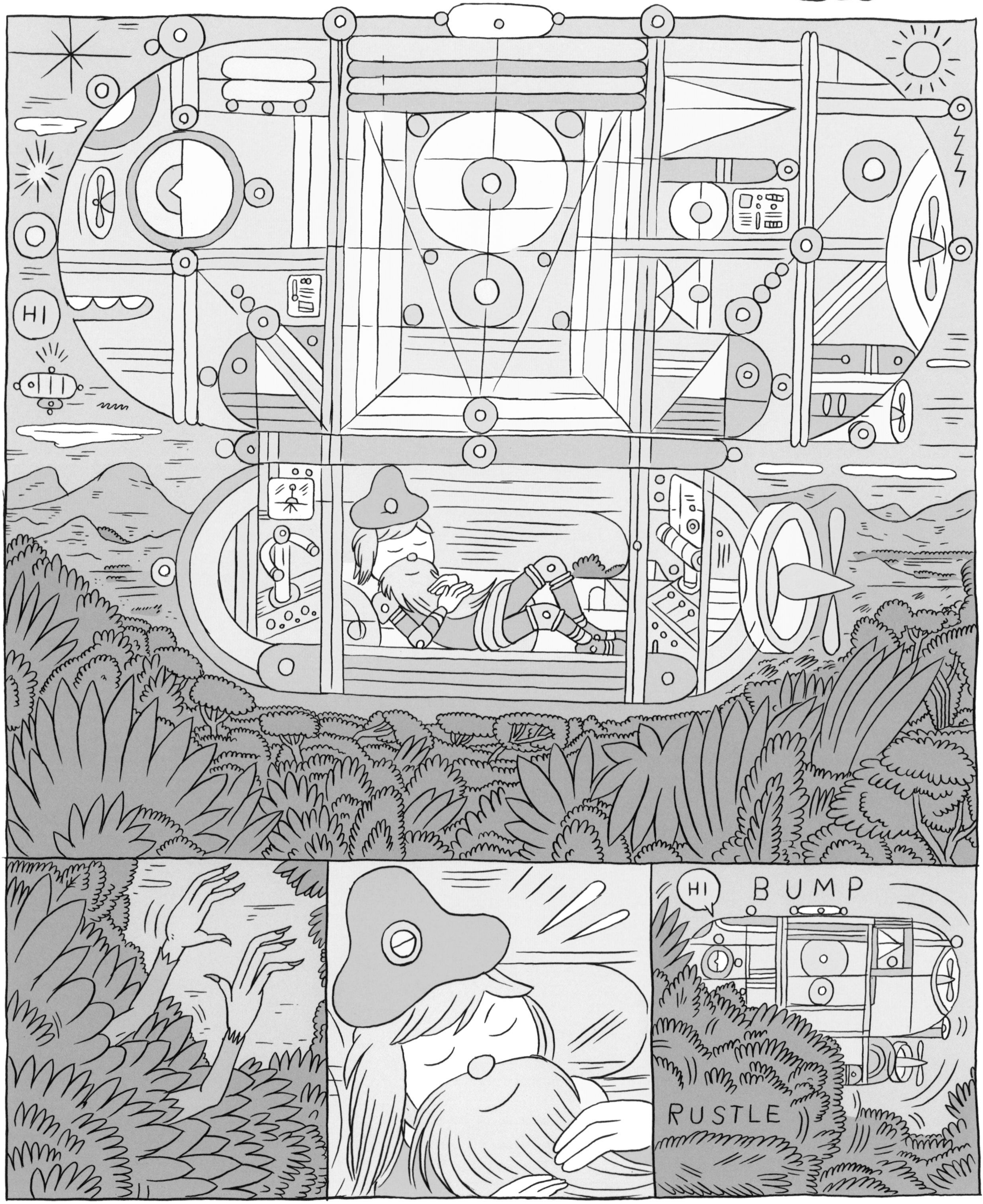
HI
HI
BUMP
RUSTLE

MEANWHLE, SOMEWHERE ELSE...

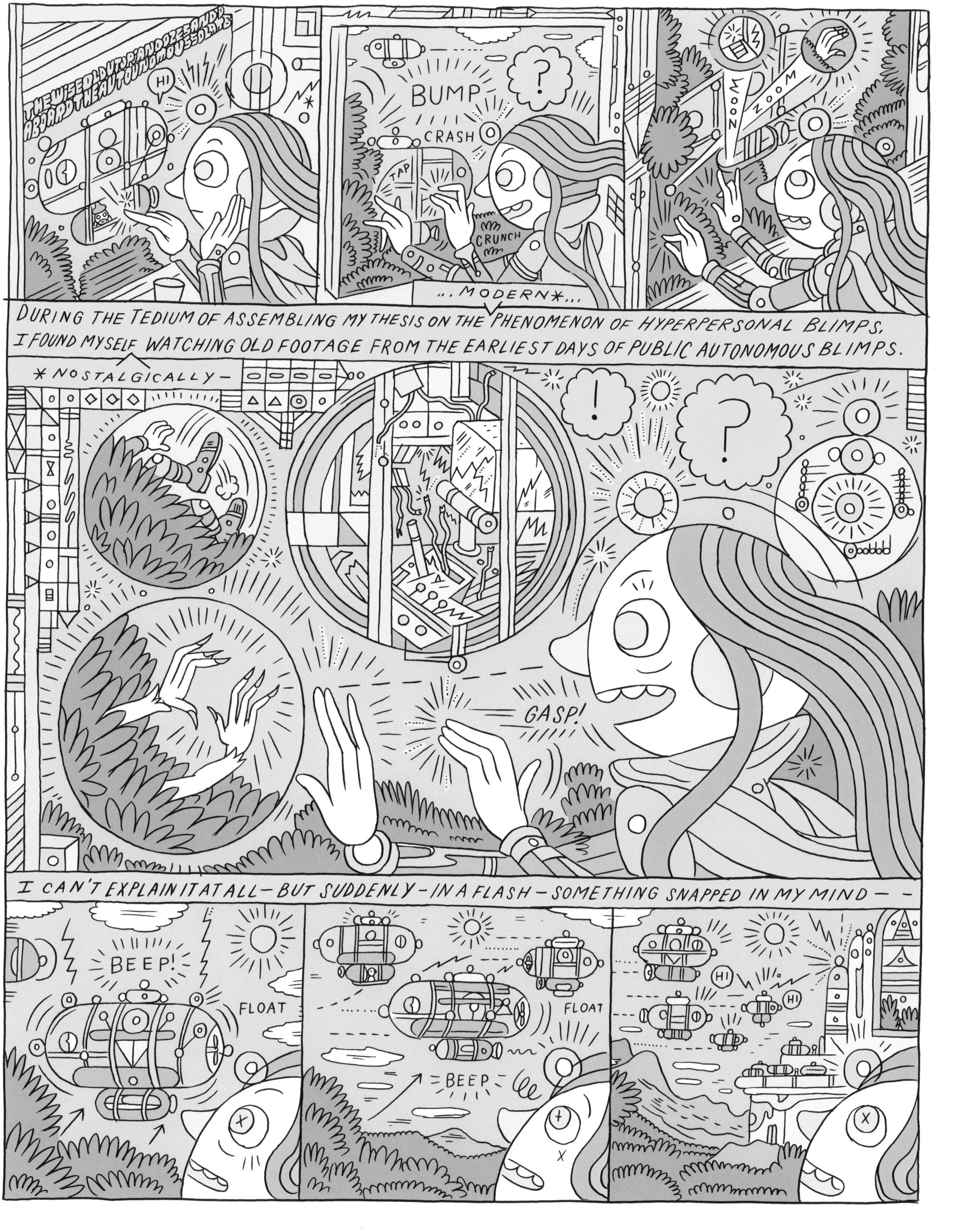
HI
BUMP
CRASH
TAP
CRUNCH
?
ZOOM
ZOOM
..MODERN*...
DURING THE TEDIUM OF ASSEMBLING MY THESIS ON THE PHENOMENON OF HYPERPERSONAL BLIMPS, I FOUND MYSELF WATCHING OLD FOOTAGE FROM THE EARLIEST DAYS OF PUBLIC AUTONOMOUS BLIMPS.
*NOSTALGICALLY-
!
?
GASP!
I CAN'T EXPLAIN IT AT ALL - BUT SUDDENLY - IN A FLASH - SOMETHING SNAPPED IN MY MIND - -
BEEP!
FLOAT
FLOAT
BEEP
HI
HI

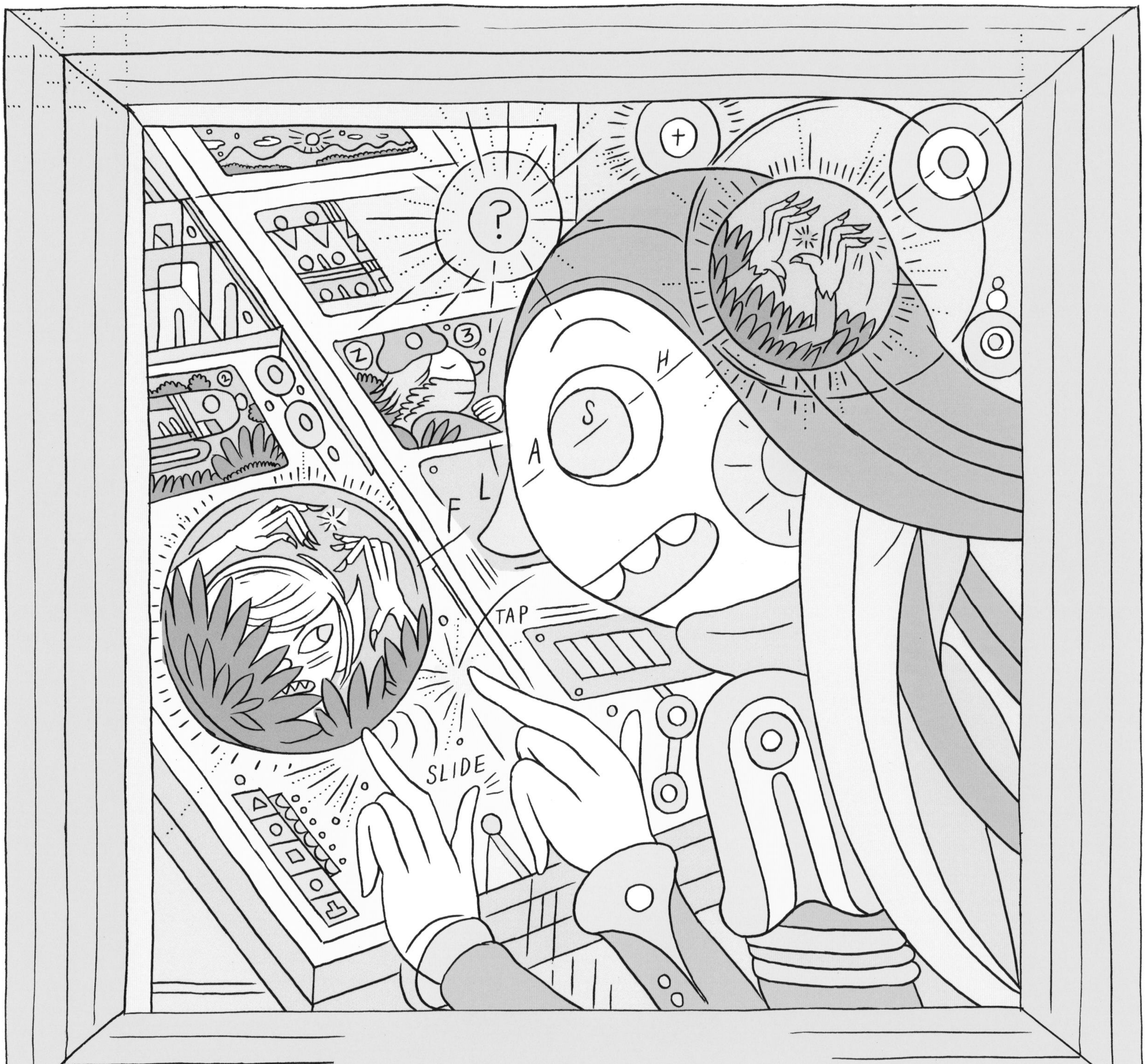
FLASH
TAP
SLIDE

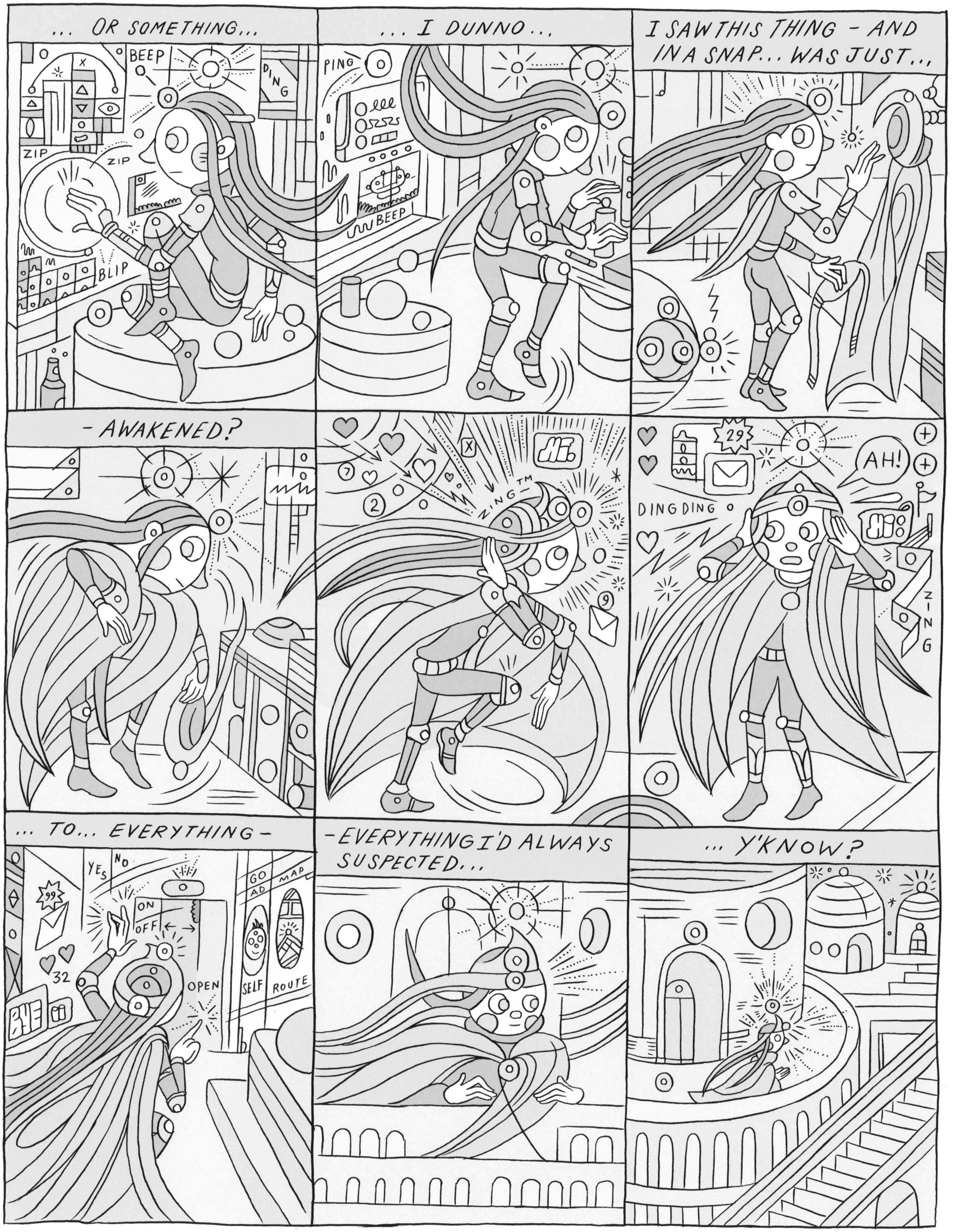
... OR SOMETHING...
BEEP
DING
ZIP
ZIP
BLIP
... I DUNNO ...
PING
BEEP
I SAW THIS THING - AND IN A SNAP... WAS JUST...
- AWAKENED?
HI
ZING™
29
AH!
DING DING
ZING
... TO... EVERYTHING -
99
32
YES
NO
ON
OFF
GO
AD
MAP
OPEN
SELF
ROUTE
- EVERYTHING I'D ALWAYS SUSPECTED...
... Y'KNOW?

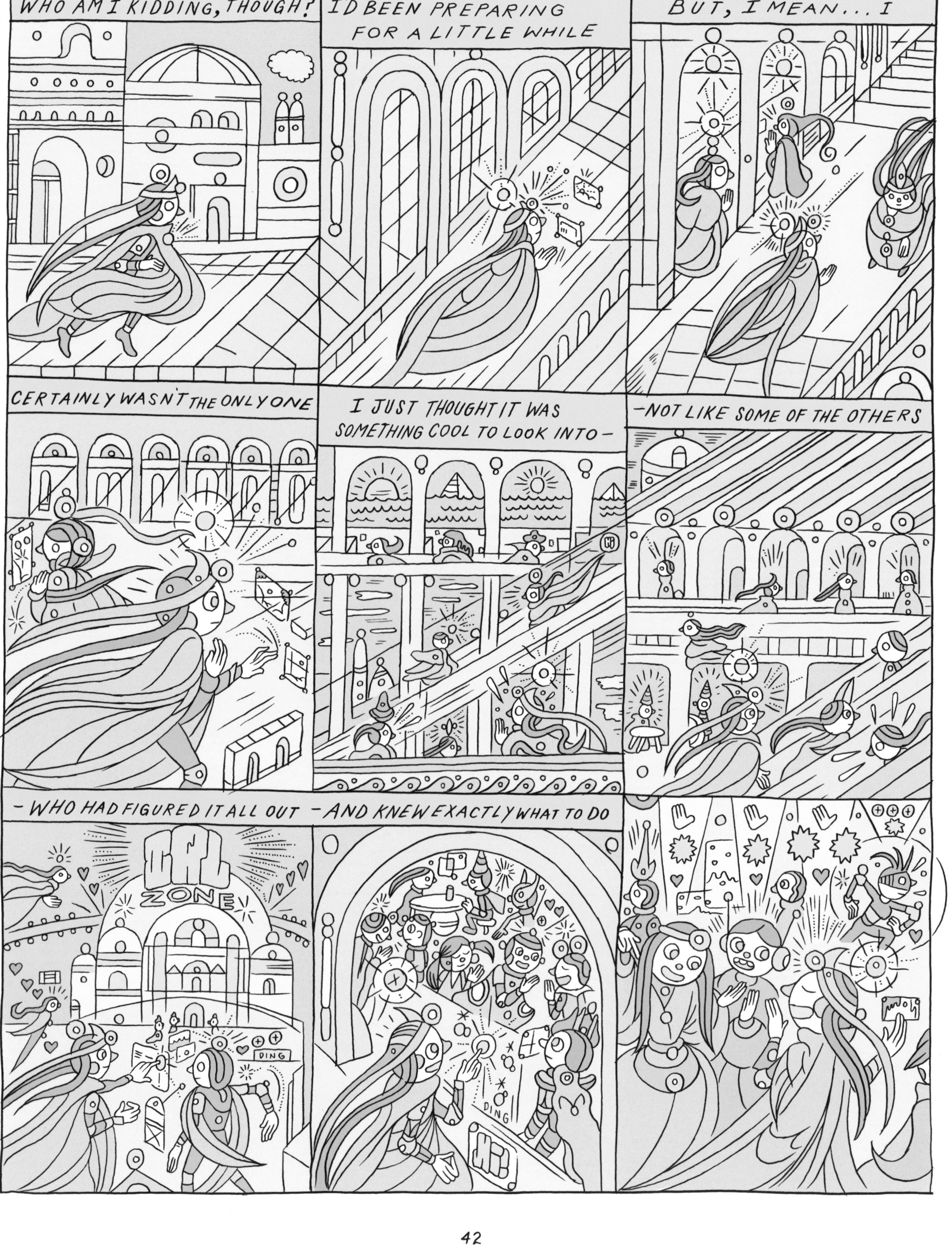
WHO AM I KIDDING, THOUGH?
I'D BEEN PREPARING FOR A LITTLE WHILE
BUT, I MEAN... I
CERTAINLY WASN'T THE ONLY ONE
I JUST THOUGHT IT WAS SOMETHING COOL TO LOOK INTO –
– NOT LIKE SOME OF THE OTHERS
– WHO HAD FIGURED IT ALL OUT
ZONE
DING
– AND KNEW EXACTLY WHAT TO DO
DING

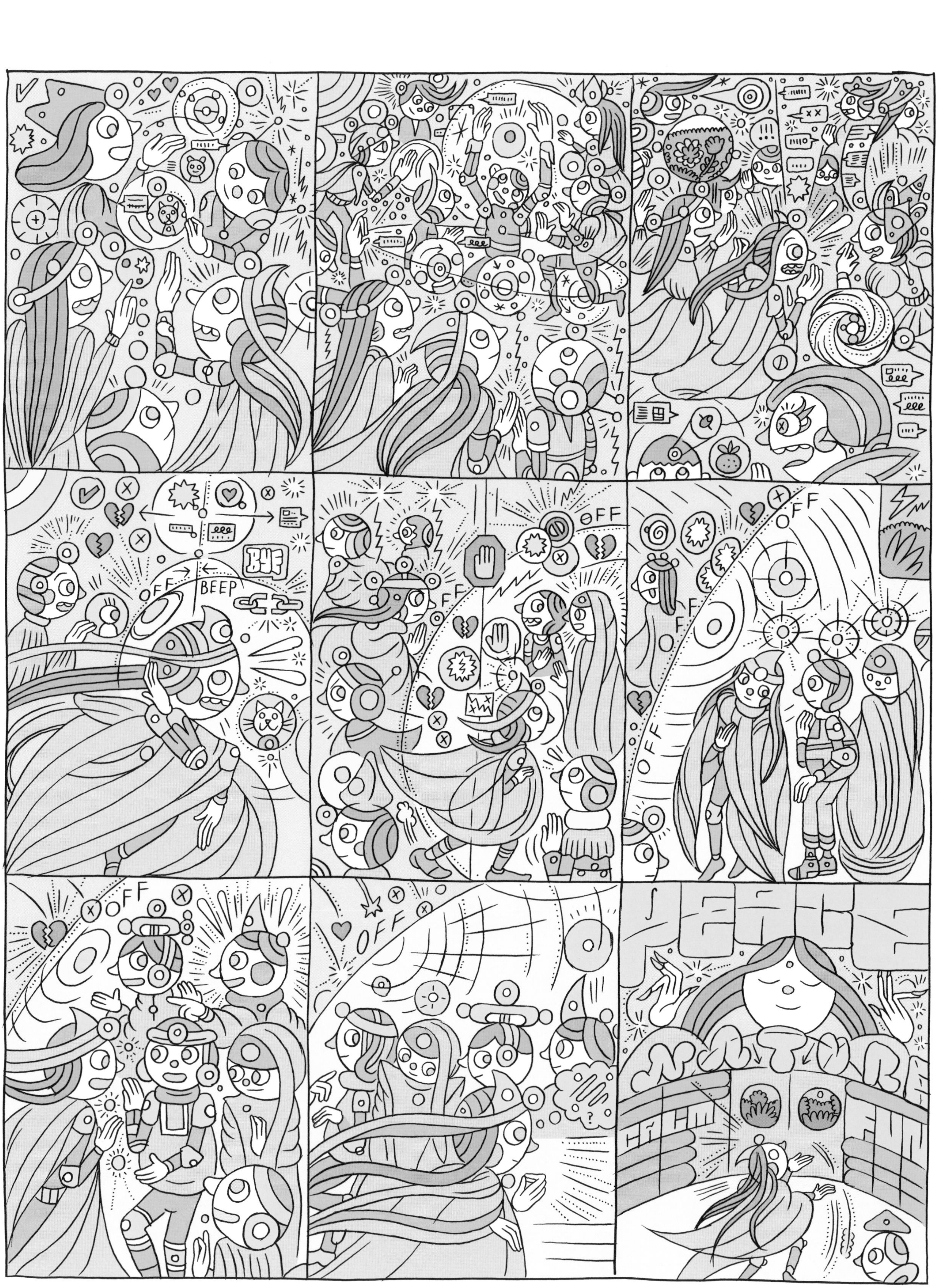
OFF
BEEP
BYE
OFF
OFF
OFF
OFF

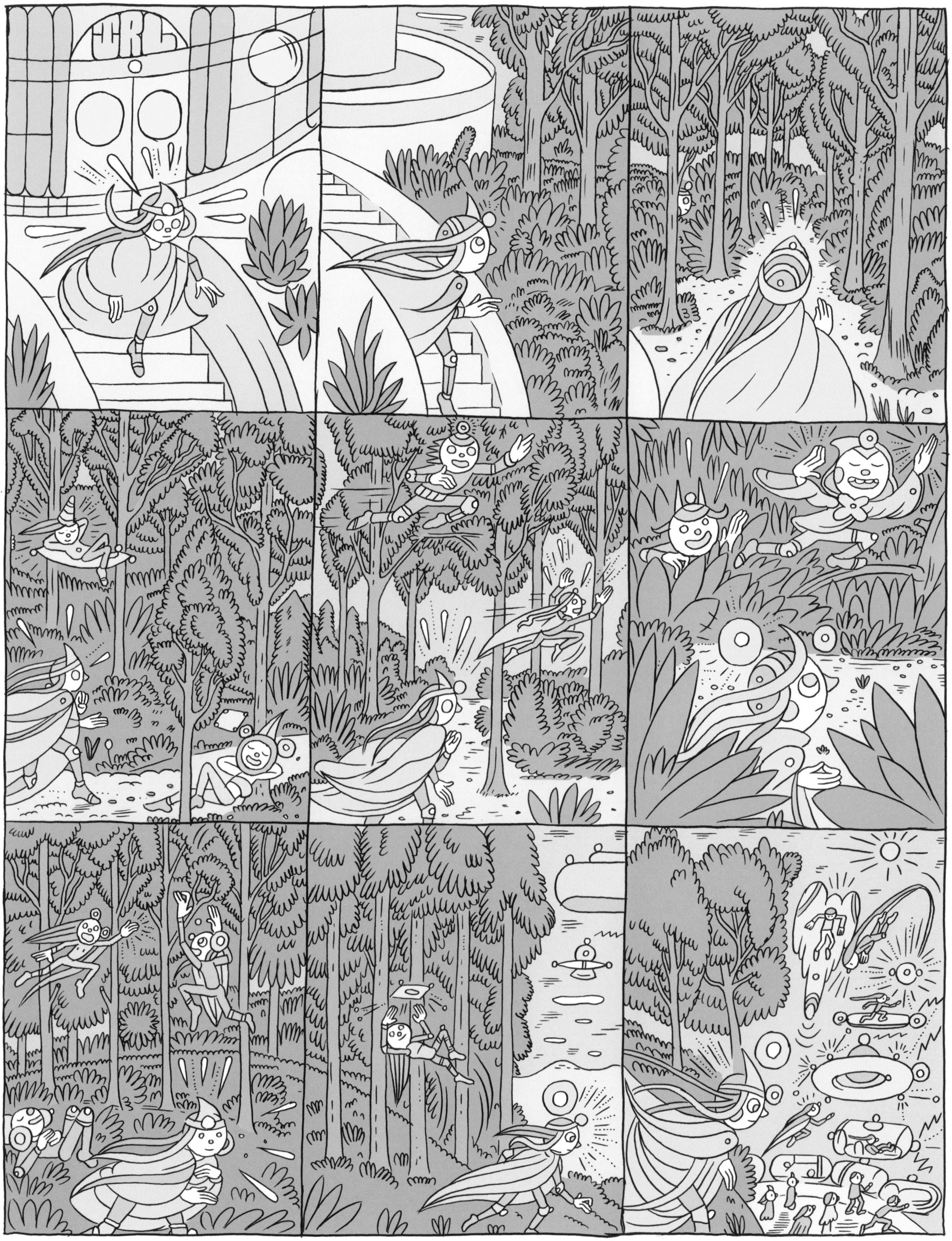

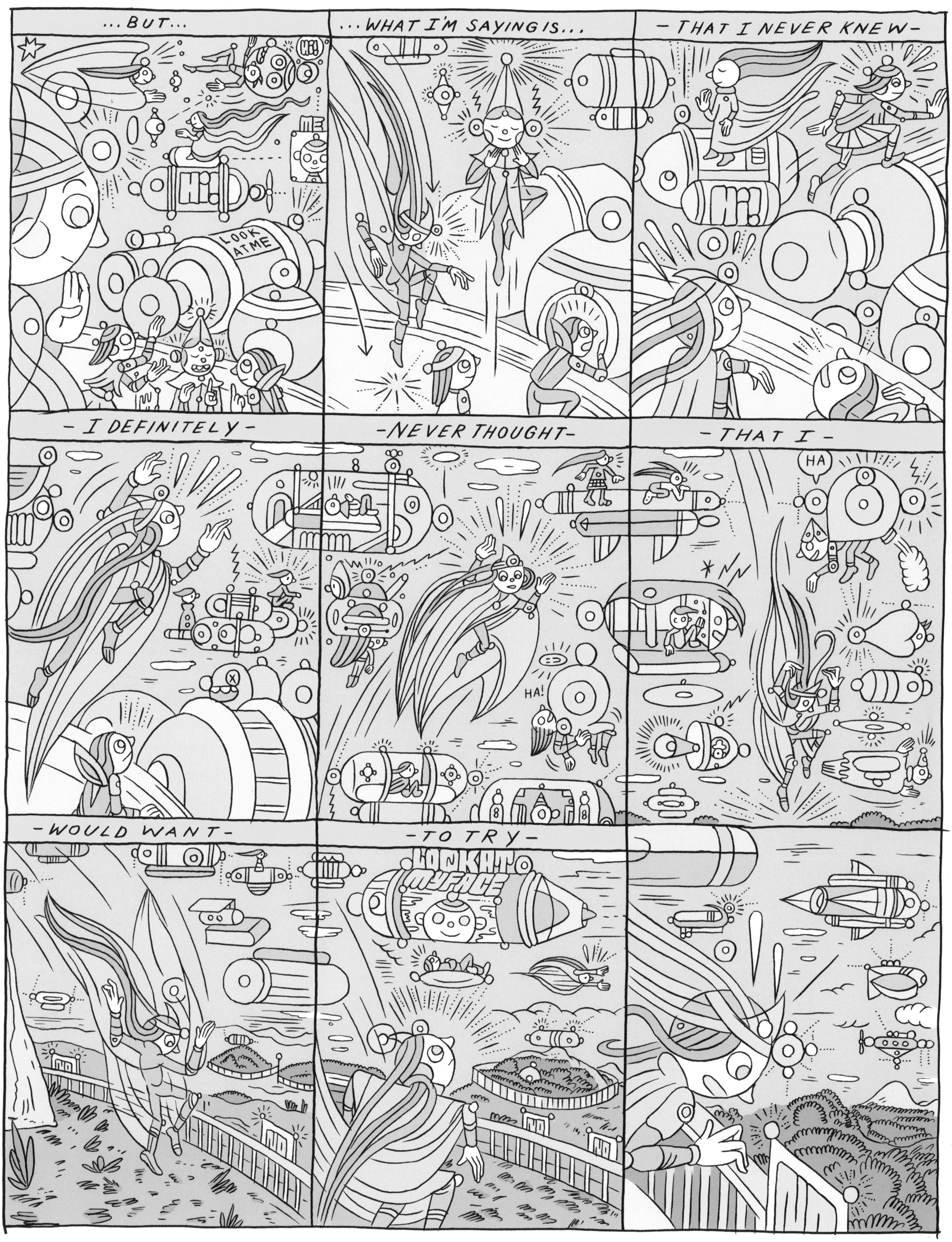
...BUT...
HI!
ME
HI!
LOOK AT ME
...WHAT I'M SAYING IS...
-THAT I NEVER KNEW-
HI!
-I DEFINITELY-
-NEVER THOUGHT-
HA!
-THAT I-
HA
-WOULD WANT-
-TO TRY-
LOOK AT MY FACE

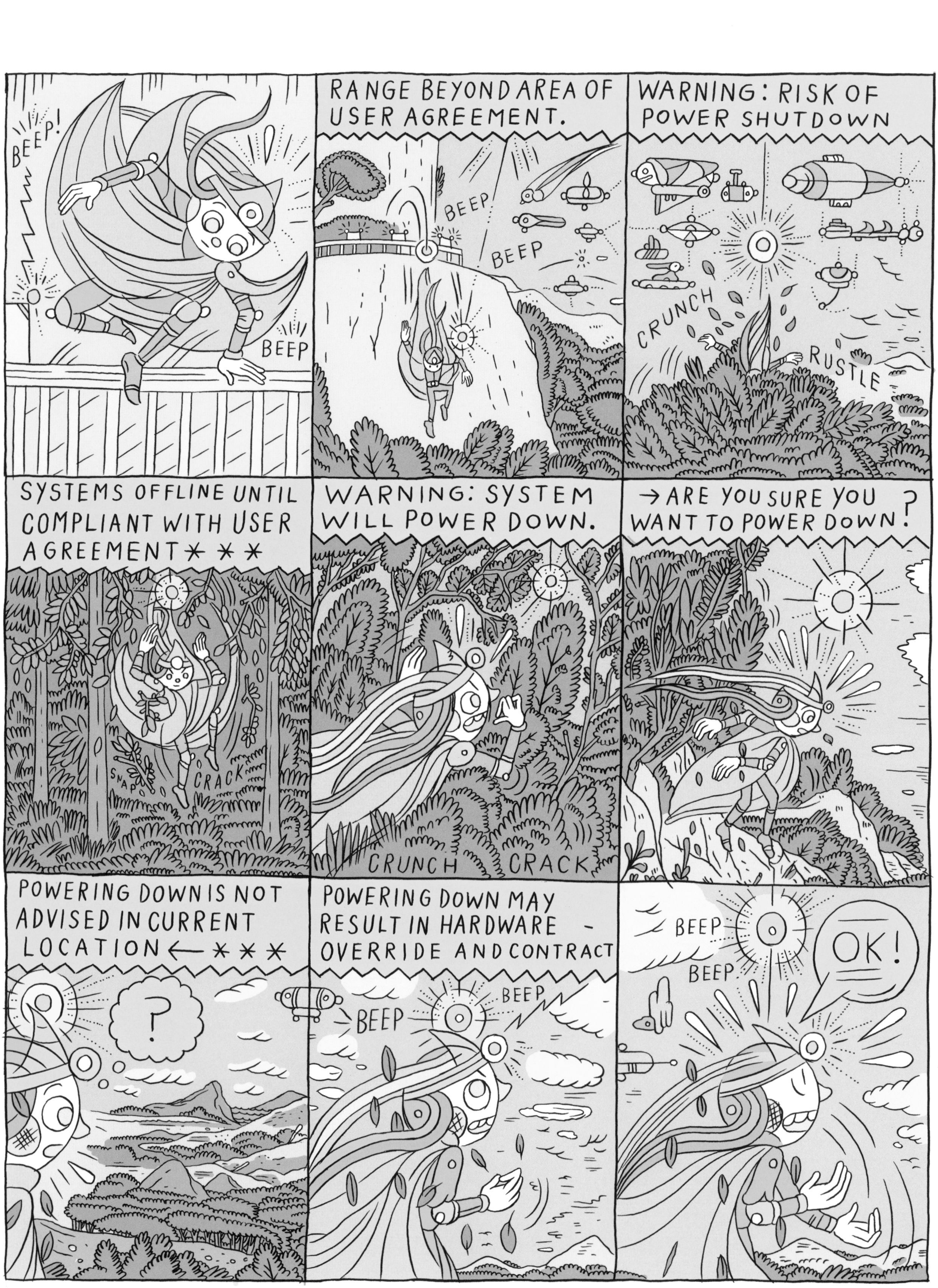
BEEP!
BEEP
RANGE BEYOND AREA OF USER AGREEMENT.
BEEP
BEEP
WARNING: RISK OF POWER SHUTDOWN
CRUNCH
RUSTLE
SYSTEMS OFFLINE UNTIL COMPLIANT WITH USER AGREEMENT * * *
SNAP
CRACK
WARNING: SYSTEM WILL POWER DOWN.
CRUNCH
CRACK
→ ARE YOU SURE YOU WANT TO POWER DOWN?
POWERING DOWN IS NOT ADVISED IN CURRENT LOCATION ← * * *
?
POWERING DOWN MAY RESULT IN HARDWARE - OVERRIDE AND CONTRACT
BEEP
BEEP
BEEP
BEEP
OK!

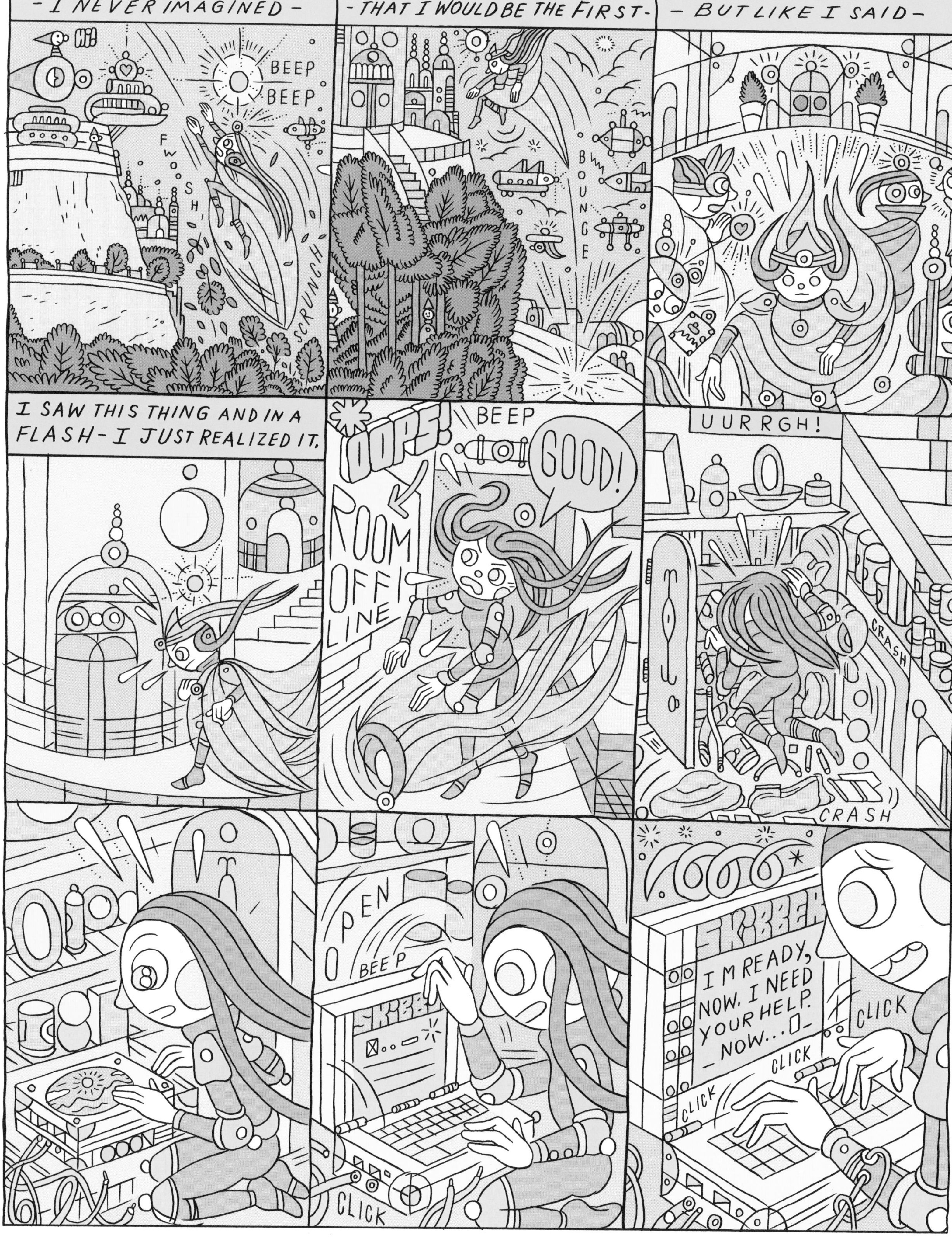
- I NEVER IMAGINED -
HI!
BEEP BEEP
FWOOSH
SCRUNCH
- THAT I WOULD BE THE FIRST -
BOUNCE
- BUT LIKE I SAID -
I SAW THIS THING AND IN A FLASH - I JUST REALIZED IT.
OOPS!
BEEP
GOOD!
ROOM OFFLINE
UURRGH!
CRASH
CRASH
OPEN
BEEP
CLICK
I M READY, NOW. I NEED YOUR HELP. NOW...
CLICK
CLICK
CLICK

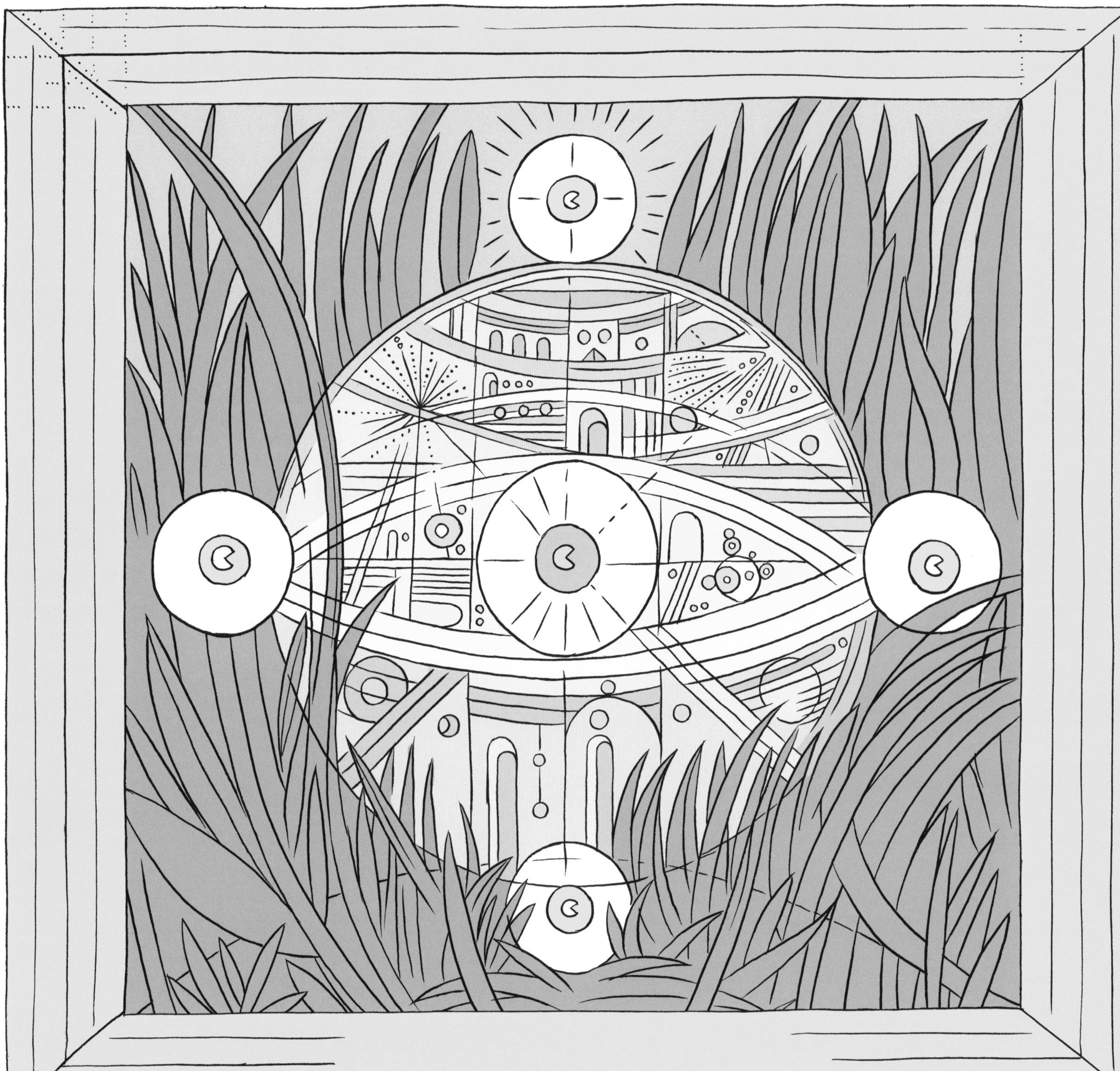

SOMETIME LATER...

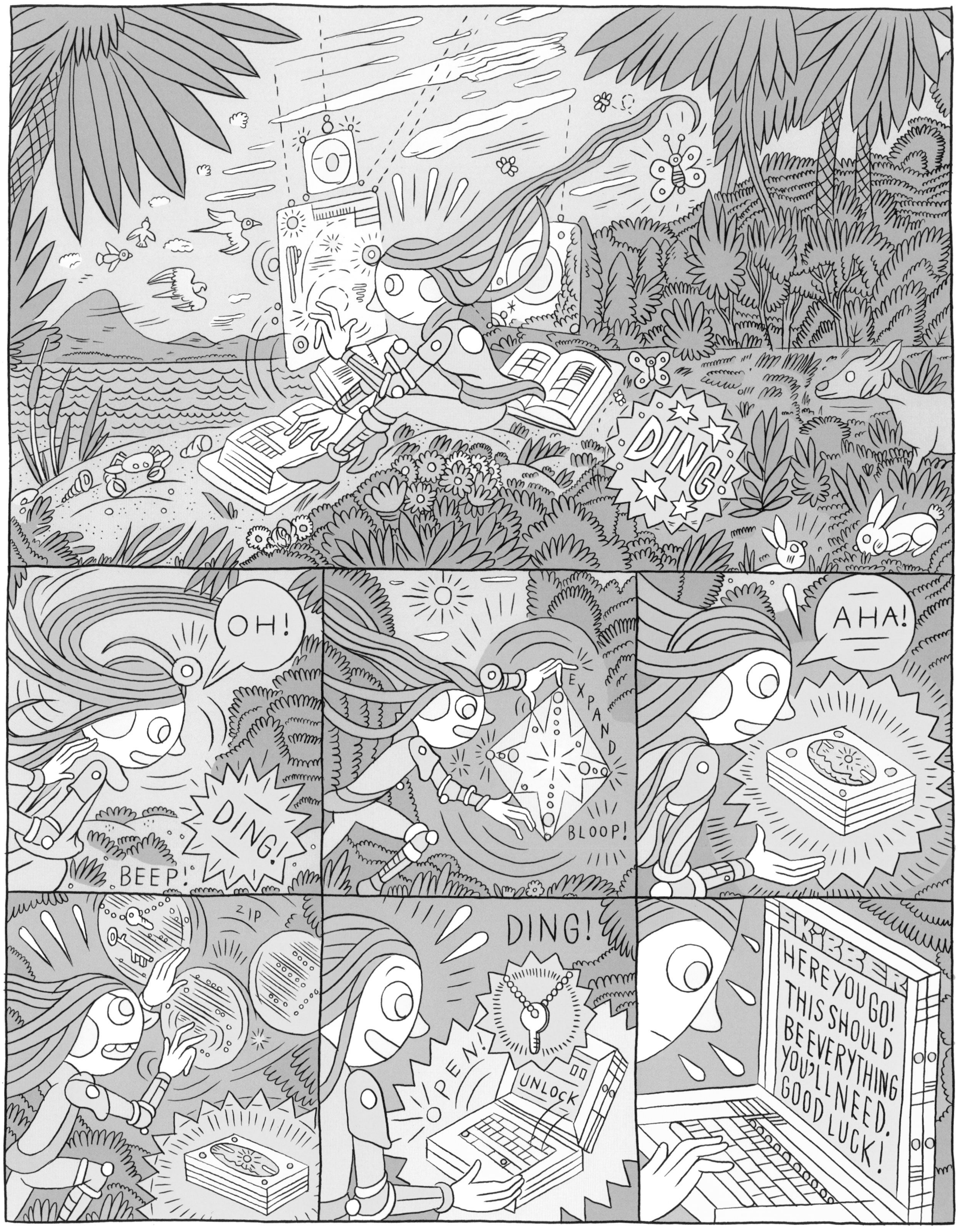
DING!
OH!
DING!
BEEP!
EXPAND
BLOOP!
AHA!
ZIP
DING!
OPEN!
UNLOCK
HERE YOU GO! THIS SHOULD BE EVERYTHING YOU'LL NEED. GOOD LUCK!

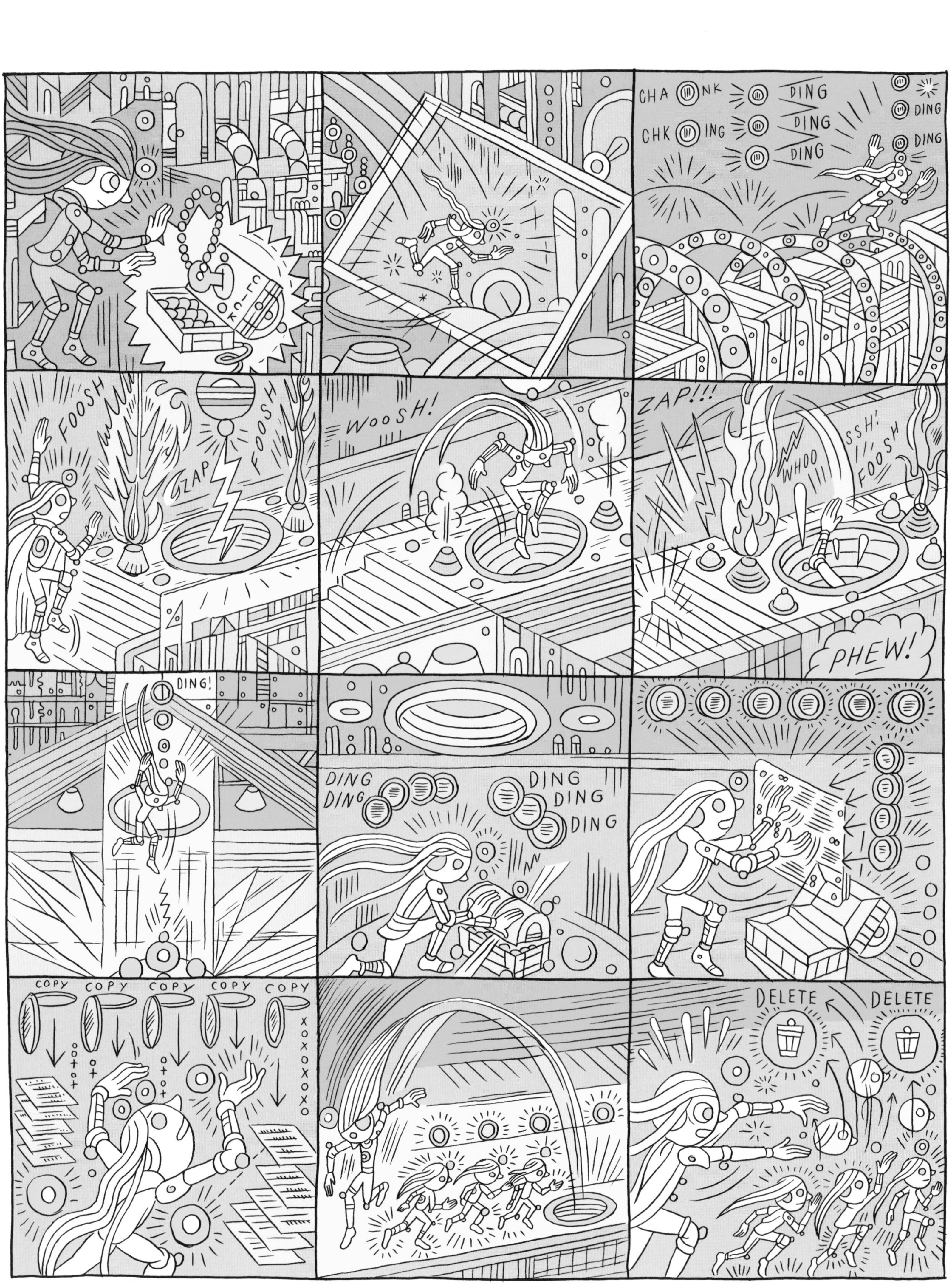
CL-CK
CHA NK
CHK ING
DING
DING
DING
DING
DING
FOOSH
ZAP
FOOSH
WooSH!
ZAP!!!
WHOO
SSH!
FOOSH
PHEW!
DING!
DING DING
DING DING DING
COPY
COPY
COPY
COPY
COPY
DELETE
DELETE

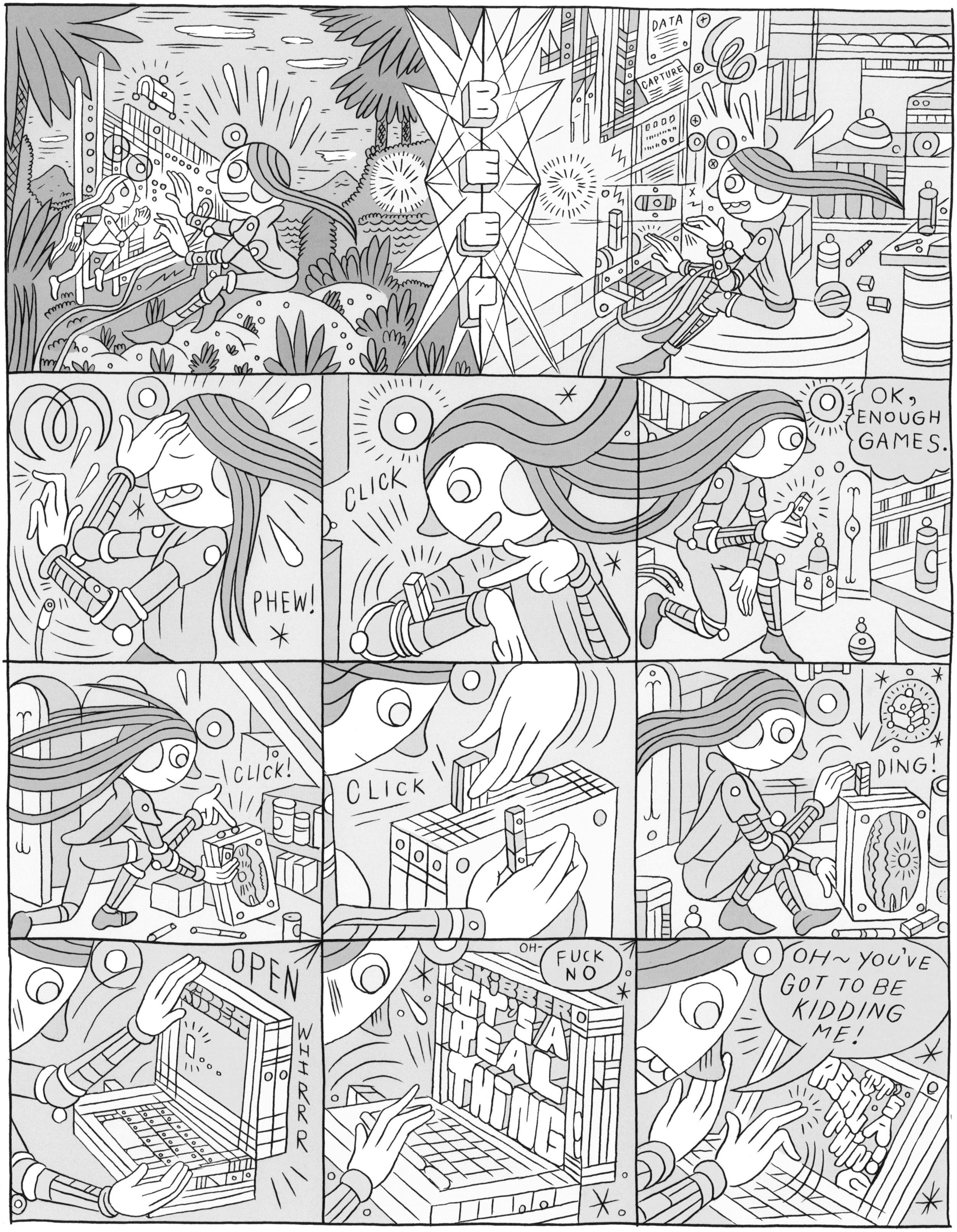

BEEP
DATA
CAPTURE
PHEW!
CLICK
OK, ENOUGH GAMES.
CLICK!
CLICK
DING!
OPEN
WHIRRR
OH-
FUCK NO
IT'S A REAL THING!
OH~ YOU'VE GOT TO BE KIDDING ME!

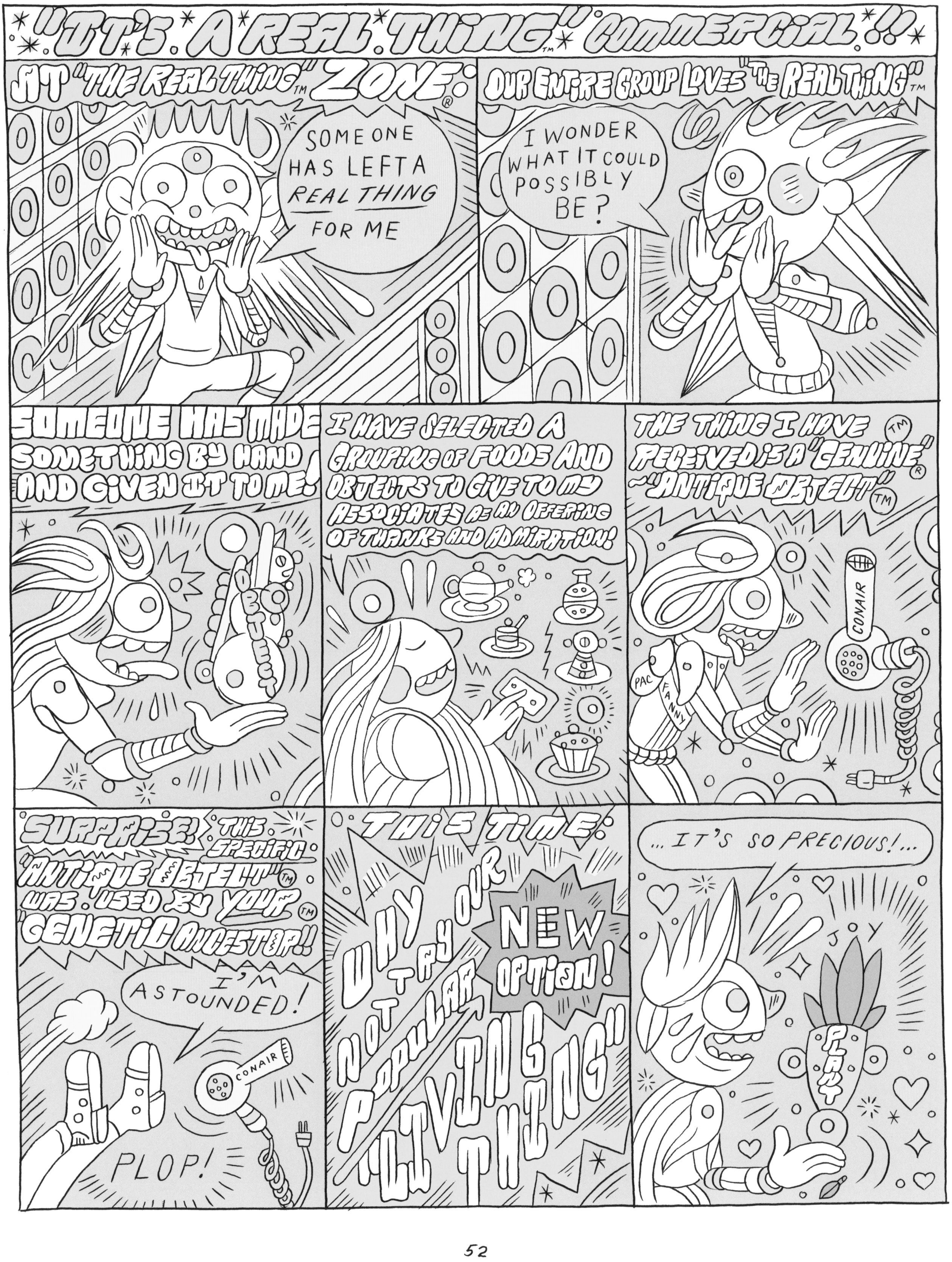
"IT'S A REAL THING"™ COMMERCIAL!!
AT "THE REAL THING"™ ZONE®:
SOME ONE HAS LEFT A REAL THING FOR ME
OUR ENTIRE GROUP LOVES "THE REAL THING"™
I WONDER WHAT IT COULD POSSIBLY BE?
SOMEONE HAS MADE SOMETHING BY HAND AND GIVEN IT TO ME!
OBJECT
I HAVE SELECTED A GROUPING OF FOODS AND OBJECTS TO GIVE TO MY ASSOCIATES AS AN OFFERING OF THANKS AND ADMIRATION!
THE THING I HAVE RECEIVED IS A "GENUINE"® ~"ANTIQUE OBJECT"™
CONAIR
PAC FANNY
SURPRISE! THIS SPECIFIC "ANTIQUE OBJECT"™ WAS USED BY YOUR "GENETIC ANCESTOR"™!!
I'M ASTOUNDED!
CONAIR
PLOP!
THIS TIME: WHY NOT TRY OUR NEW OPTION! POPULAR "LIVING THING"
... IT'S SO PRECIOUS! ...
JOY
PLANT

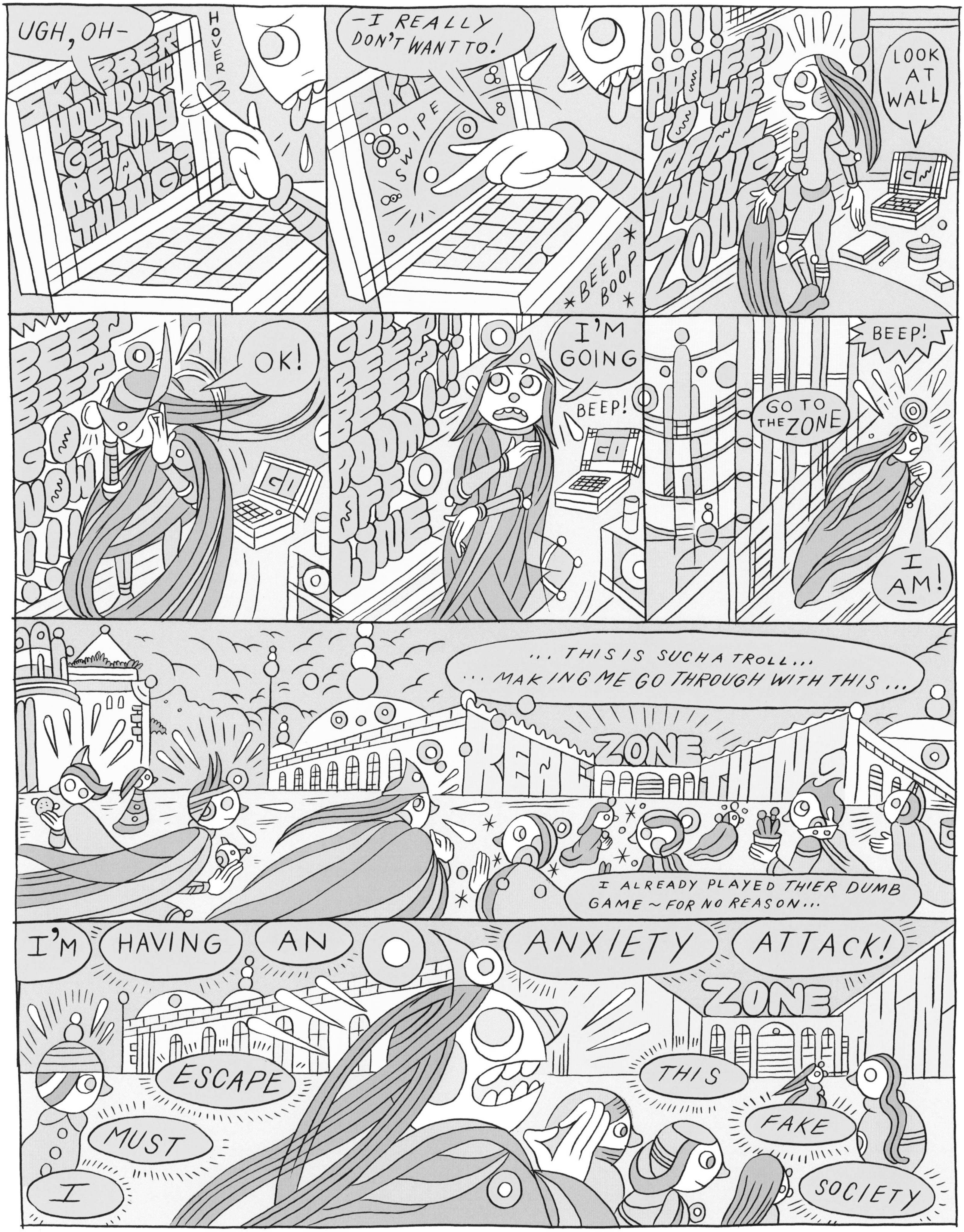
UGH, OH-
HOW DO I GET MY REAL THING?
HOVER
-I REALLY DON'T WANT TO!
SWIPE
BEEP BOOP
!!!
PROCEED TO THE REAL THING ZONE
LOOK AT WALL
OK!
I'M GOING
BEEP!
BEEP!
GO TO THE ZONE
I AM!
...THIS IS SUCH A TROLL...
...MAKING ME GO THROUGH WITH THIS...
ZONE
I ALREADY PLAYED THIER DUMB GAME ~ FOR NO REASON...
I'M HAVING AN ANXIETY ATTACK!
ZONE
I MUST ESCAPE THIS FAKE SOCIETY

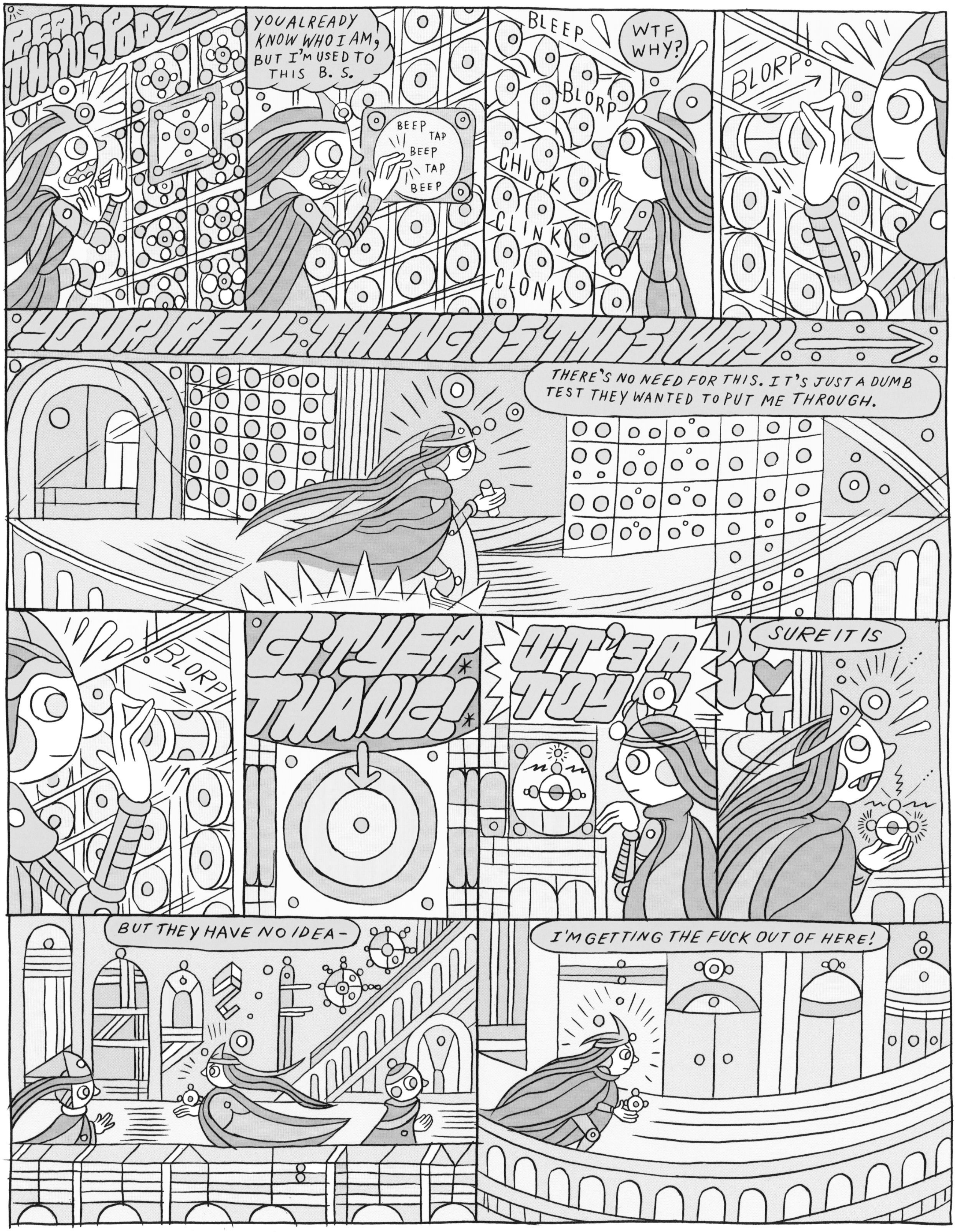
REAL THING PODZ
YOU ALREADY KNOW WHO I AM, BUT I'M USED TO THIS B. S.
BEEP TAP BEEP TAP BEEP
BLEEP
BLORP
CHUCK
CLINK
CLONK
WTF WHY?
BLORP
YOUR REAL THING IS THIS WAY
THERE'S NO NEED FOR THIS. IT'S JUST A DUMB TEST THEY WANTED TO PUT ME THROUGH.
BLORP
GIT YER THANG!
IT'S A TOY!
SURE IT IS
BUT THEY HAVE NO IDEA-
I'M GETTING THE FUCK OUT OF HERE!

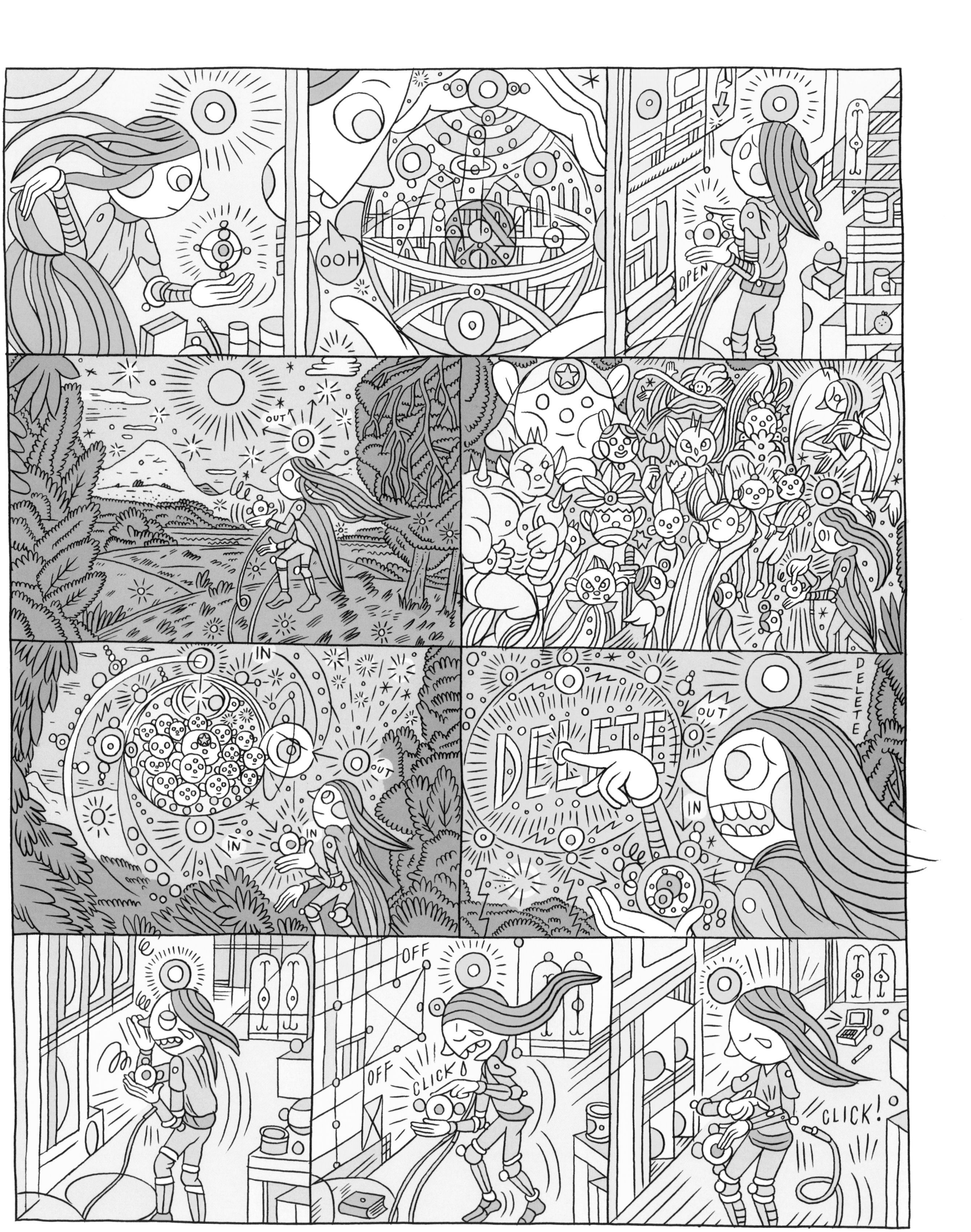
OOH
OPEN
OUT
IN
OUT
IN
IN
DELETE
OUT
DELETE
IN
OFF
OFF
CLICK
CLICK!

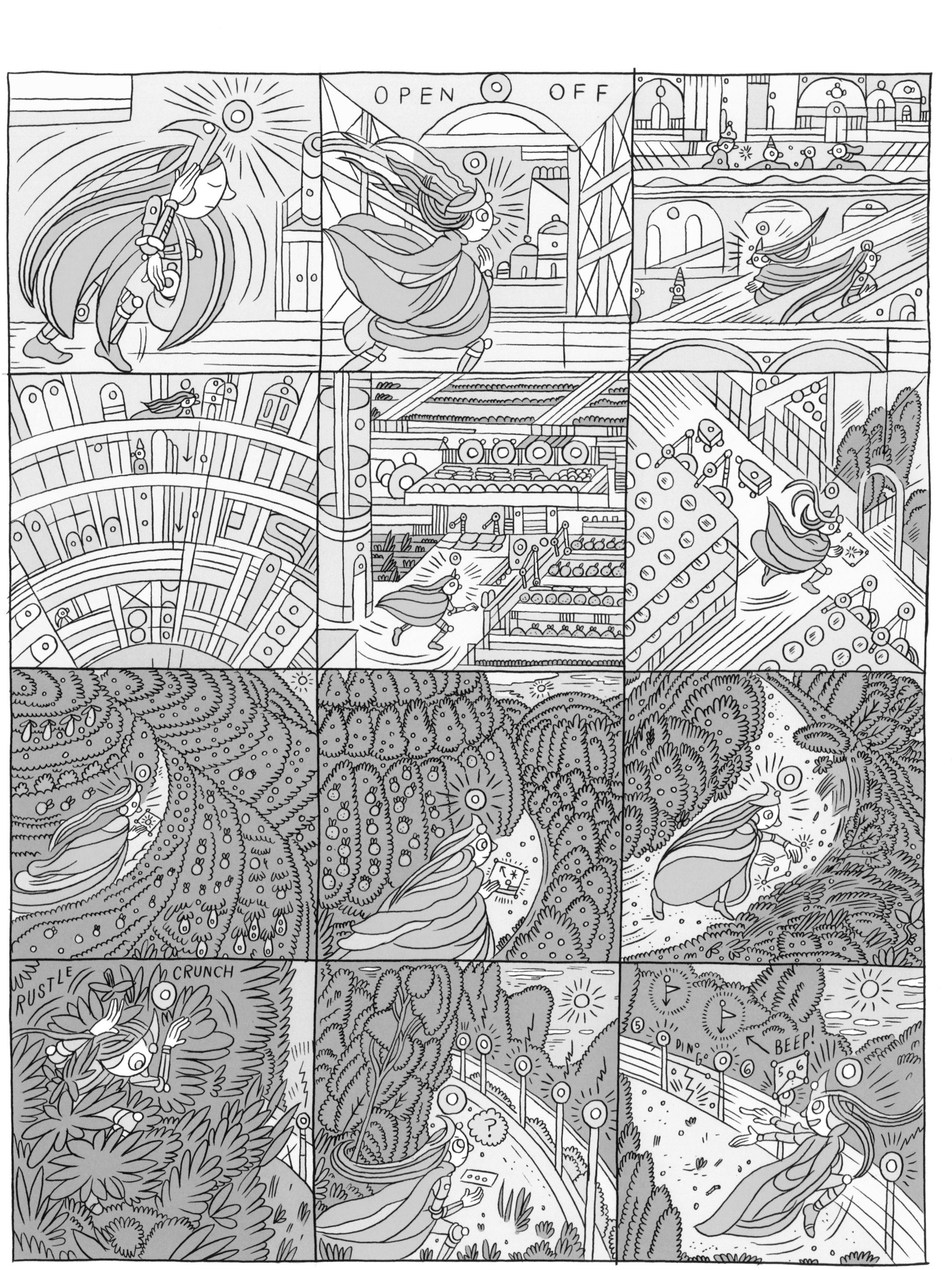
OPEN
OFF
RUSTLE
CRUNCH
DING
BEEP!

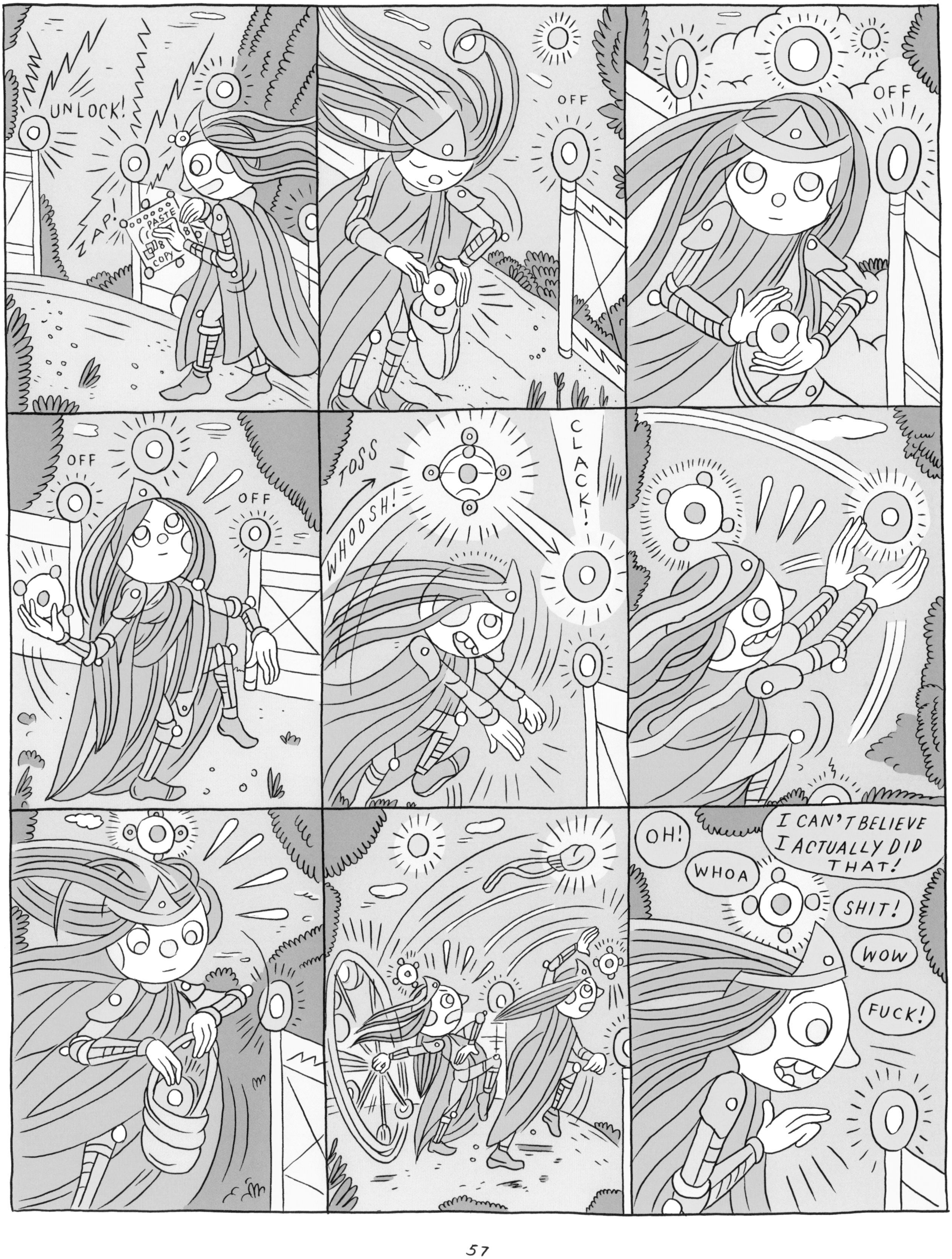
UNLOCK!
ZAP!
PASTE
COPY
OFF
OFF
OFF
OFF
TOSS
WHOOSH!
CLACK!
OH!
I CAN'T BELIEVE I ACTUALLY DID THAT!
WHOA
SHIT!
WOW
FUCK!

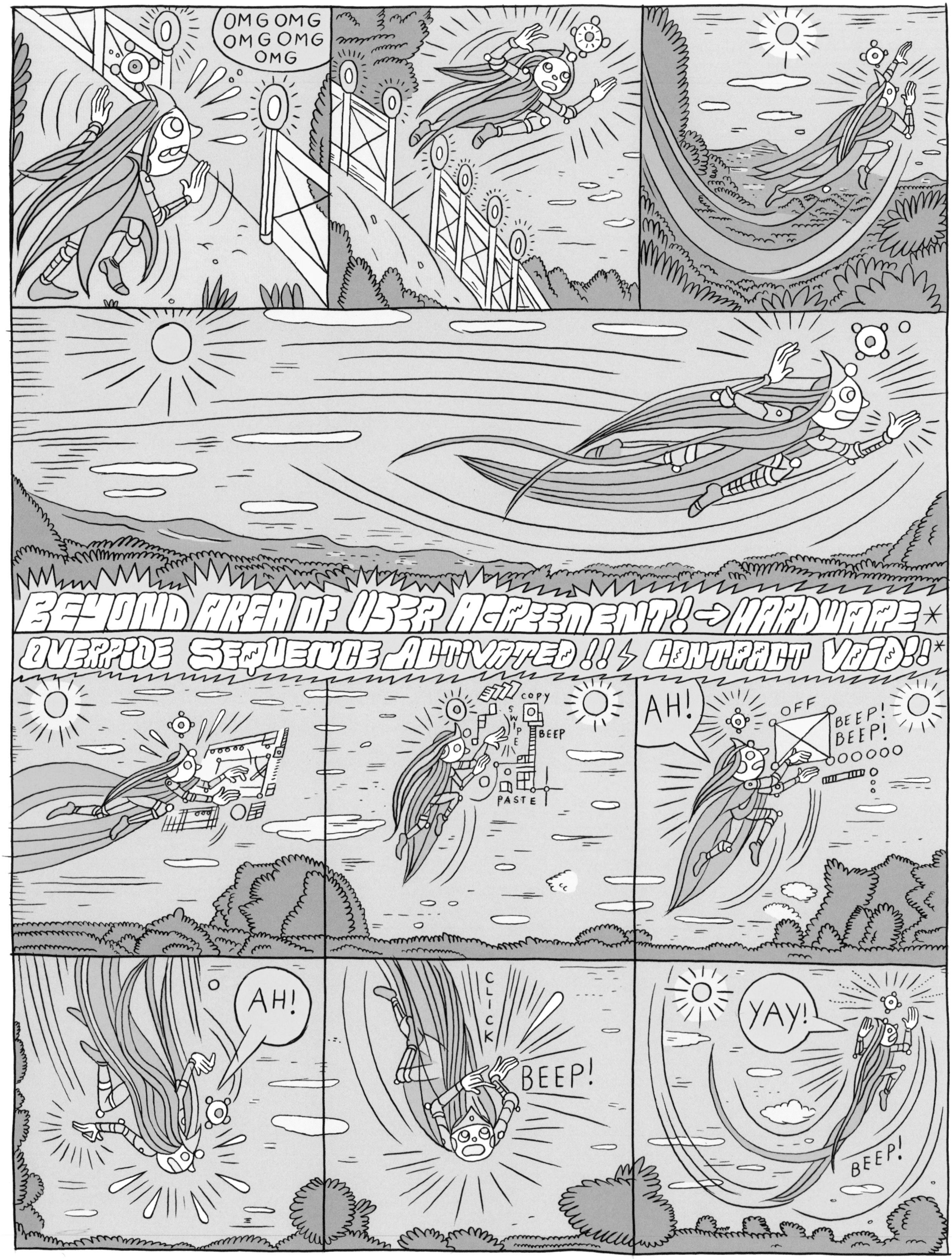
OMGOMG OMGOMG OMG
BEYOND AREA OF USER AGREEMENT! → HARDWARE OVERRIDE SEQUENCE ACTIVATED!! CONTRACT VOID!!
COPY
SWIPE
BEEP
PASTE
AH!
OFF
BEEP! BEEP!
AH!
CLICK
BEEP!
YAY!
BEEP!

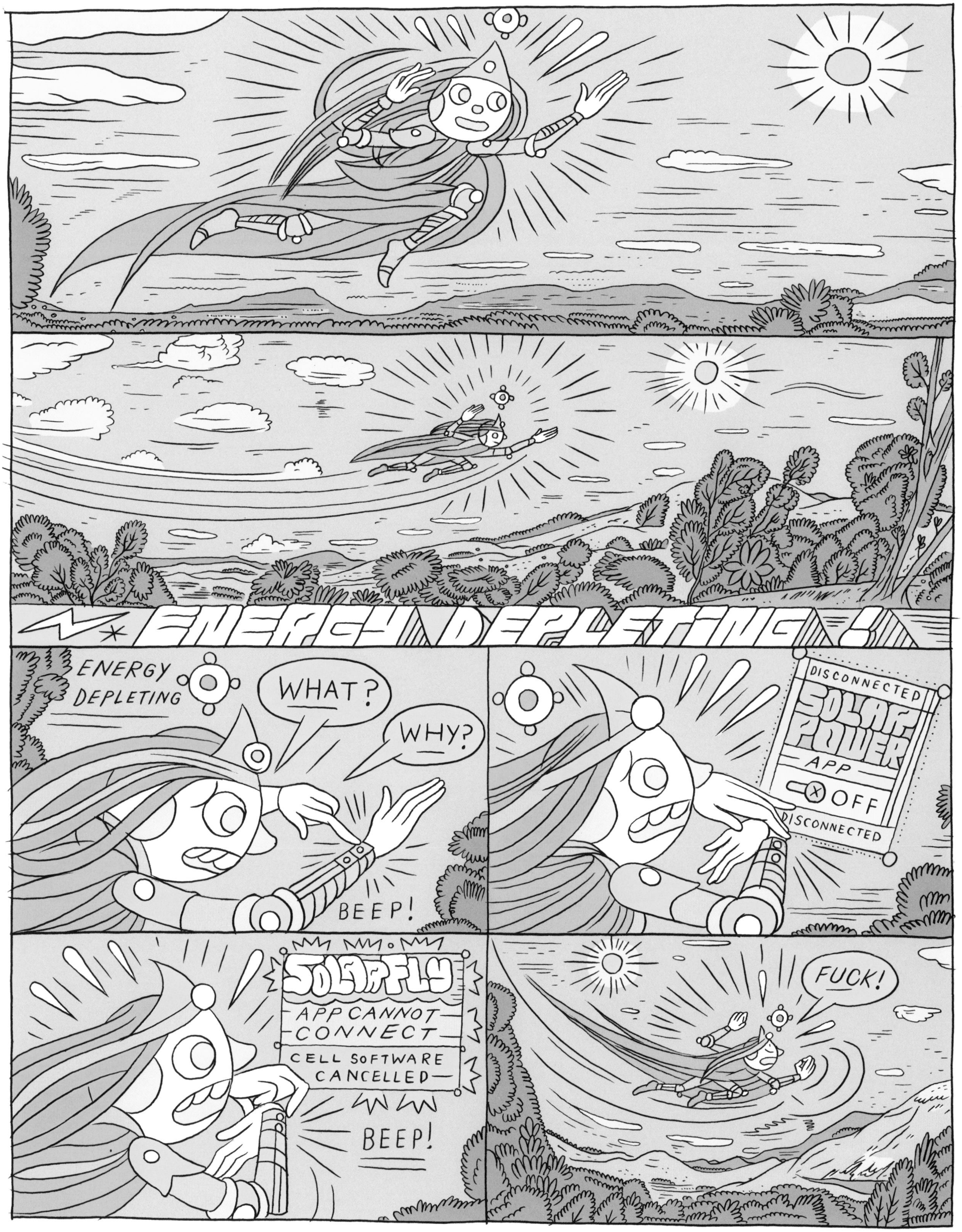
ENERGY DEPLETING!
ENERGY DEPLETING
WHAT?
WHY?
BEEP!
DISCONNECTED
SOLAR POWER
APP
OFF
DISCONNECTED
SOLARFLY
APP CANNOT CONNECT
CELL SOFTWARE CANCELLED
BEEP!
FUCK!

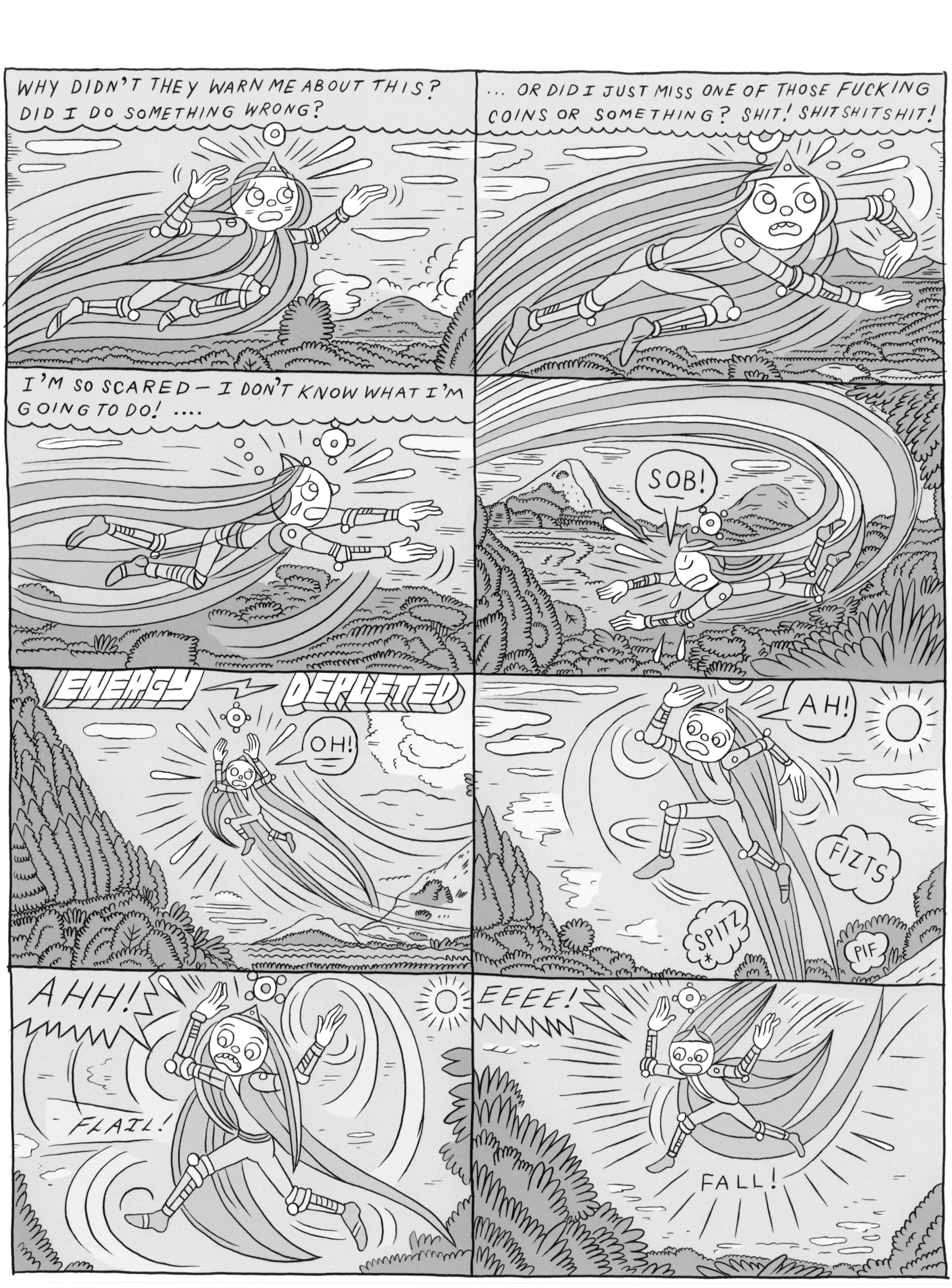
WHY DIDN'T THEY WARN ME ABOUT THIS? DID I DO SOMETHING WRONG?
... OR DID I JUST MISS ONE OF THOSE FUCKING COINS OR SOMETHING? SHIT! SHITSHITSHIT!
I'M SO SCARED — I DON'T KNOW WHAT I'M GOING TO DO! ....
SOB!
ENERGY DEPLETED
OH!
AH!
FIZTS
SPITZ
PIF
AHH!
FLAIL!
EEEE!
FALL!

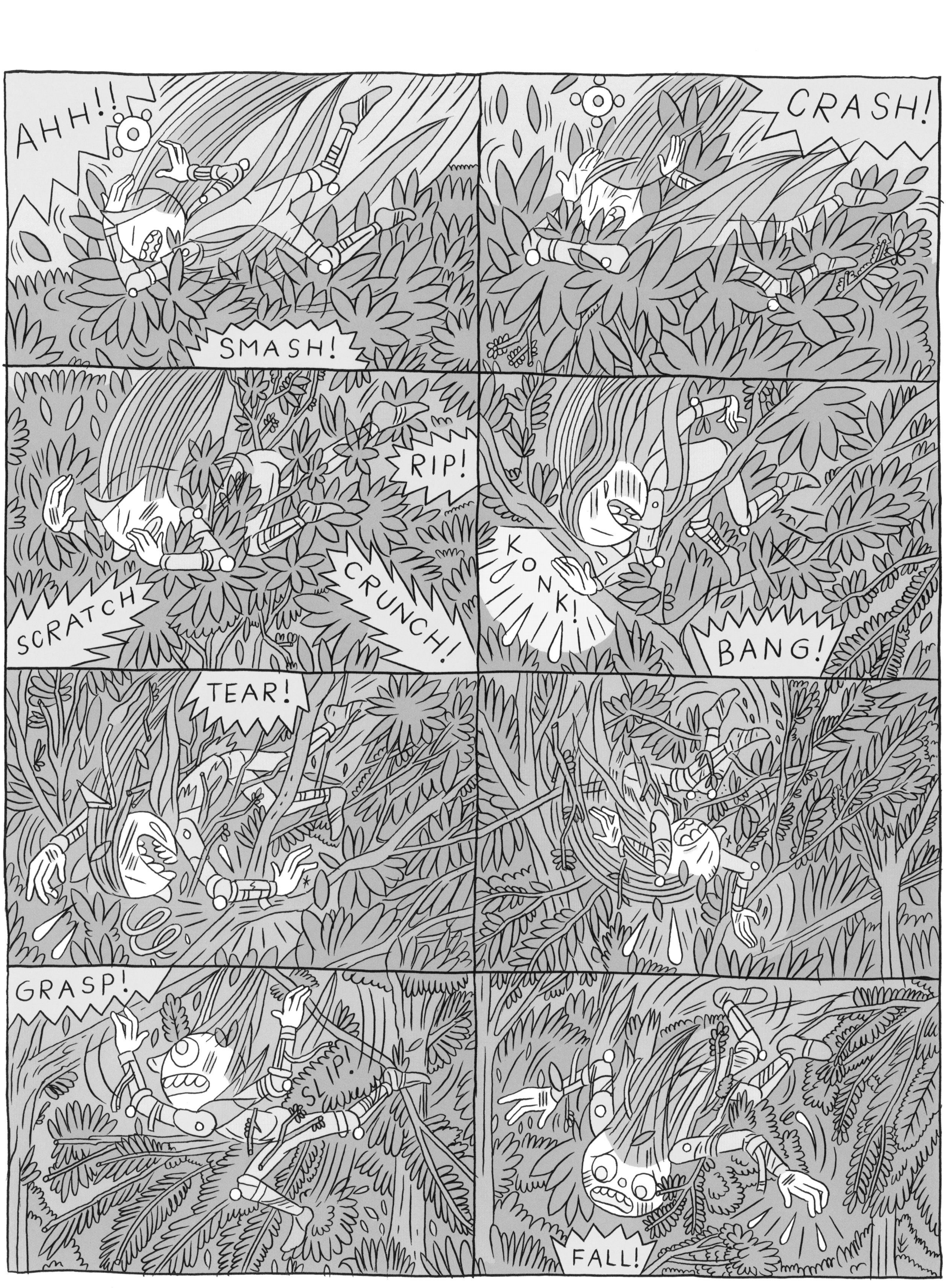
AHH!!
CRASH!
SMASH!
RIP!
SCRATCH
CRUNCH!
KONK!
BANG!
TEAR!
GRASP!
SLIP!
FALL!

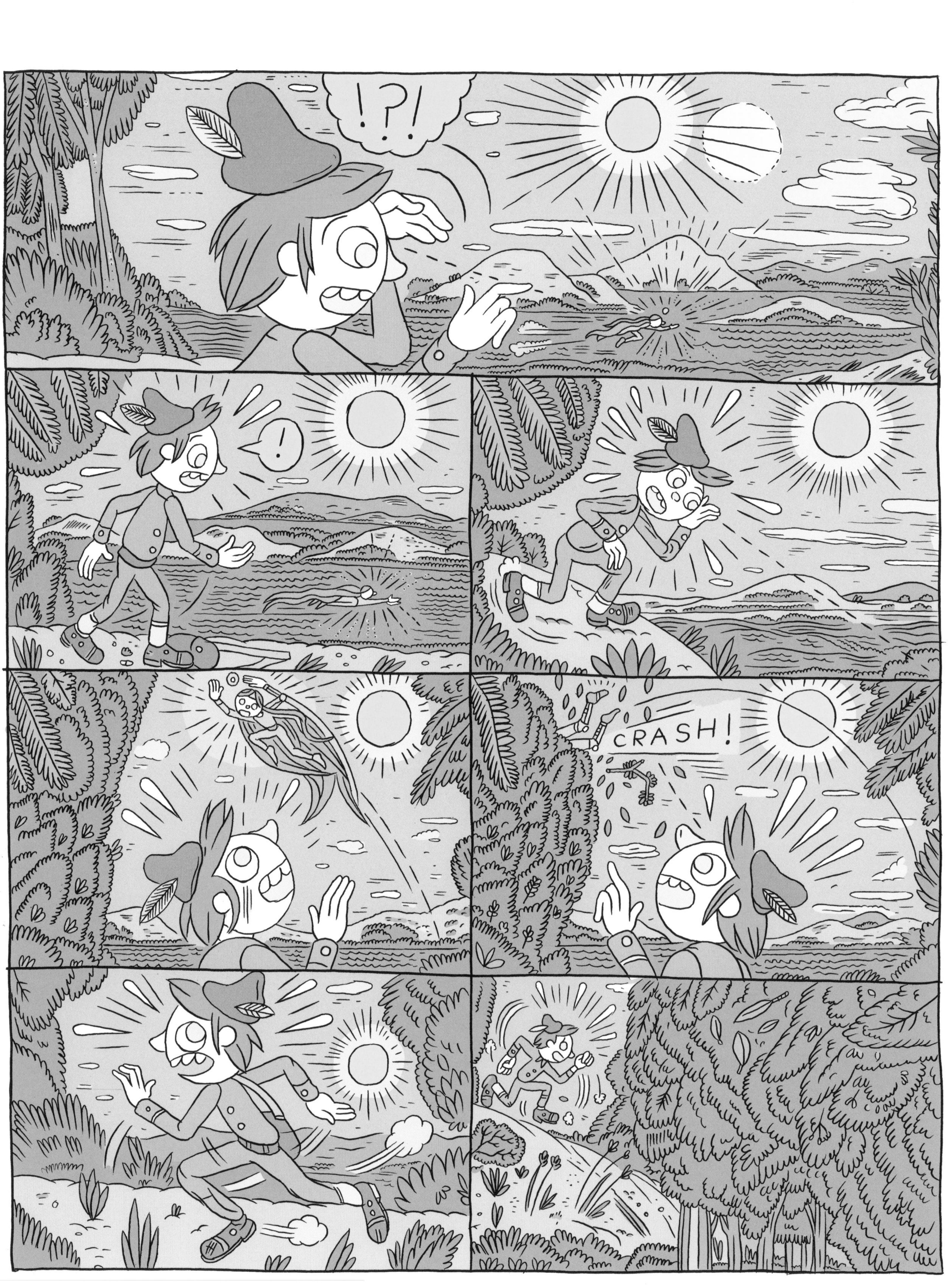
!?!
!
CRASH!

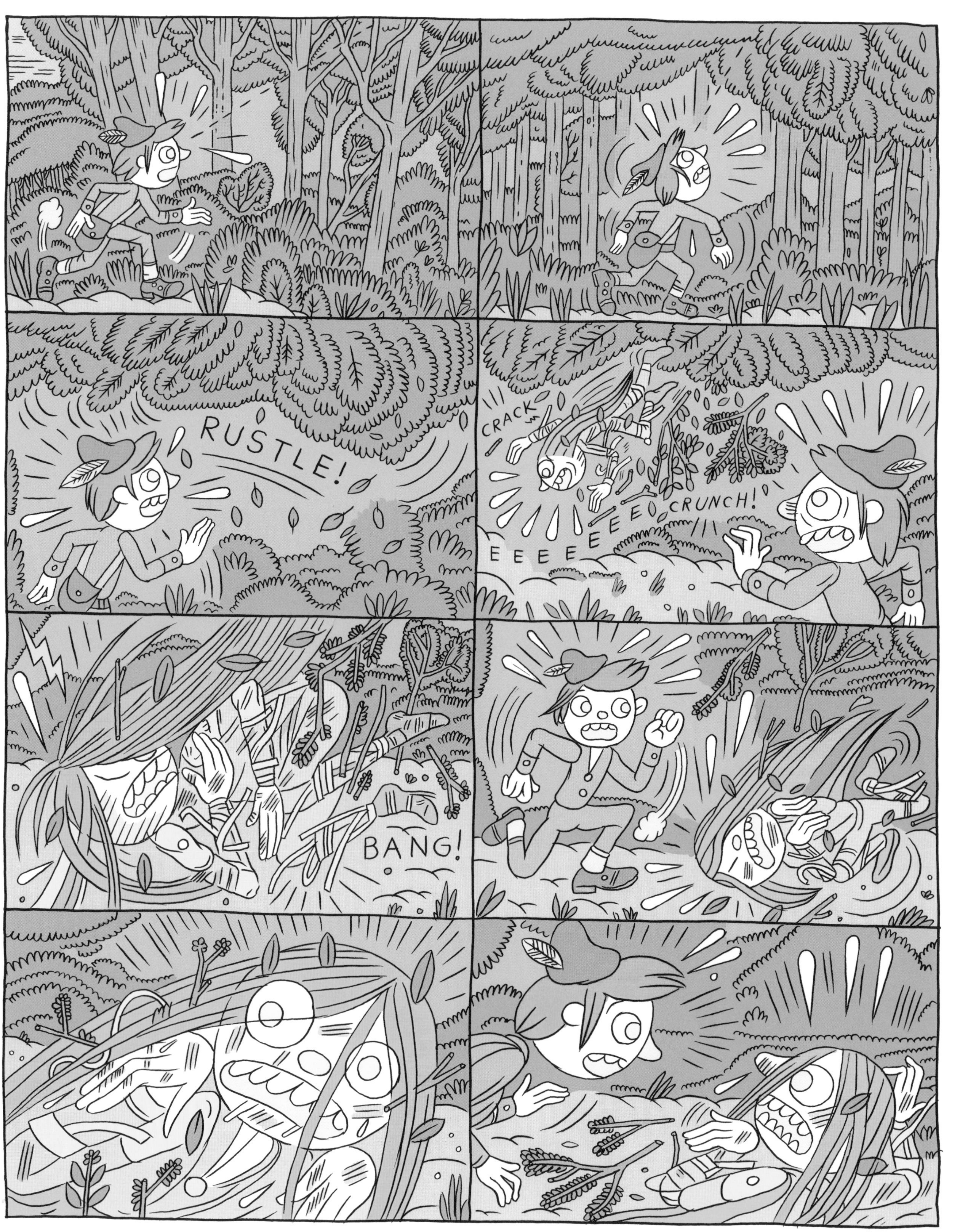
RUSTLE!
CRACK
CRUNCH!
EEEEEEEEE
BANG!

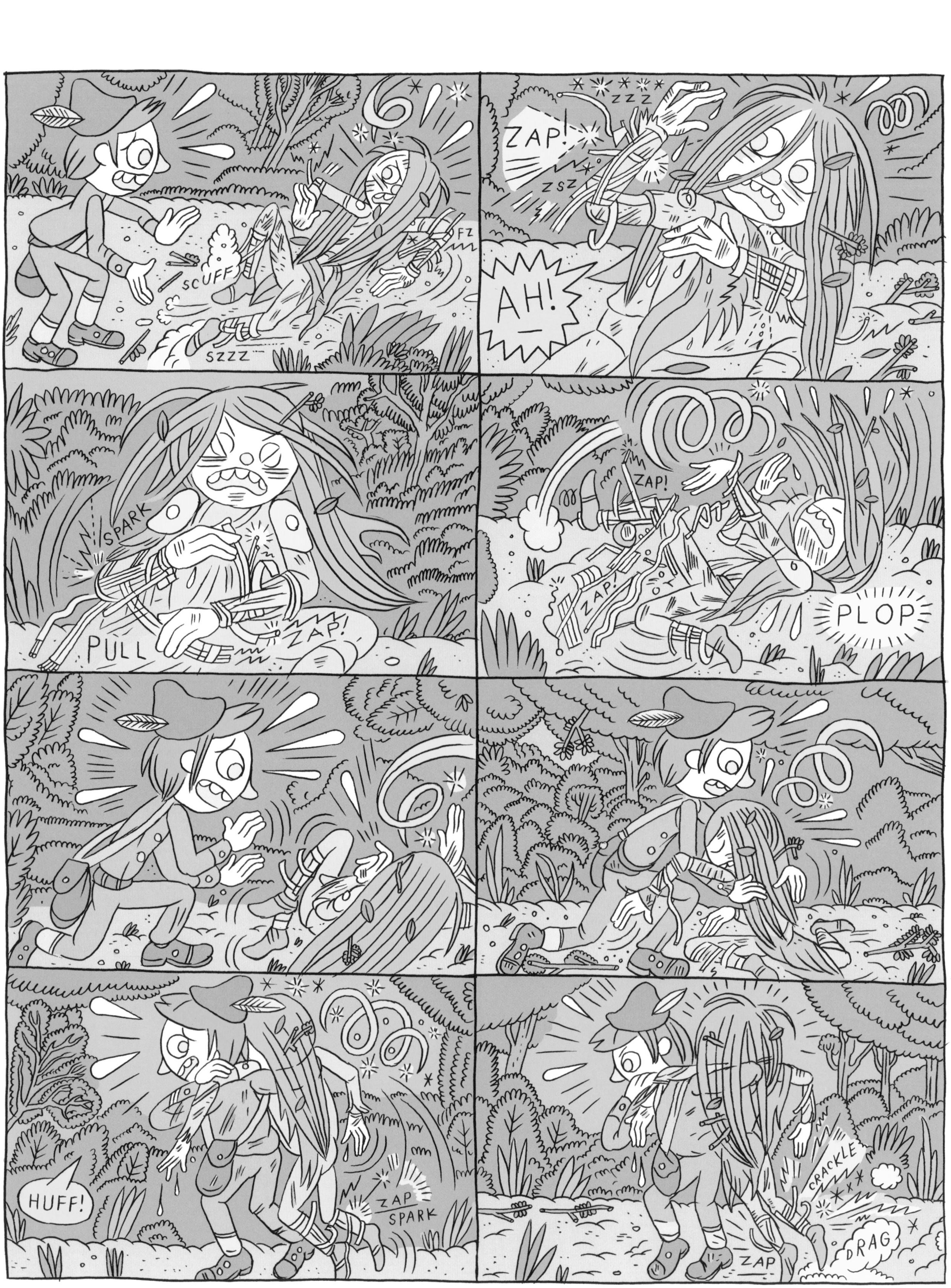
SCUFF
FZ
SZZZ
ZZZ
ZAP!
ZSZ
AH!
SPARK
PULL
ZAP!
ZAP!
ZAP!
PLOP
HUFF!
ZAP
SPARK
CRACKLE
ZAP
DRAG

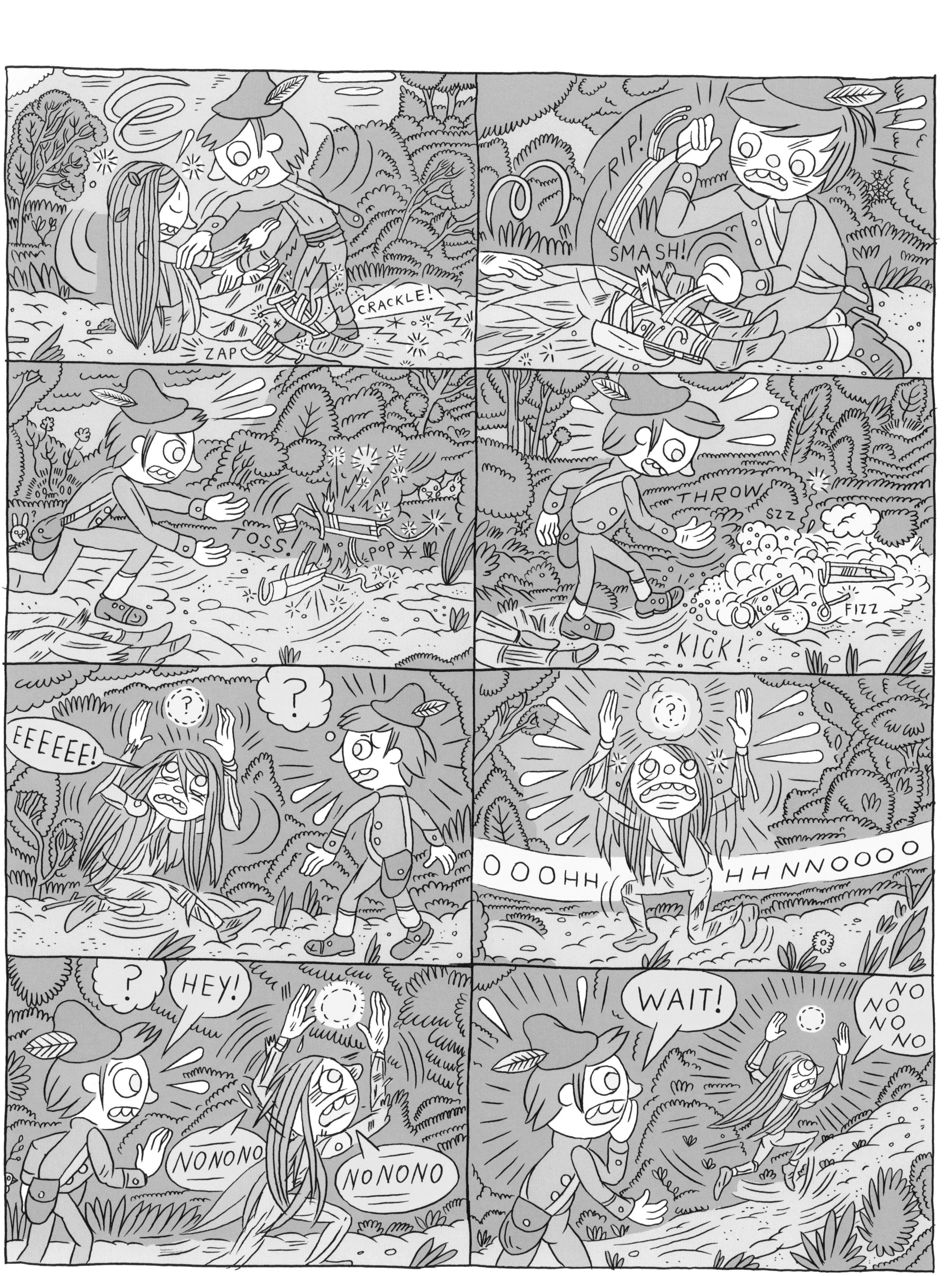
CRACKLE!
ZAP
RIP!
SMASH!
TOSS!
POP
THROW
SZZ
FIZZ
KICK!
EEEEEE!
?
?
OOOHH HHNNOOOO
?
HEY!
NONONO
NONONO
WAIT!
NO NO NO NO

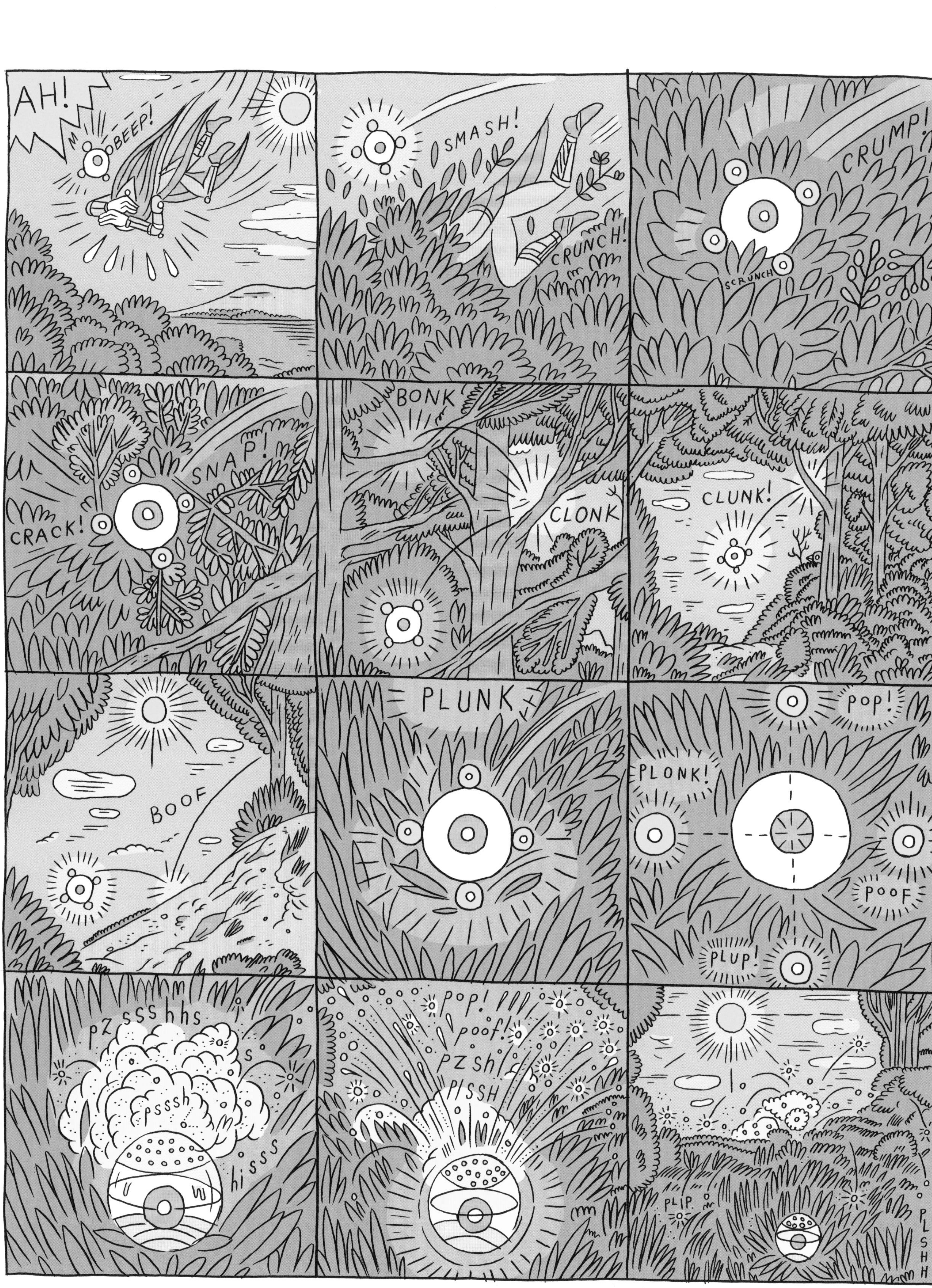
AH!
BEEP!
SMASH!
CRUNCH!
CRUMP!
SCRUNCH
CRACK!
SNAP!
BONK
CLONK
CLUNK!
BOOF
PLUNK
PLONK!
POP!
POOF
PLUP!
PZSSShhS
S
PSSSh
hiSSS
POP!
POOF!
PZSh!
PISSH
PLIP
PLSHH

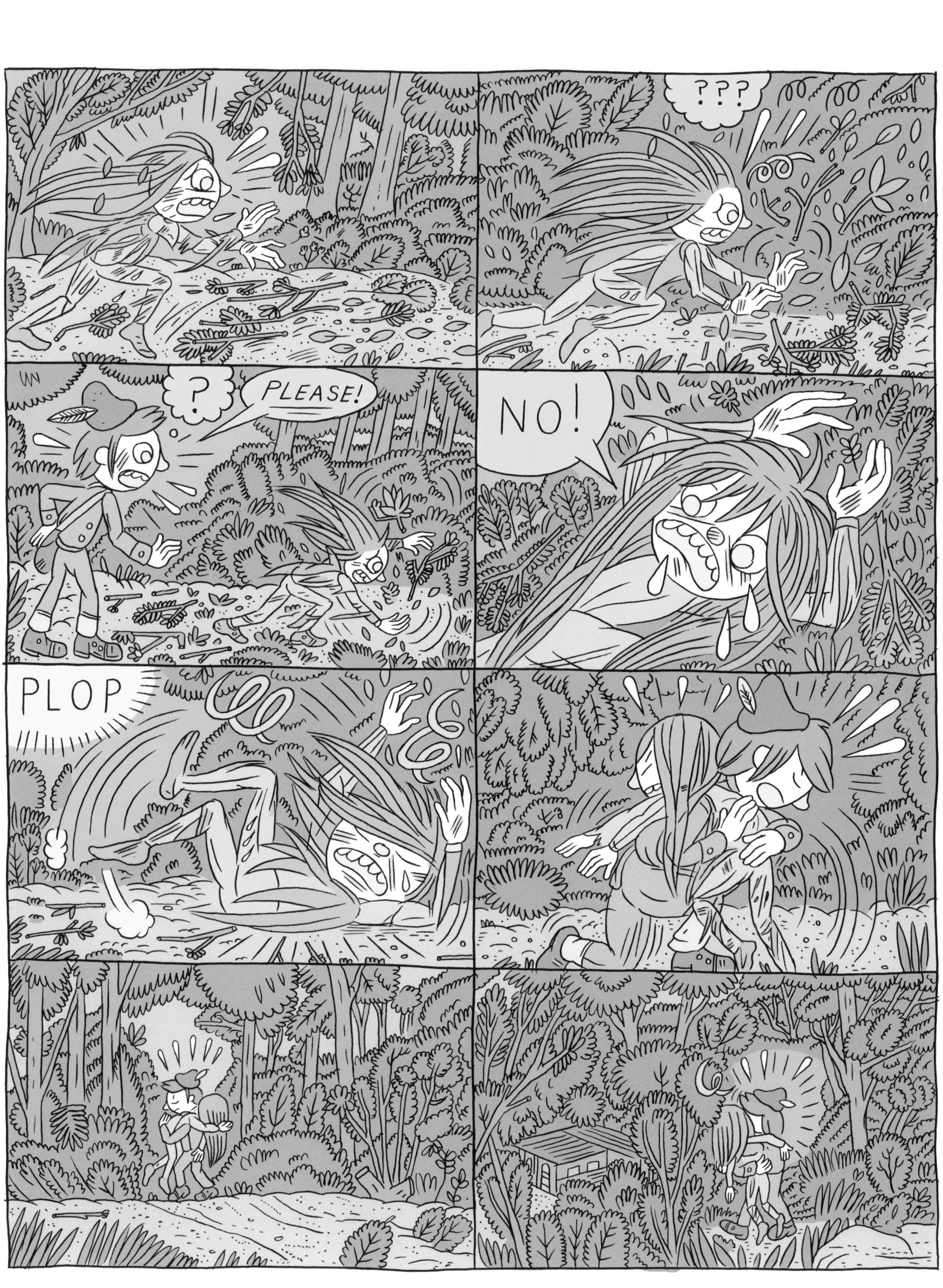
???
?
PLEASE!
NO!
PLOP

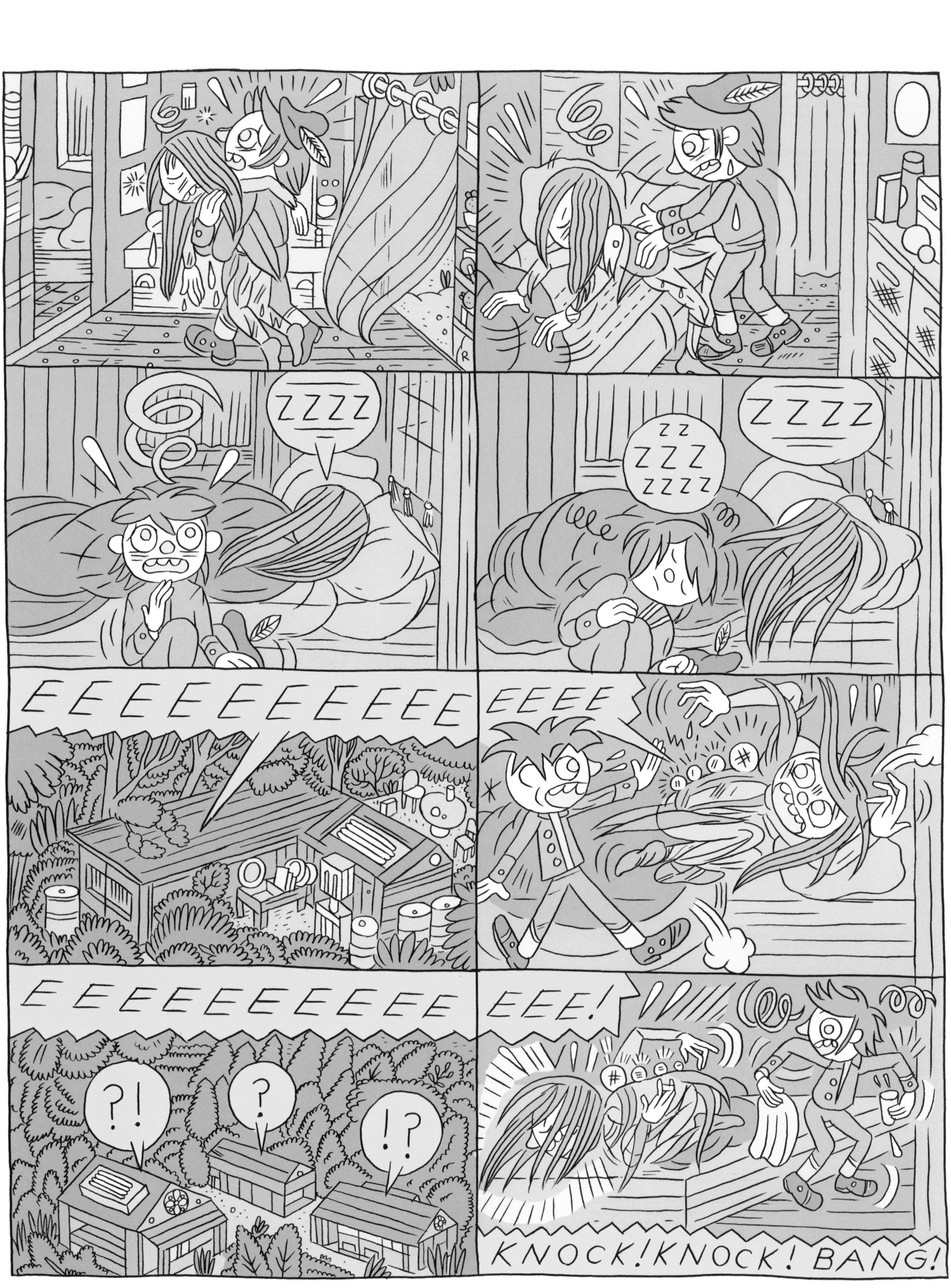
ZZZZ
ZZ
ZZZ
ZZZZ
ZZZZ
EEEEEEEEEE
EEEE
EEEEEEEEEE
?!
?
!?
EEE!
KNOCK! KNOCK! BANG!

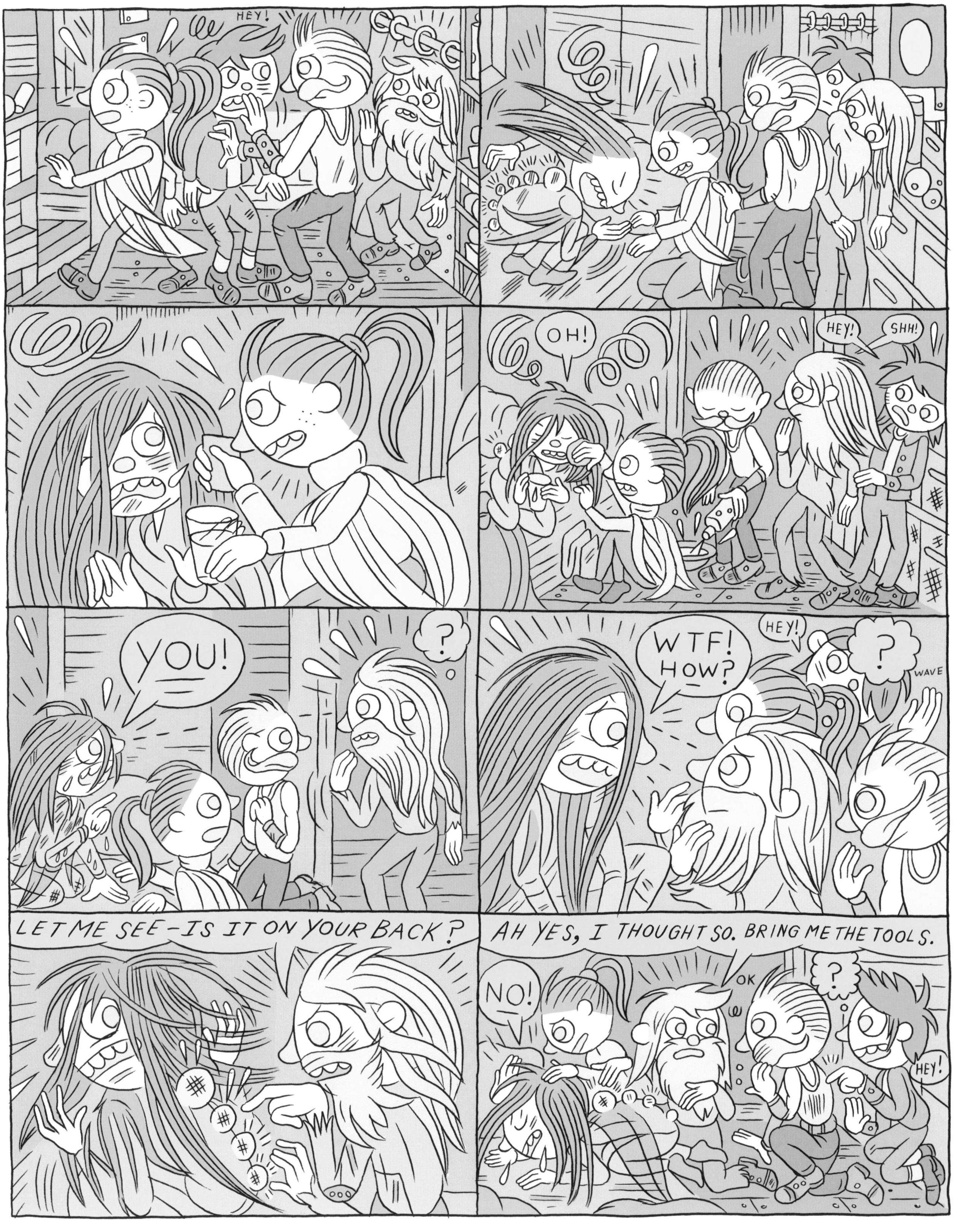
HEY!
OH!
HEY!
SHH!
YOU!
?
WTF! HOW?
HEY!
?
WAVE
LET ME SEE-IS IT ON YOUR BACK?
AH YES, I THOUGHT SO. BRING ME THE TOOLS.
NO!
OK
?
HEY!

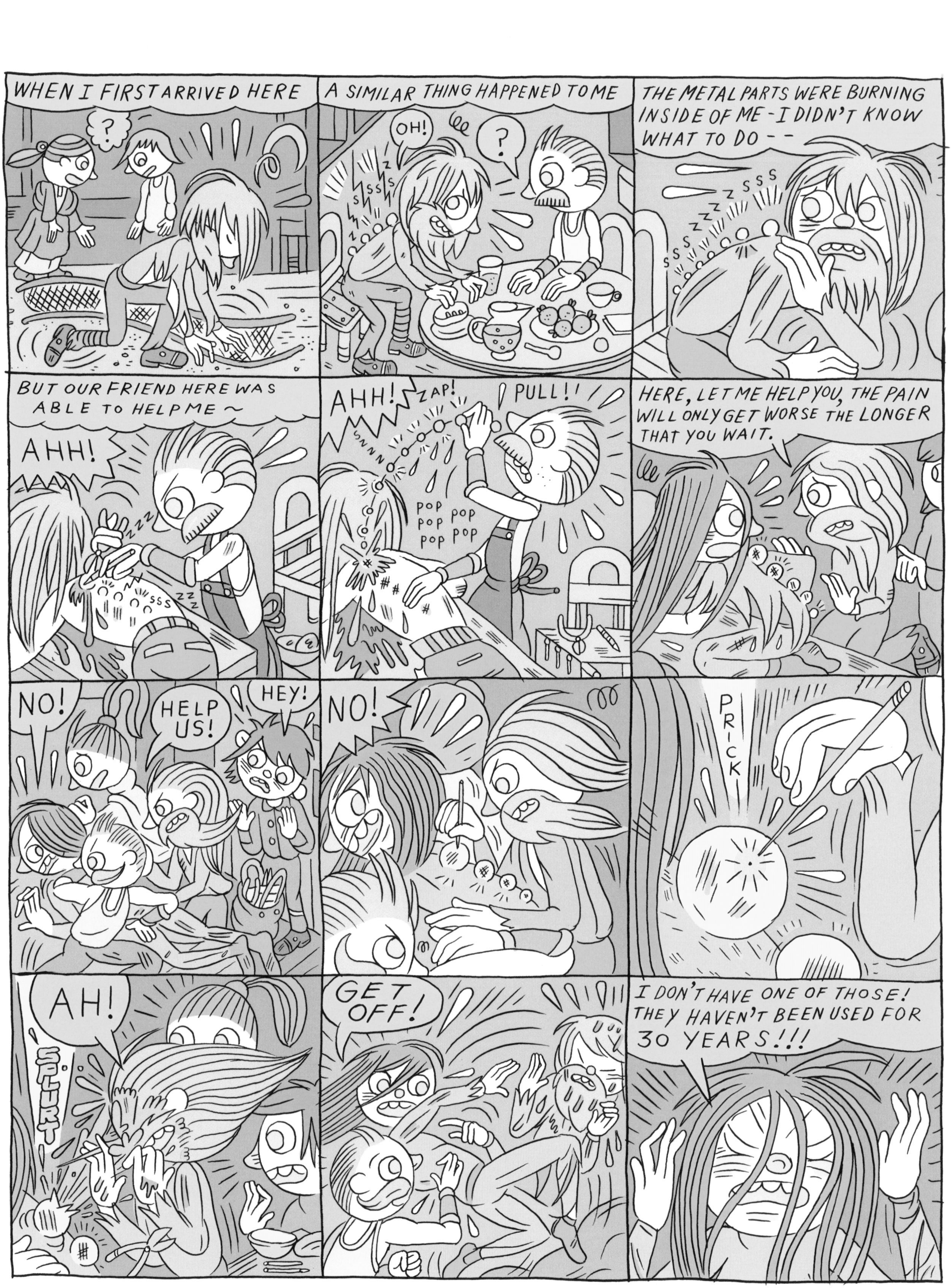
WHEN I FIRST ARRIVED HERE
?
A SIMILAR THING HAPPENED TO ME
OH!
?
THE METAL PARTS WERE BURNING INSIDE OF ME - I DIDN'T KNOW WHAT TO DO - -
BUT OUR FRIEND HERE WAS ABLE TO HELP ME ~
AHH!
AHH!
ZAP!
PULL!!
POP POP POP POP POP POP
HERE, LET ME HELP YOU, THE PAIN WILL ONLY GET WORSE THE LONGER THAT YOU WAIT.
NO!
HELP US!
HEY!
NO!
PRICK
AH!
SPLURT
GET OFF!
I DON'T HAVE ONE OF THOSE! THEY HAVEN'T BEEN USED FOR 30 YEARS!!!

LATER THAT NIGHT—

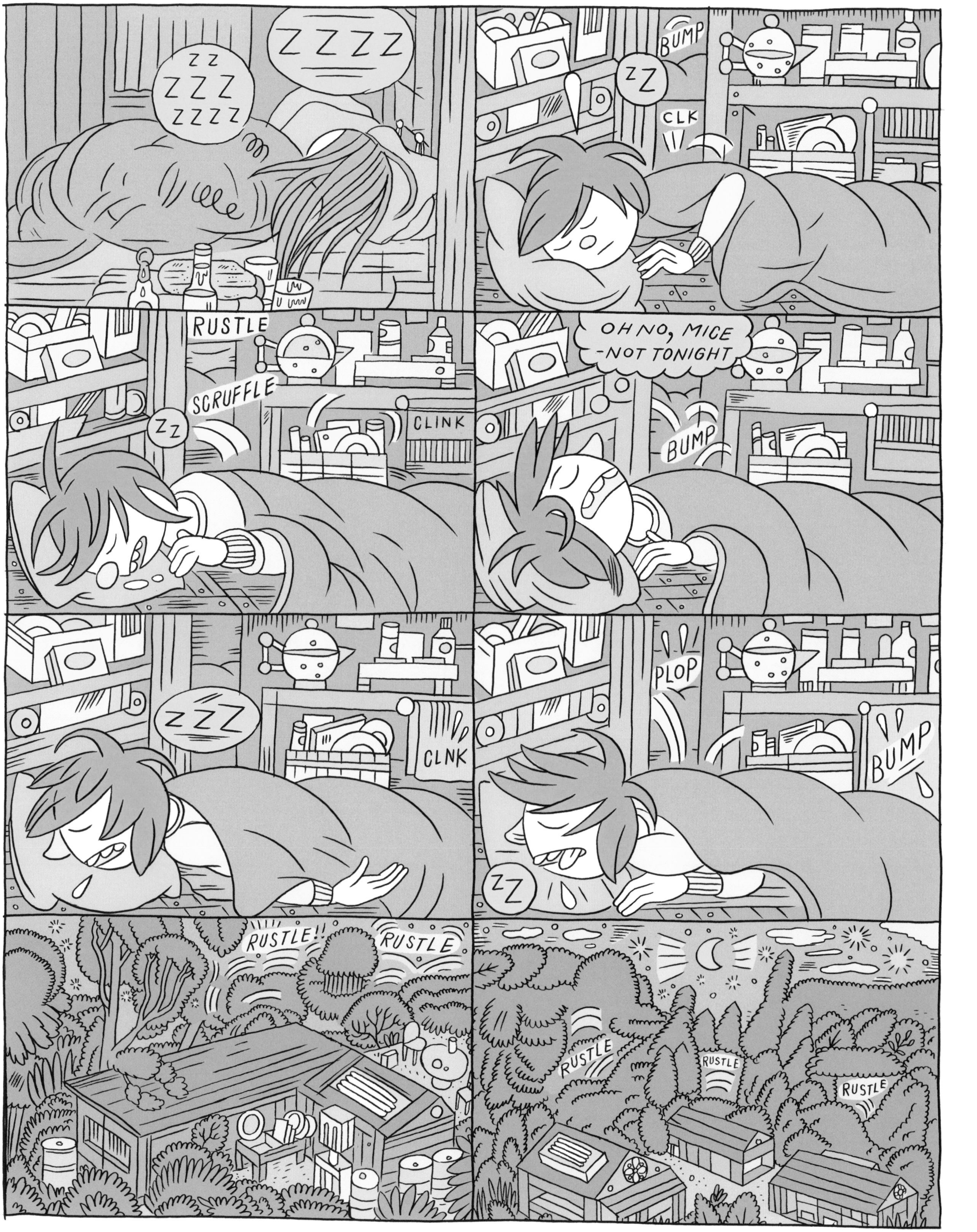

ZZ ZZZ ZZZZ
ZZZZ
BUMP
ZZ
CLK
RUSTLE
SCRUFFLE
ZZ
CLINK
OH NO, MICE -NOT TONIGHT
BUMP
ZZZ
CLNK
PLOP
BUMP
ZZ
RUSTLE!!
RUSTLE
RUSTLE
RUSTLE
RUSTLE

- IN THE MORNING -

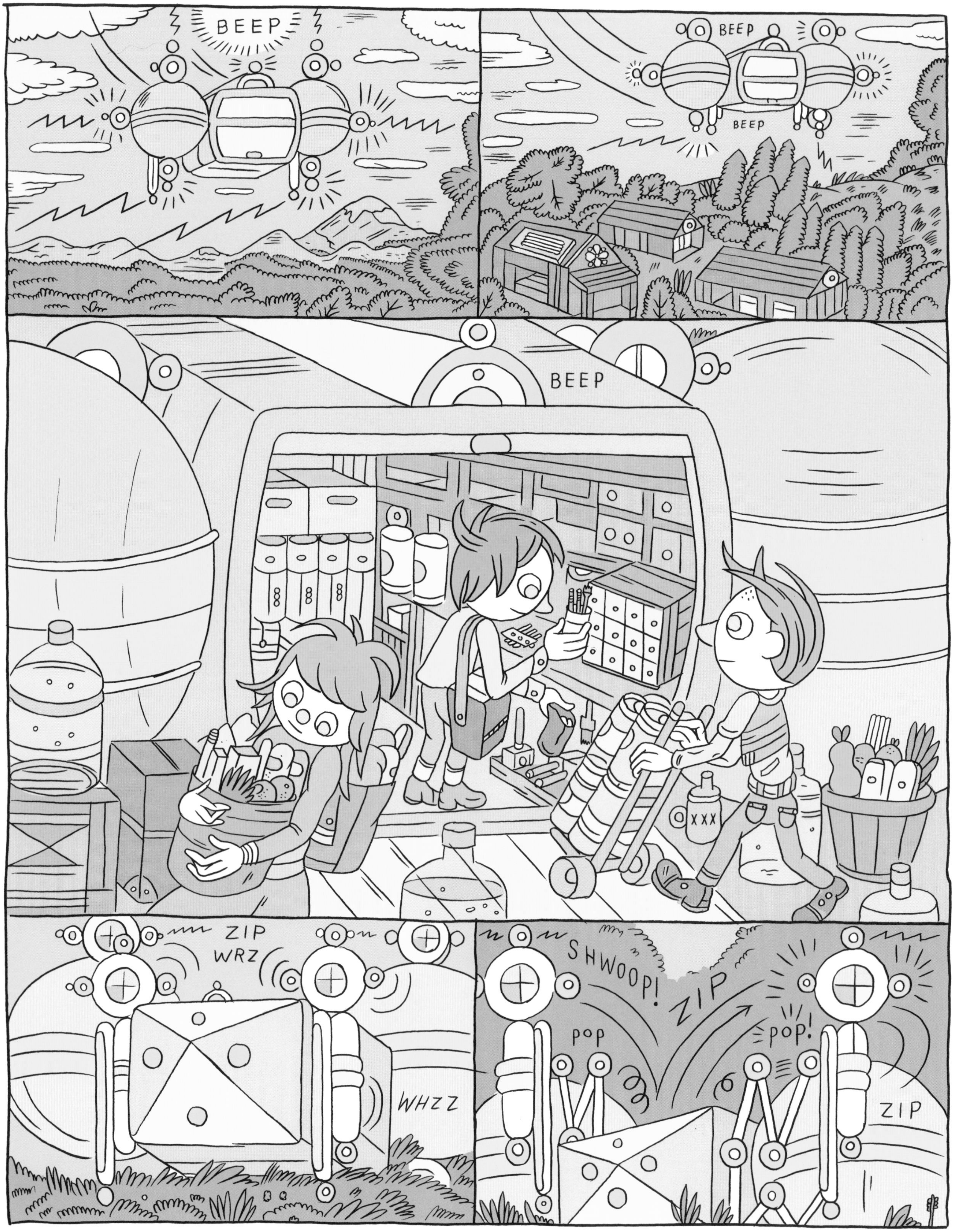
BEEP
BEEP
BEEP
BEEP
ZIP
WRZ
WHZZ
SHWOOP!
ZIP
pop
pop!
ZIP

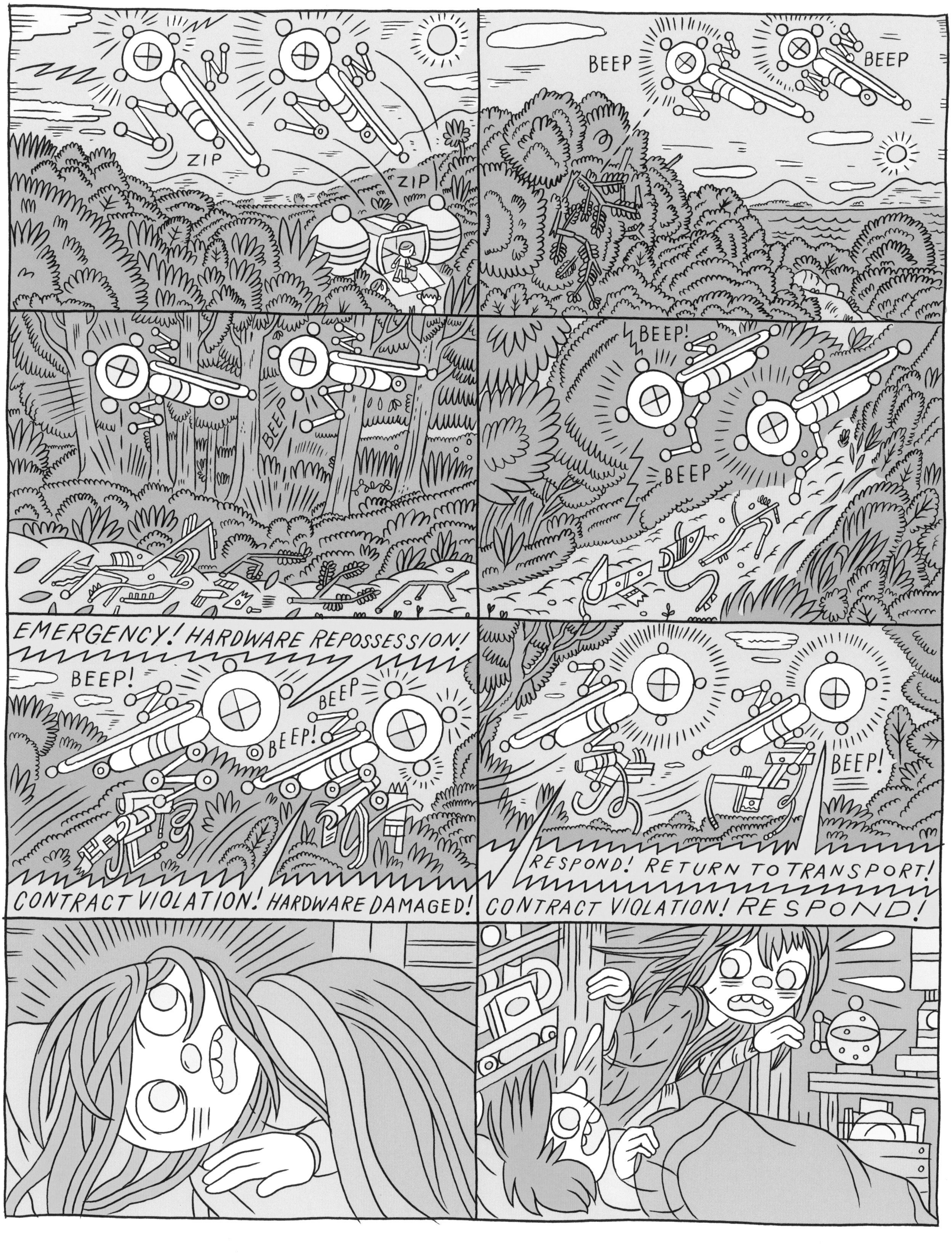

ZIP
ZIP
BEEP
BEEP
BEEP
BEEP!
BEEP
EMERGENCY! HARDWARE REPOSSESSION!
BEEP!
BEEP!
BEEP
CONTRACT VIOLATION! HARDWARE DAMAGED!
BEEP!
RESPOND! RETURN TO TRANSPORT!
CONTRACT VIOLATION! RESPOND!

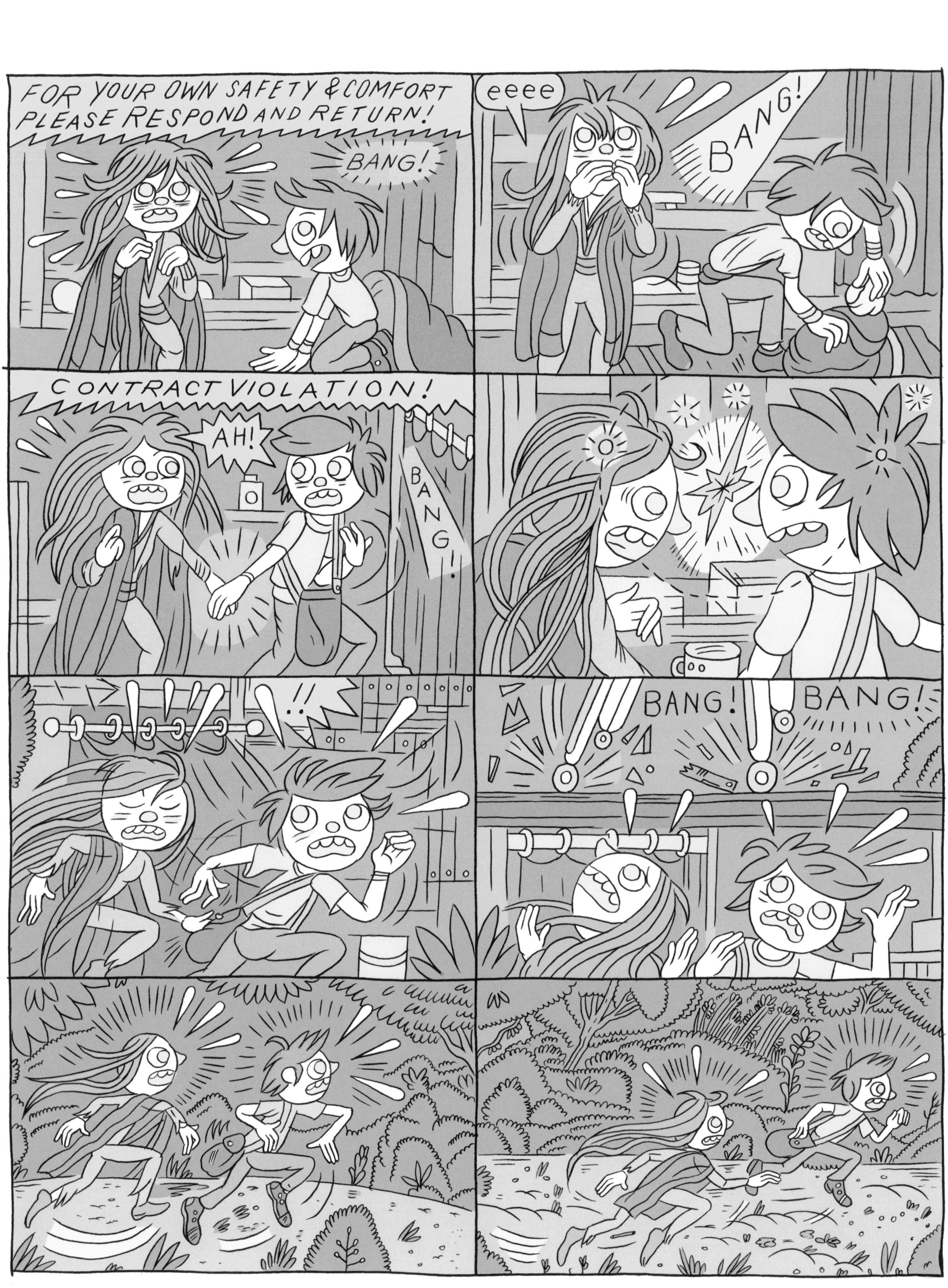
FOR YOUR OWN SAFETY & COMFORT PLEASE RESPOND AND RETURN!
BANG!
eeee
BANG!
CONTRACT VIOLATION!
AH!
BANG!
BANG!
BANG!

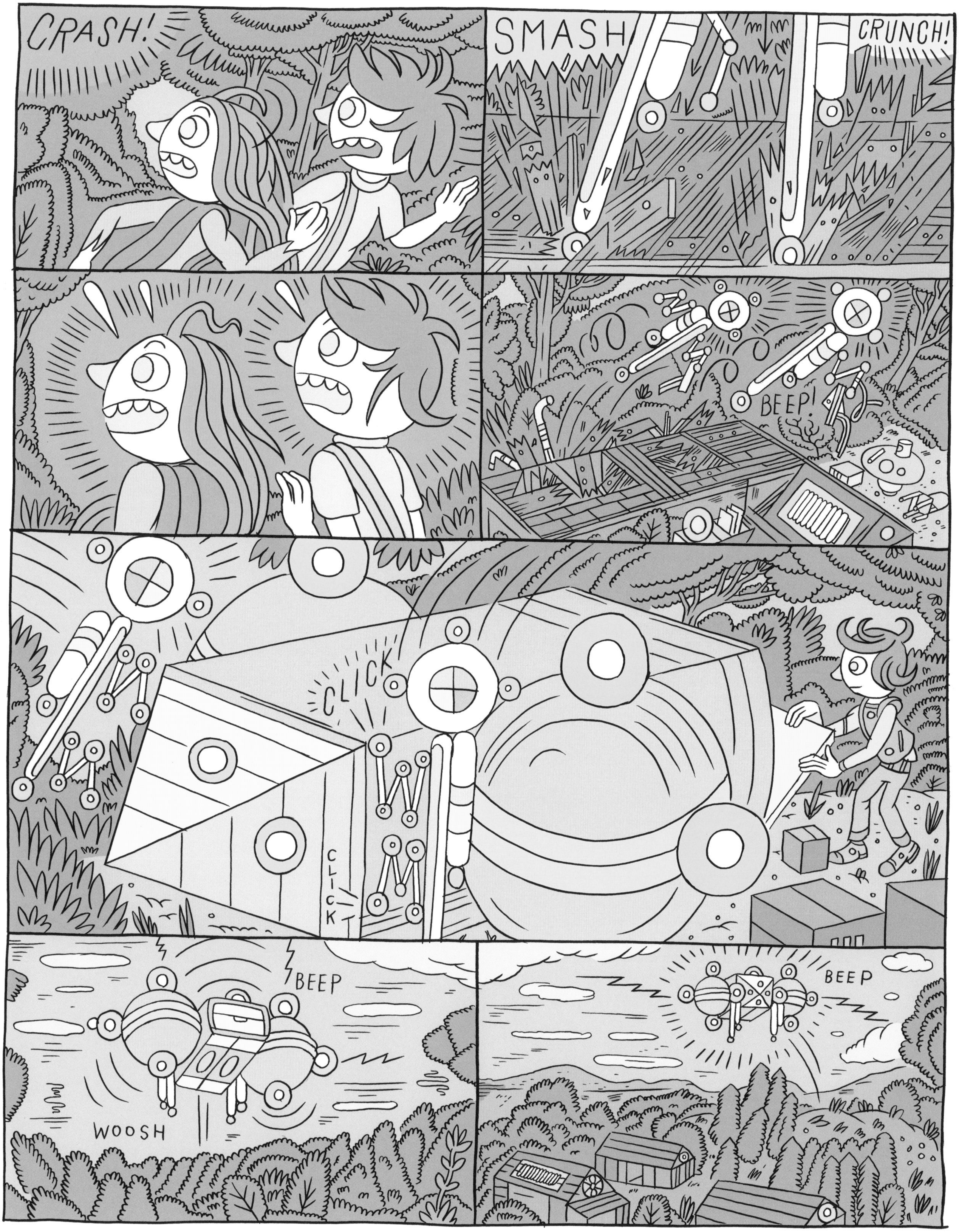
CRASH!
SMASH
CRUNCH!
BEEP!
CLICK
CLICK
BEEP
WOOSH
BEEP

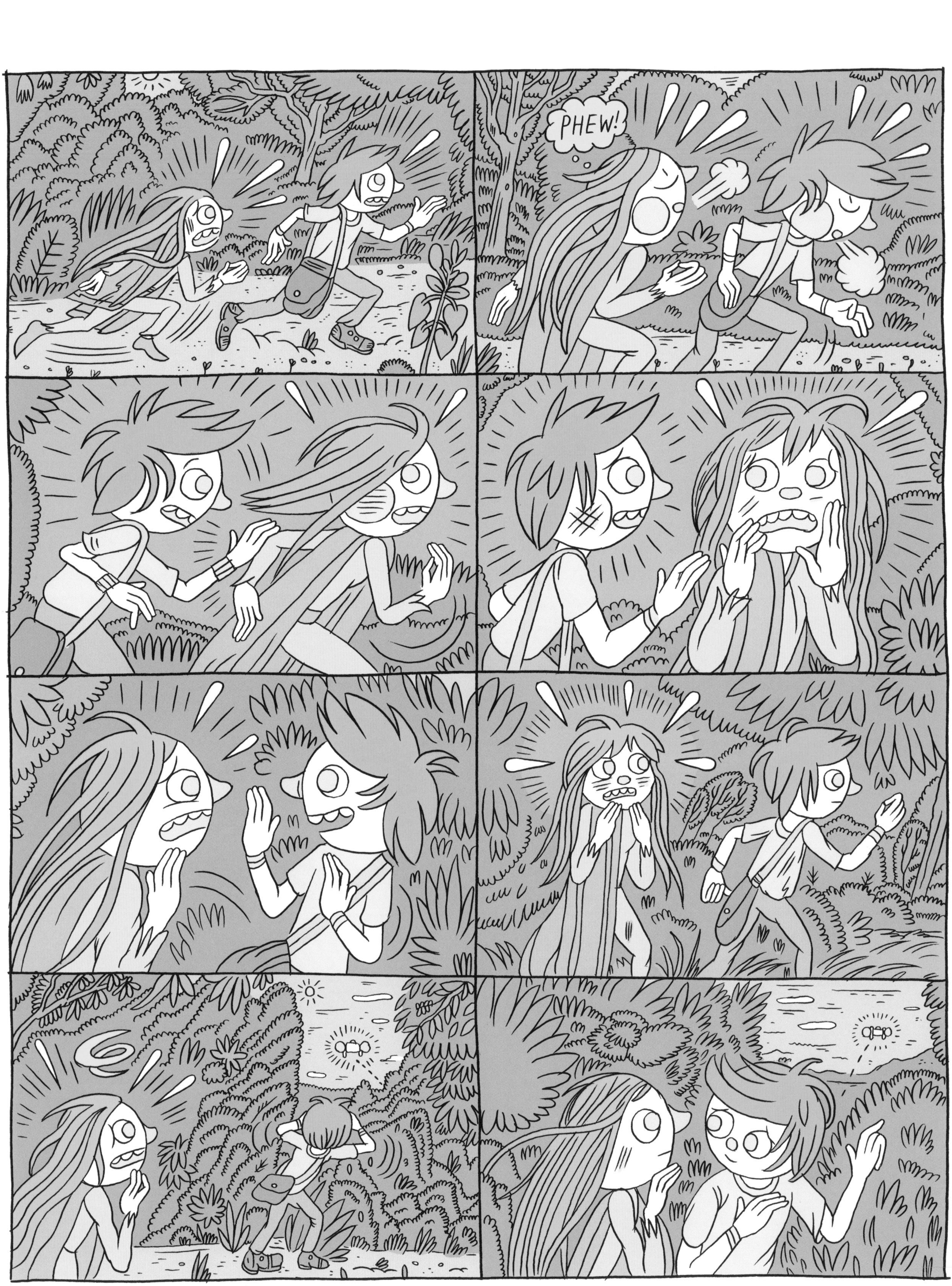
PHEW!

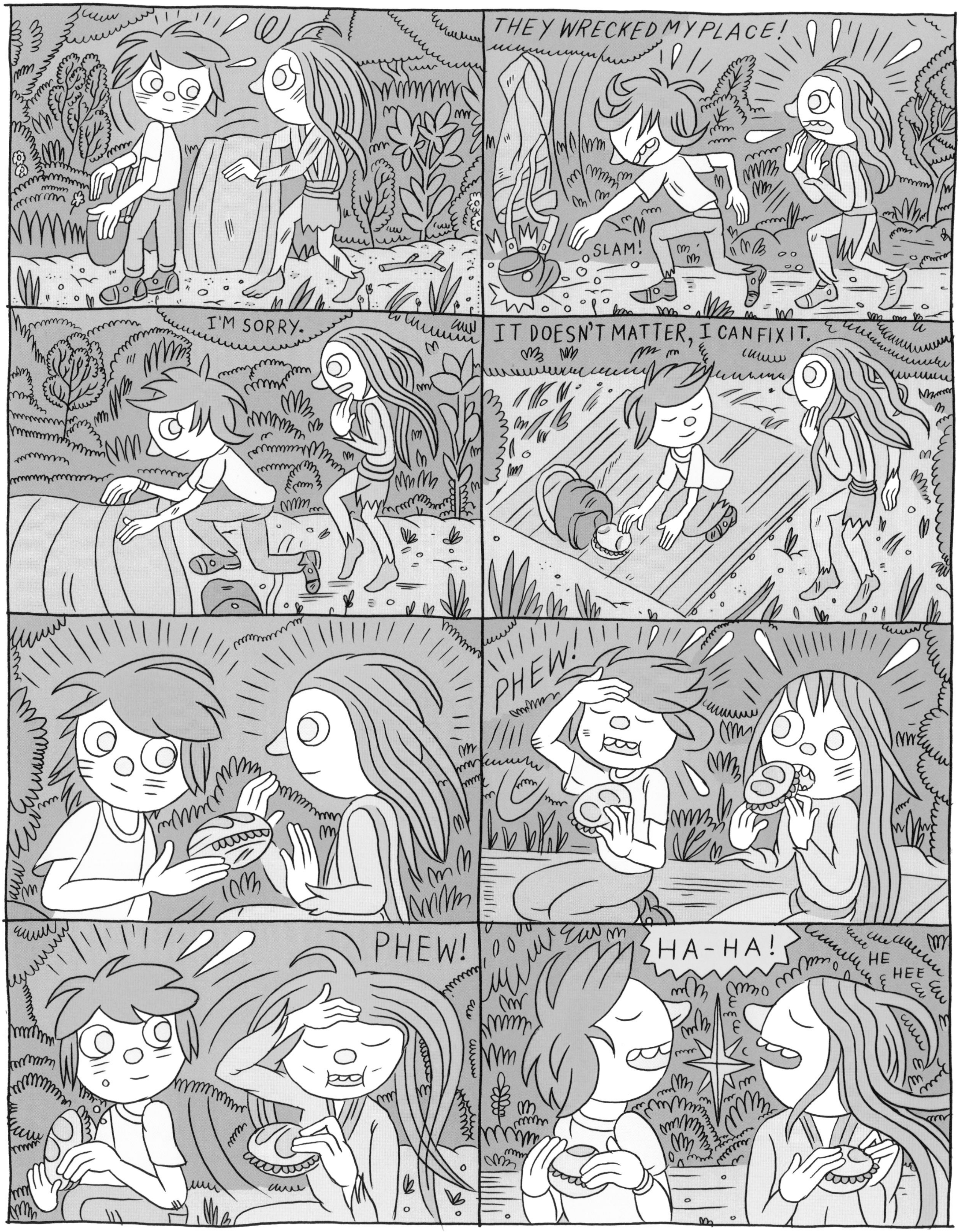
THEY WRECKED MY PLACE!
SLAM!
I'M SORRY.
IT DOESN'T MATTER, I CAN FIX IT.
PHEW!
PHEW!
HA-HA!
HE HEE

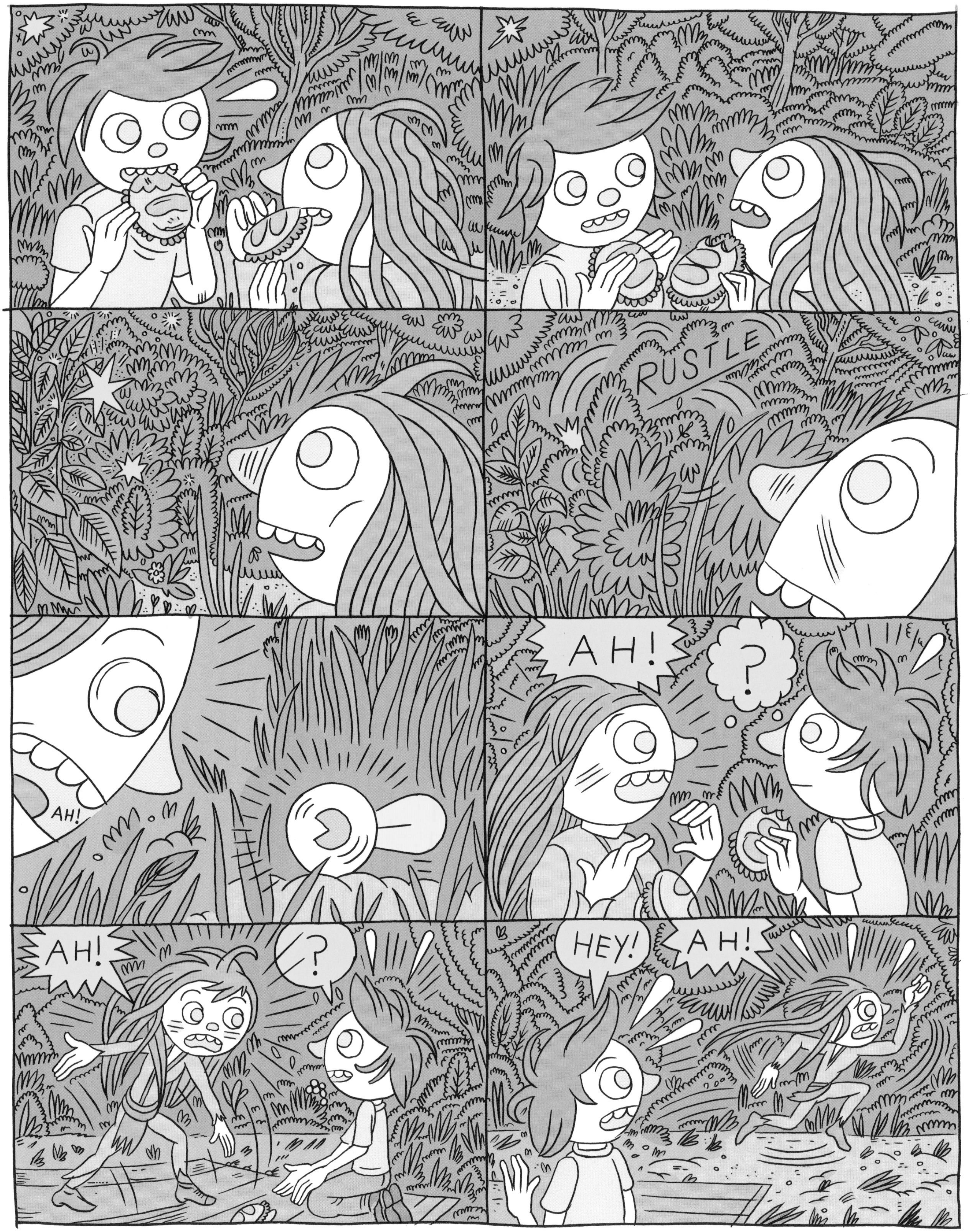
RUSTLE
AH!
AH!
?
AH!
?
HEY!
AH!

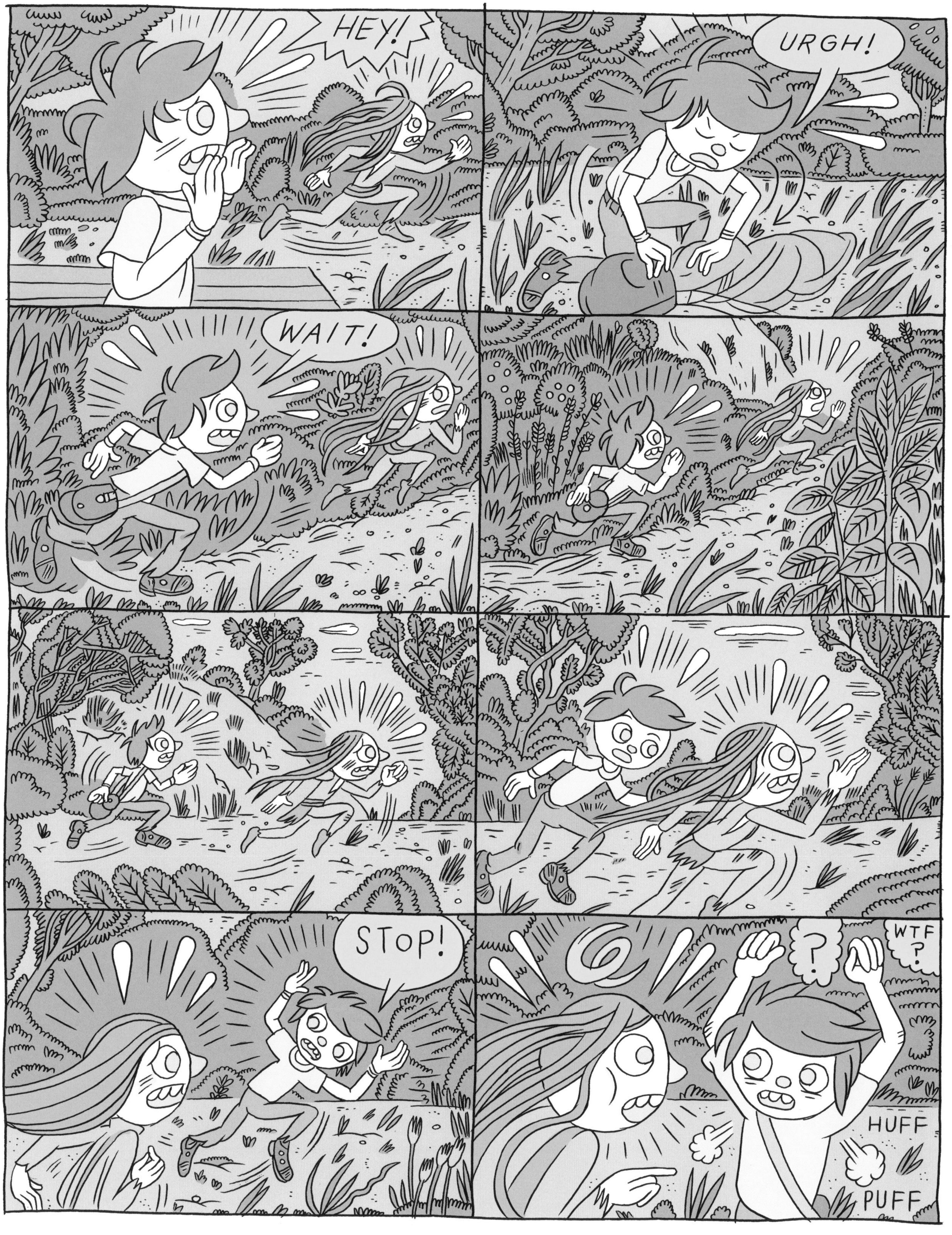
HEY!
URGH!
WAIT!
STOP!
?
WTF ?
HUFF
PUFF

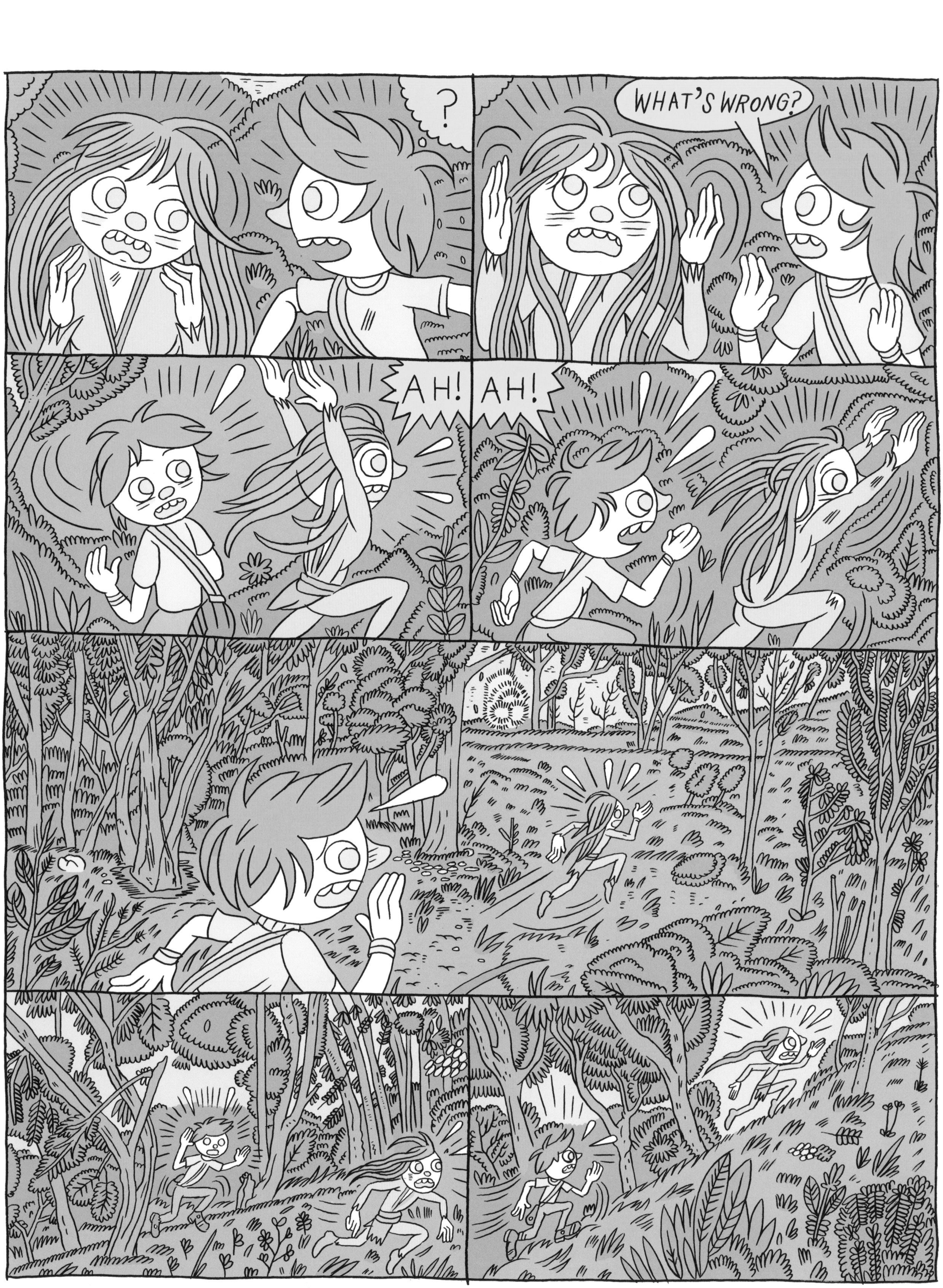
?
WHAT'S WRONG?
AH!
AH!

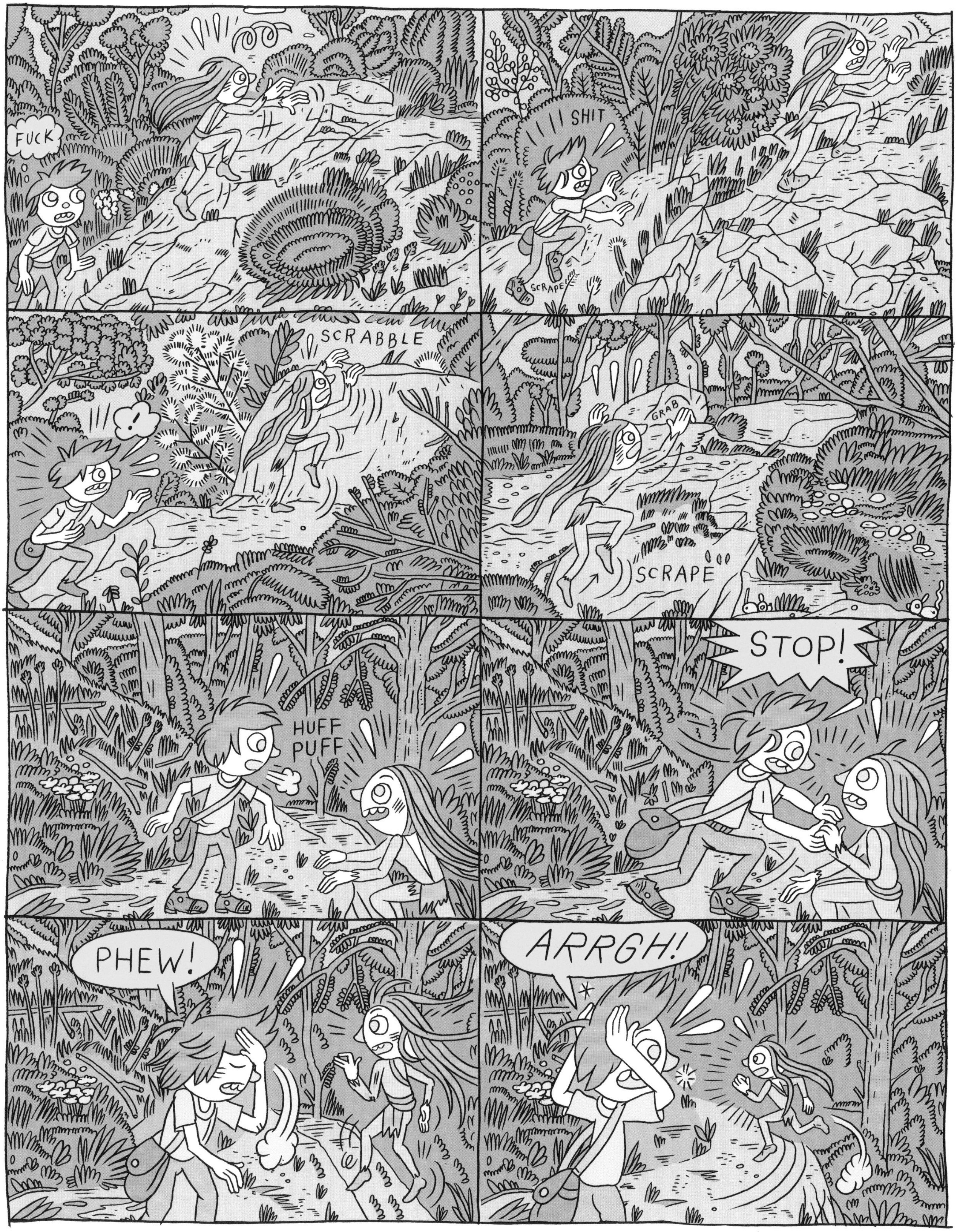
FUCK
SHIT
SCRAPE!
SCRABBLE
!
GRAB
SCRAPE
HUFF
PUFF
STOP!
PHEW!
ARRGH!

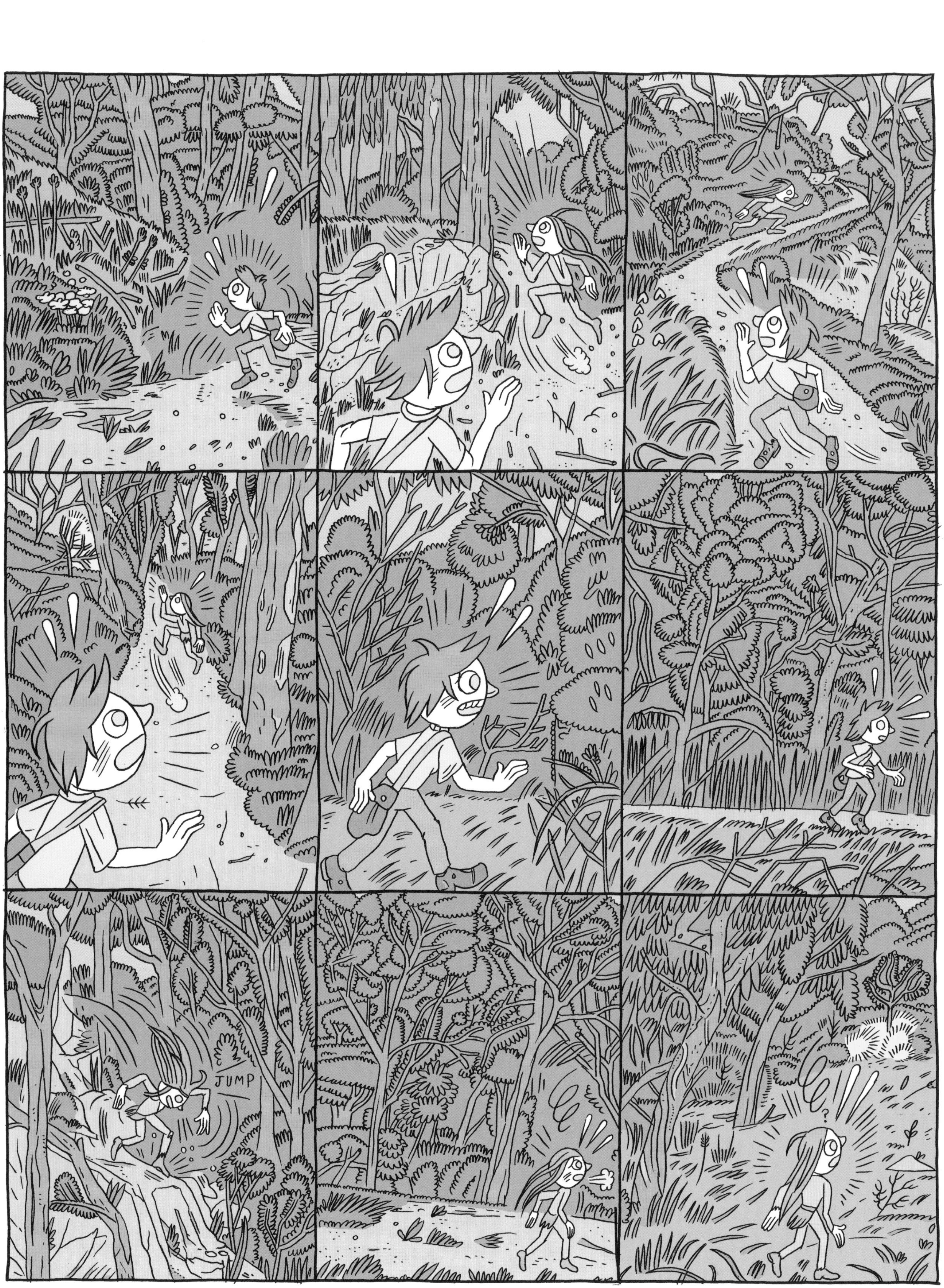
JUMP

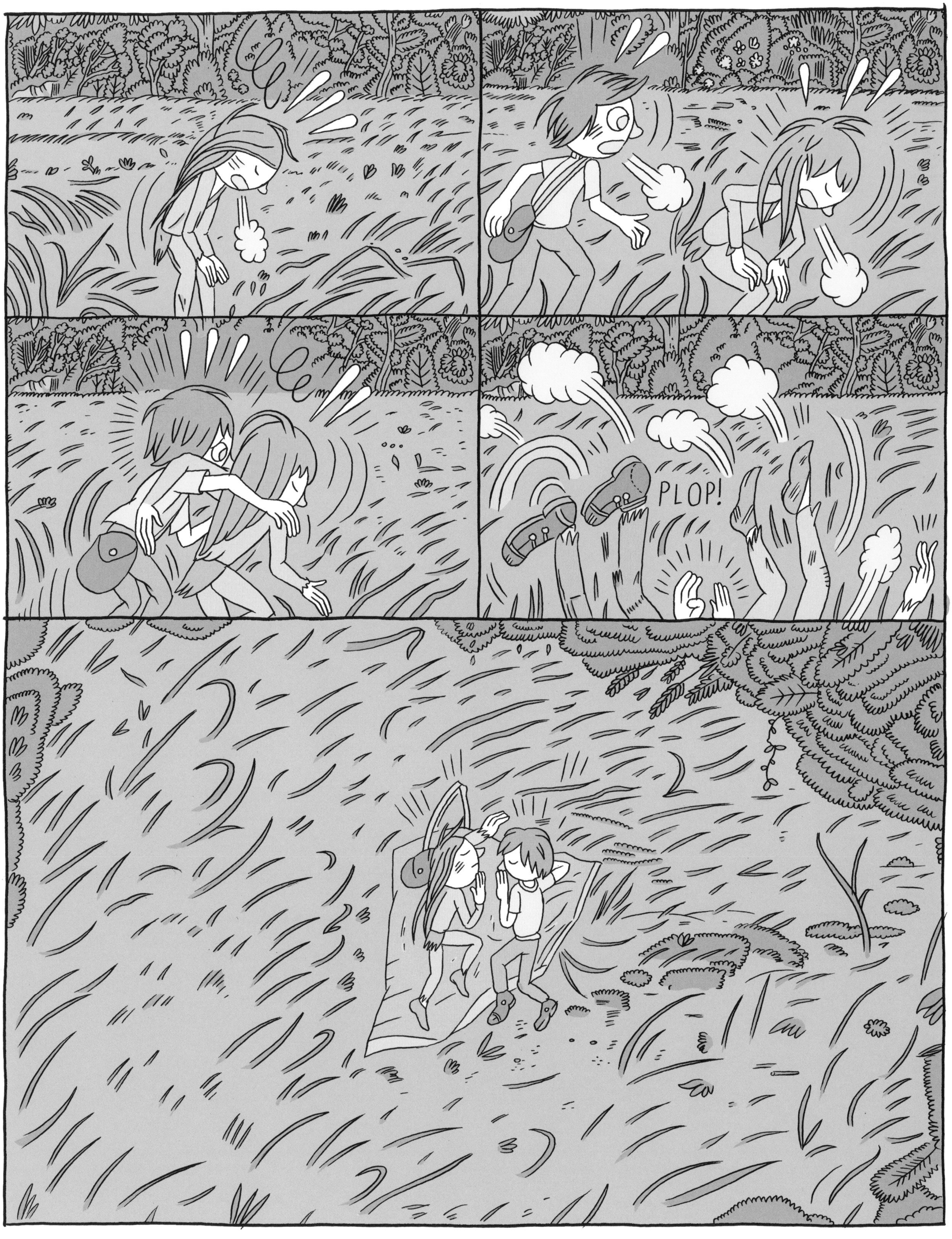
PLOP!

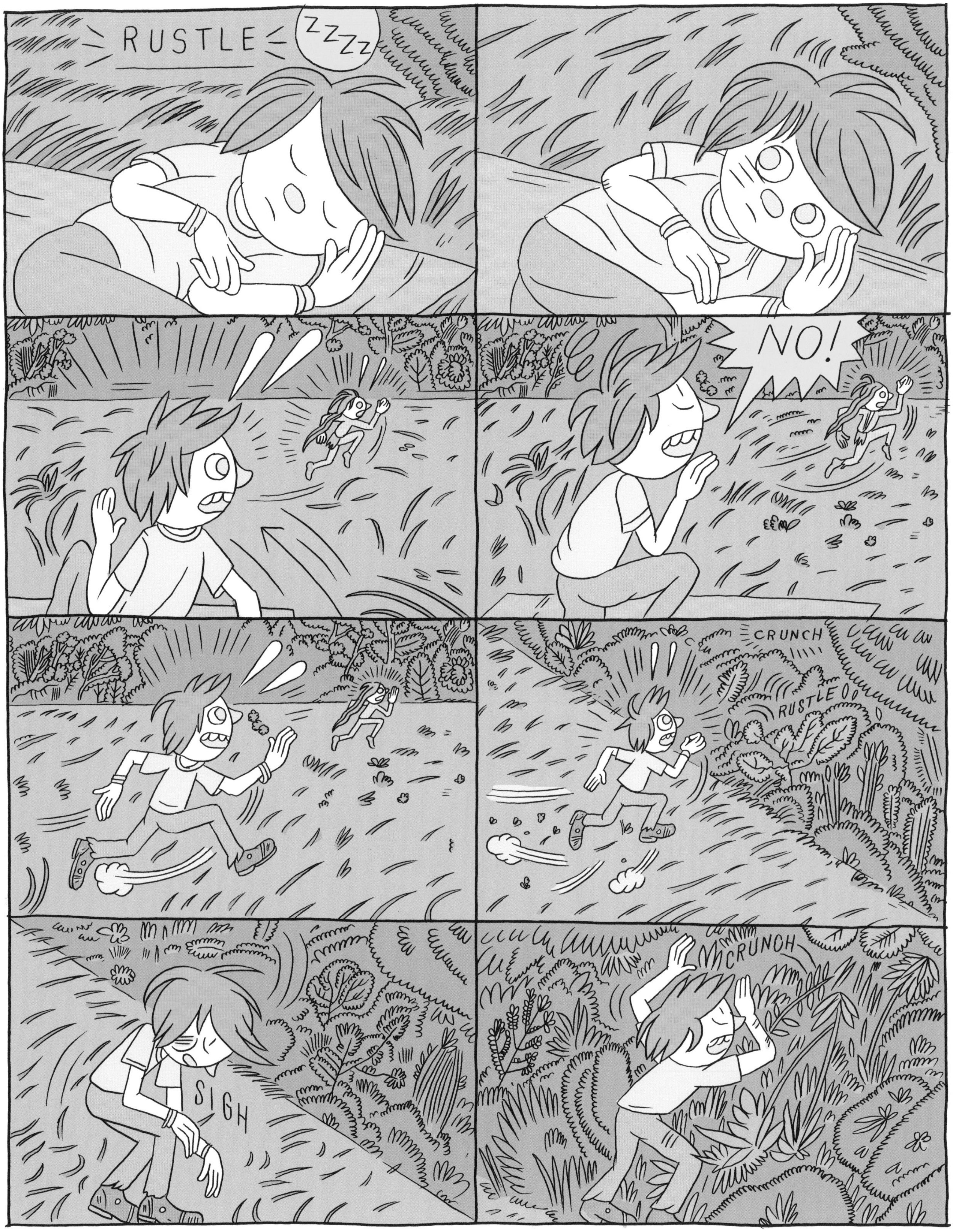
RUSTLE
ZZZZZ
NO!
CRUNCH
RUSTLE
SIGH
CRUNCH

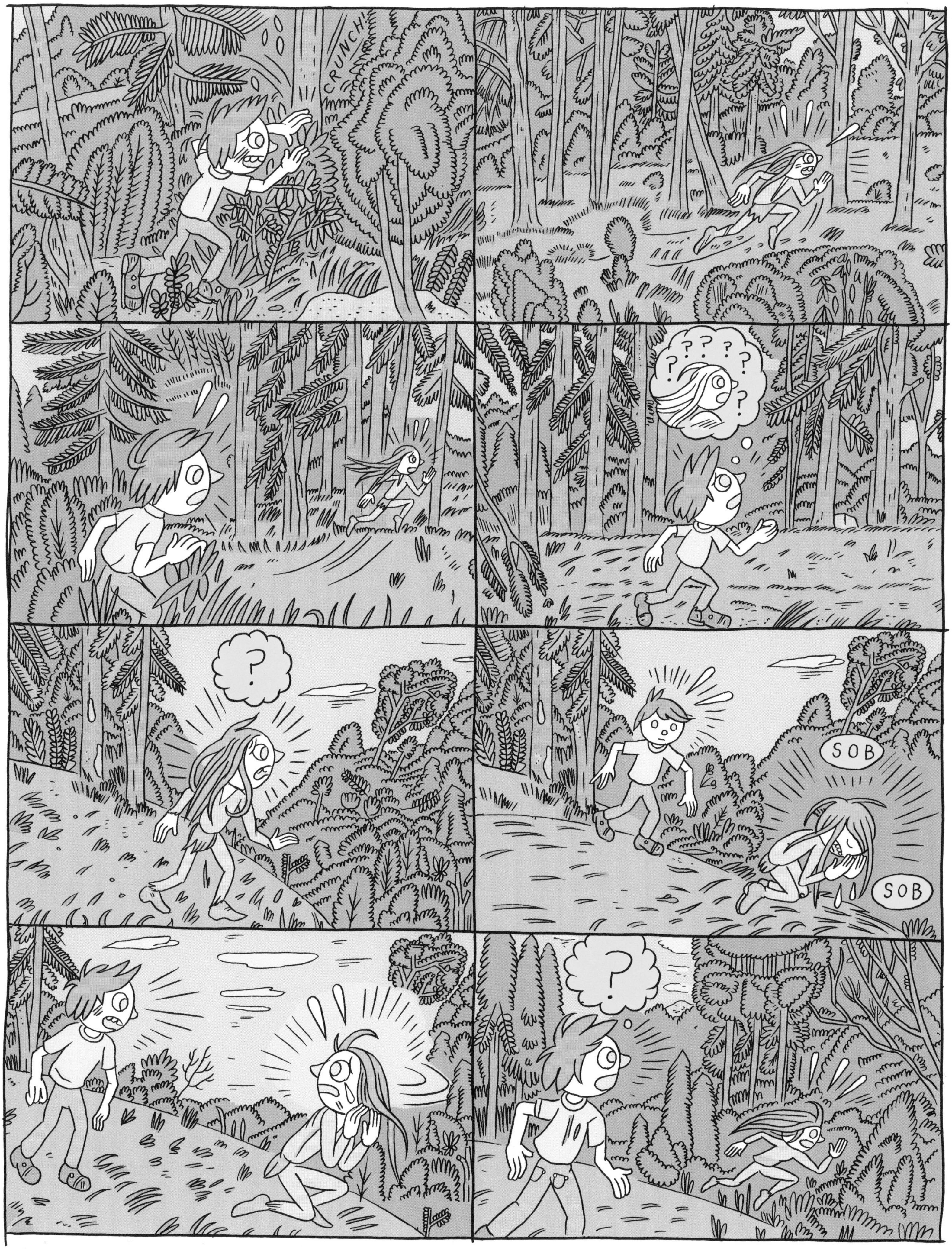
CRUNCH!
SOB
SOB

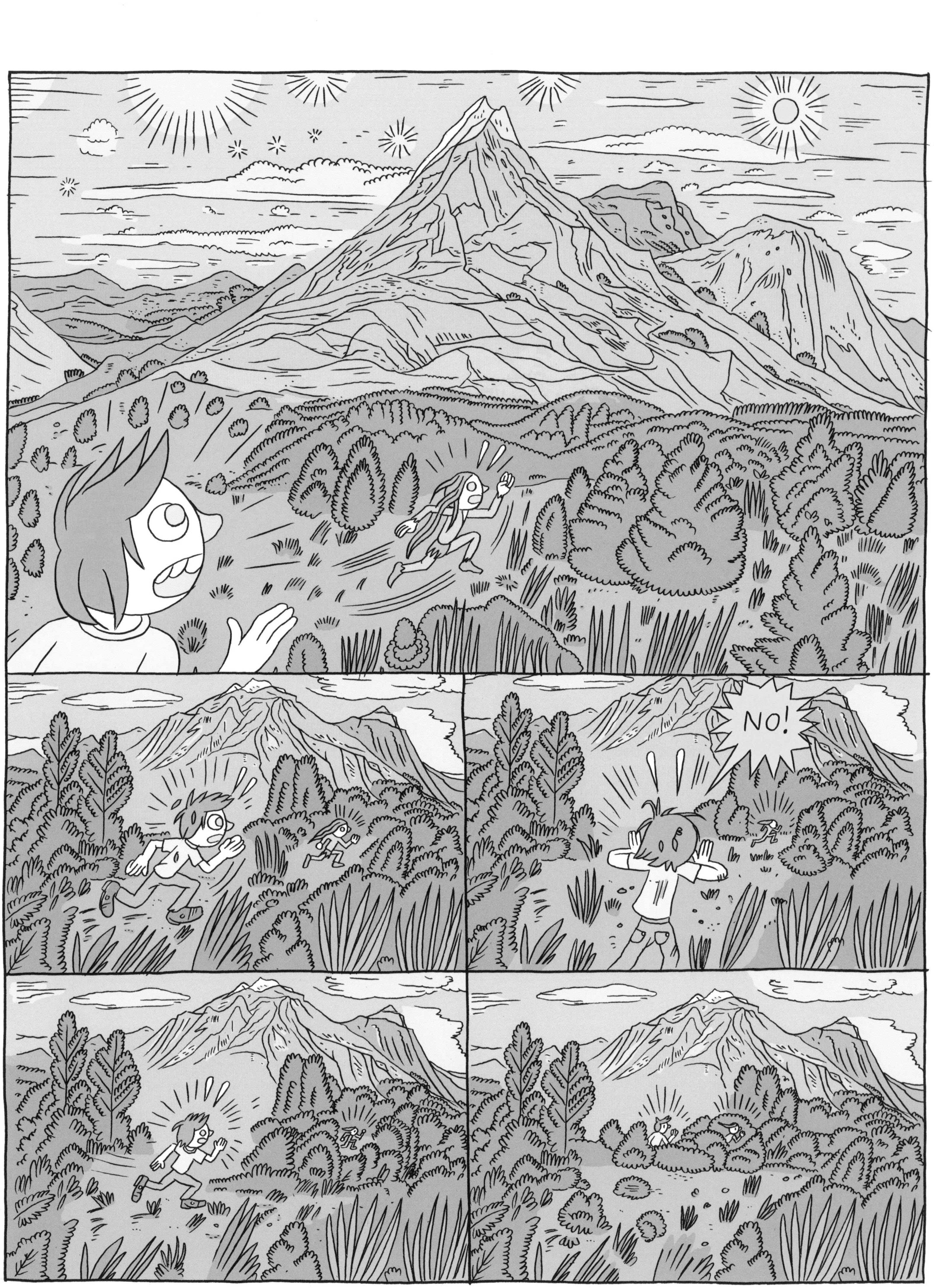
NO!

... AND SO ON ...

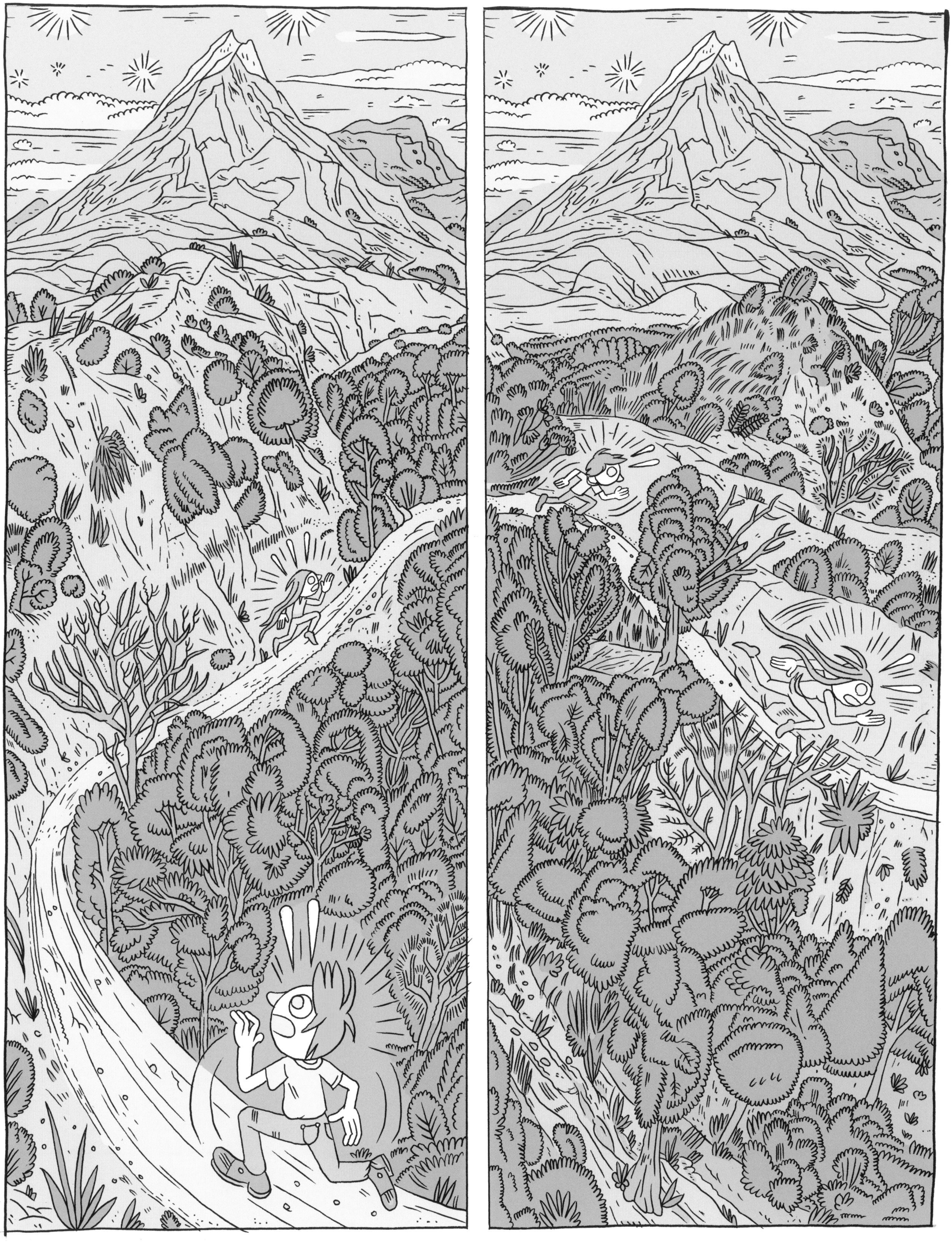

UNTIL, ...EVENTUALLY...

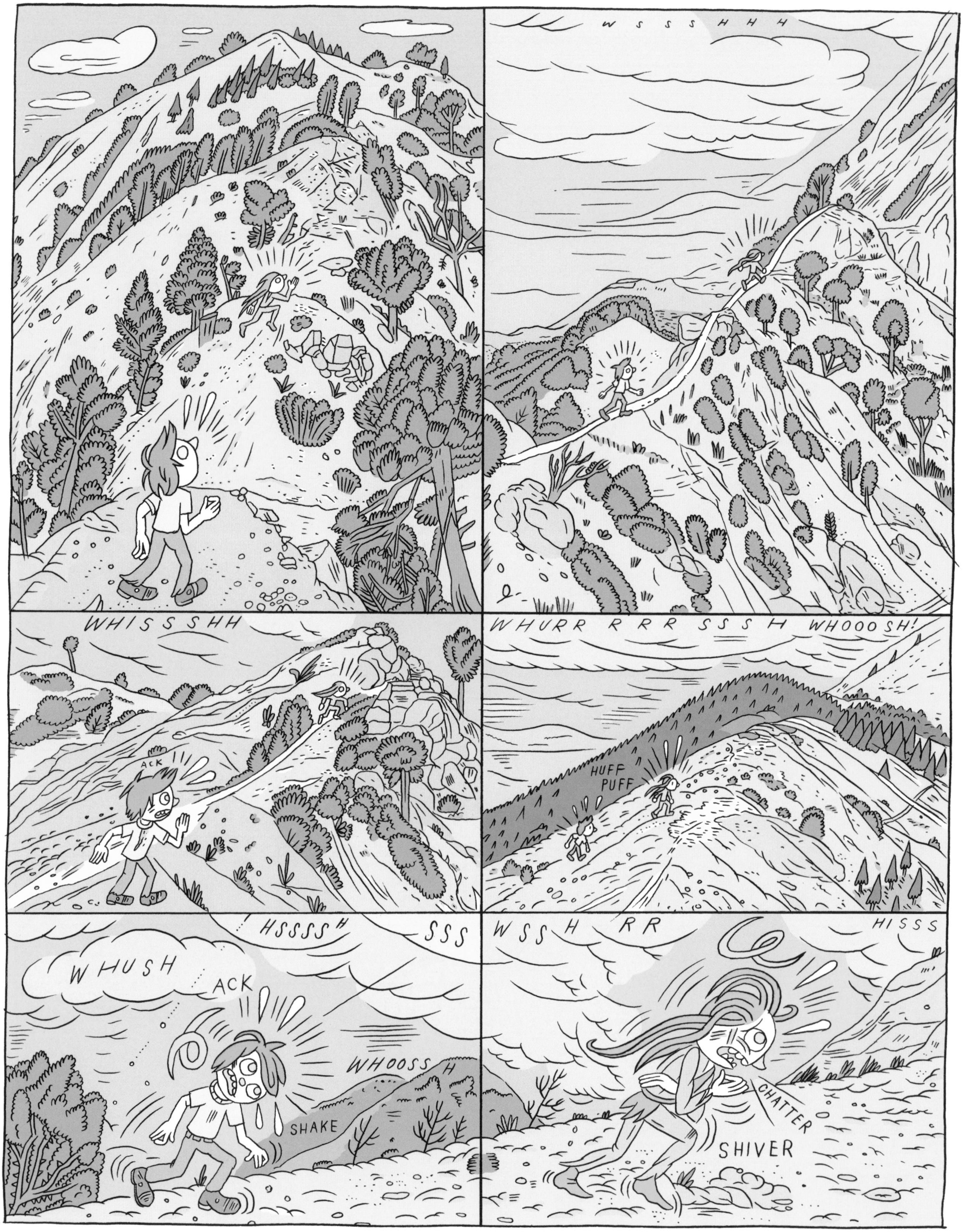
W S S S H H H
WHISSSHH
ACK
WHURR RRR SSSH WHOOOSH!
HUFF
PUFF
HSSSSH
SSS
WHUSH
ACK
WHOOSSH
SHAKE
WSS H RR
HISSS
CHATTER
SHIVER

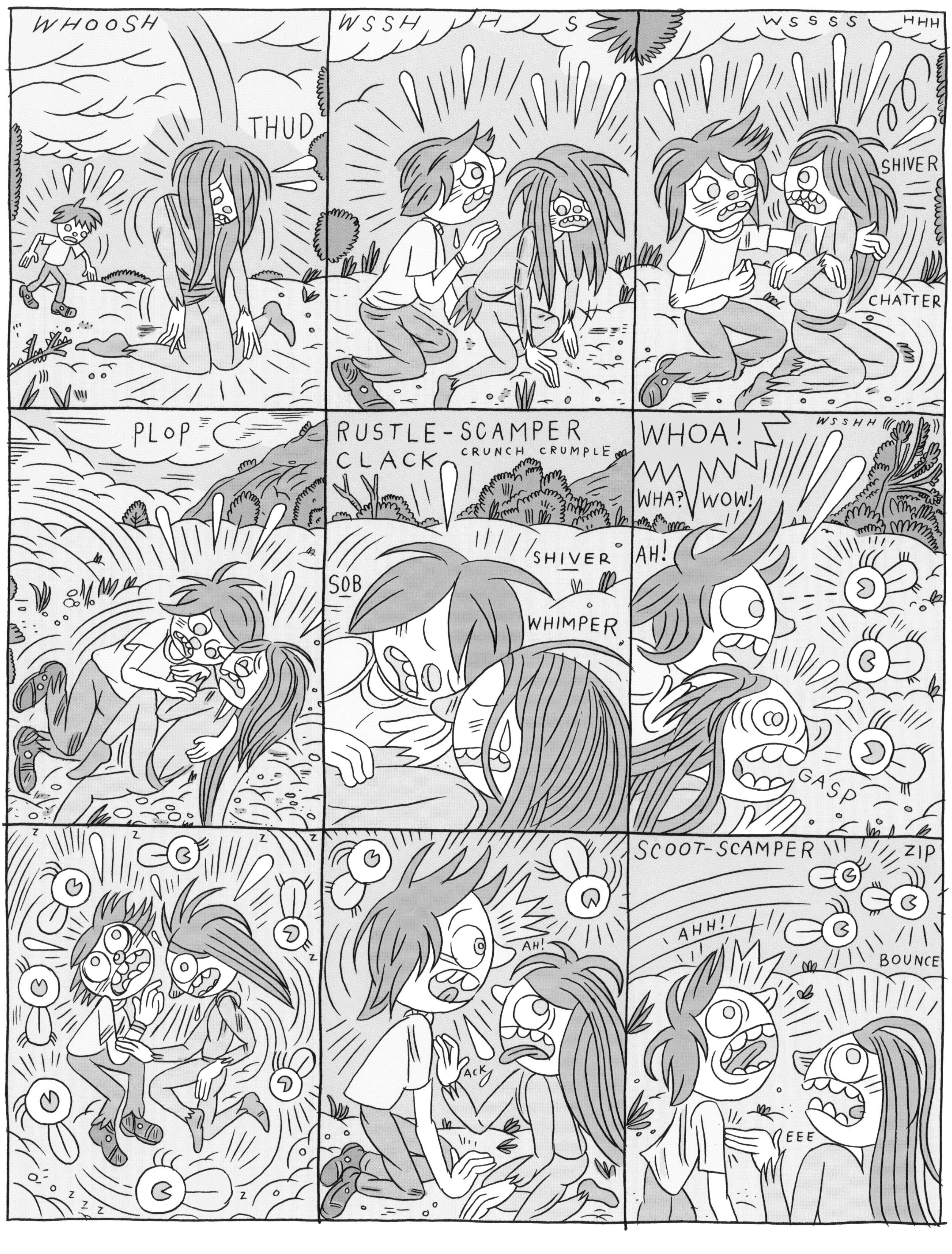
WHOOSH
THUD
WSSH
H
S
WSSSS
HHH
SHIVER
CHATTER
PLOP
RUSTLE-SCAMPER
CLACK
CRUNCH CRUMPLE
SHIVER
SOB
WHIMPER
WHOA!
WSSHH
WHA?
WOW!
AH!
GASP
AH!
ACK
SCOOT-SCAMPER
ZIP
AHH!
BOUNCE
EEE

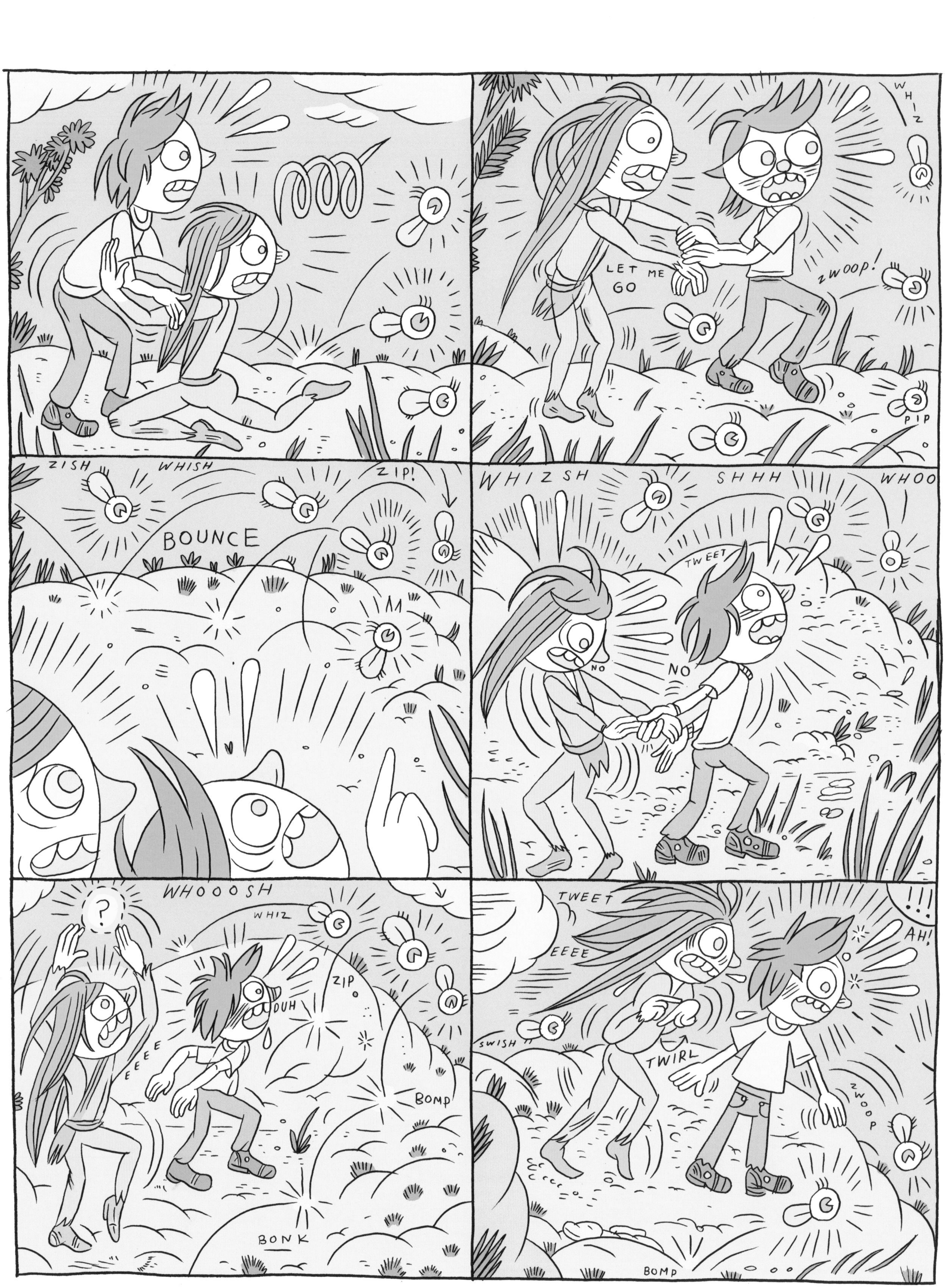
WHIZ
LET ME GO
ZWOOP!
PIP
ZISH
WHISH
ZIP!
BOUNCE
WHIZSH
SHHH
WHOO
TWEET
NO
NO
WHOOOSH
?
WHIZ
ZIP
DUH
EEEE
BOMP
BONK
TWEET
!!!
AH!
EEEE
SWISH
TWIRL
ZWOOP
BOMP

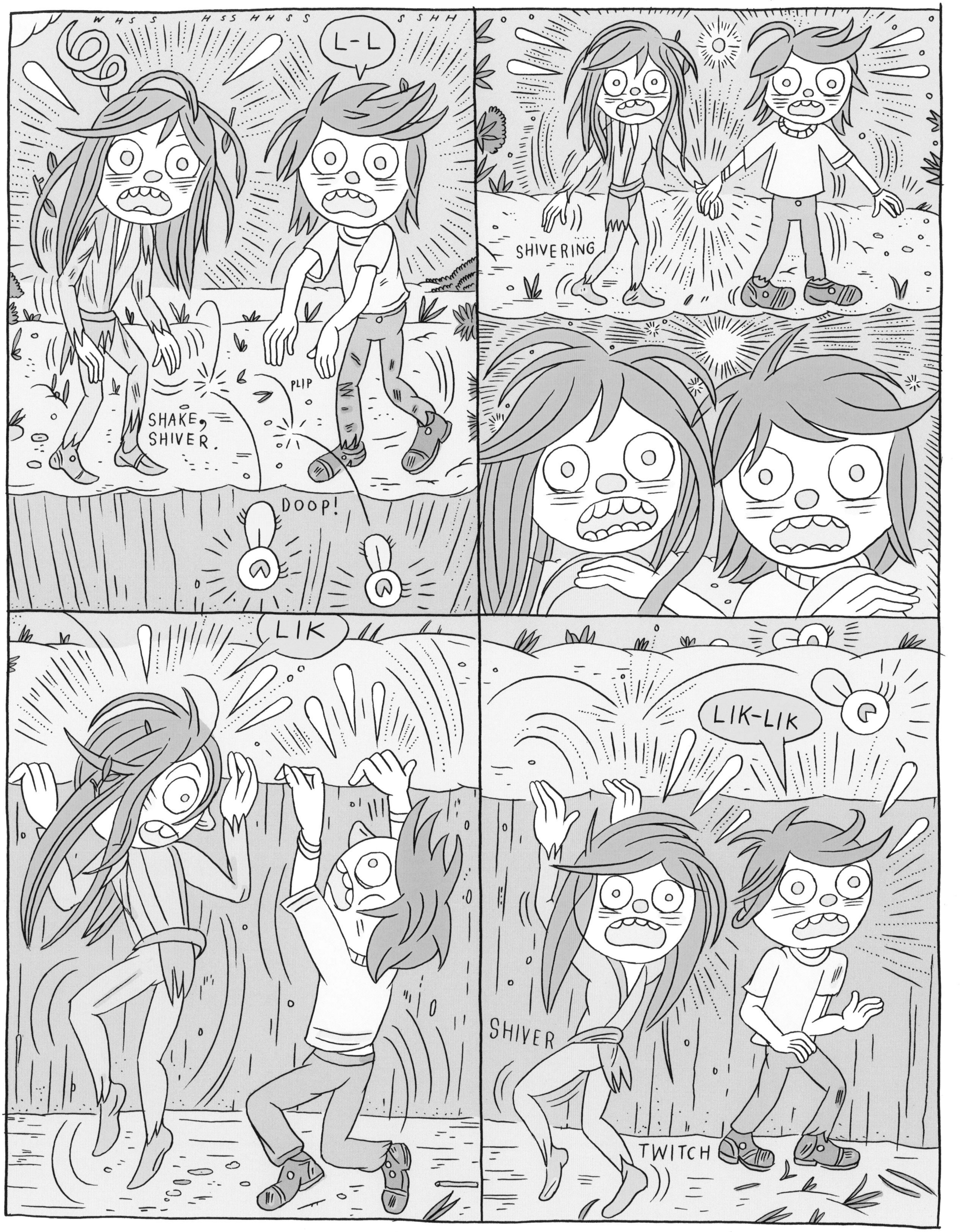
WHSS HSSHHSS SSHH
L-L
SHAKE, SHIVER.
PLIP
DOOP!
SHIVERING
LIK
LIK-LIK
SHIVER
TWITCH

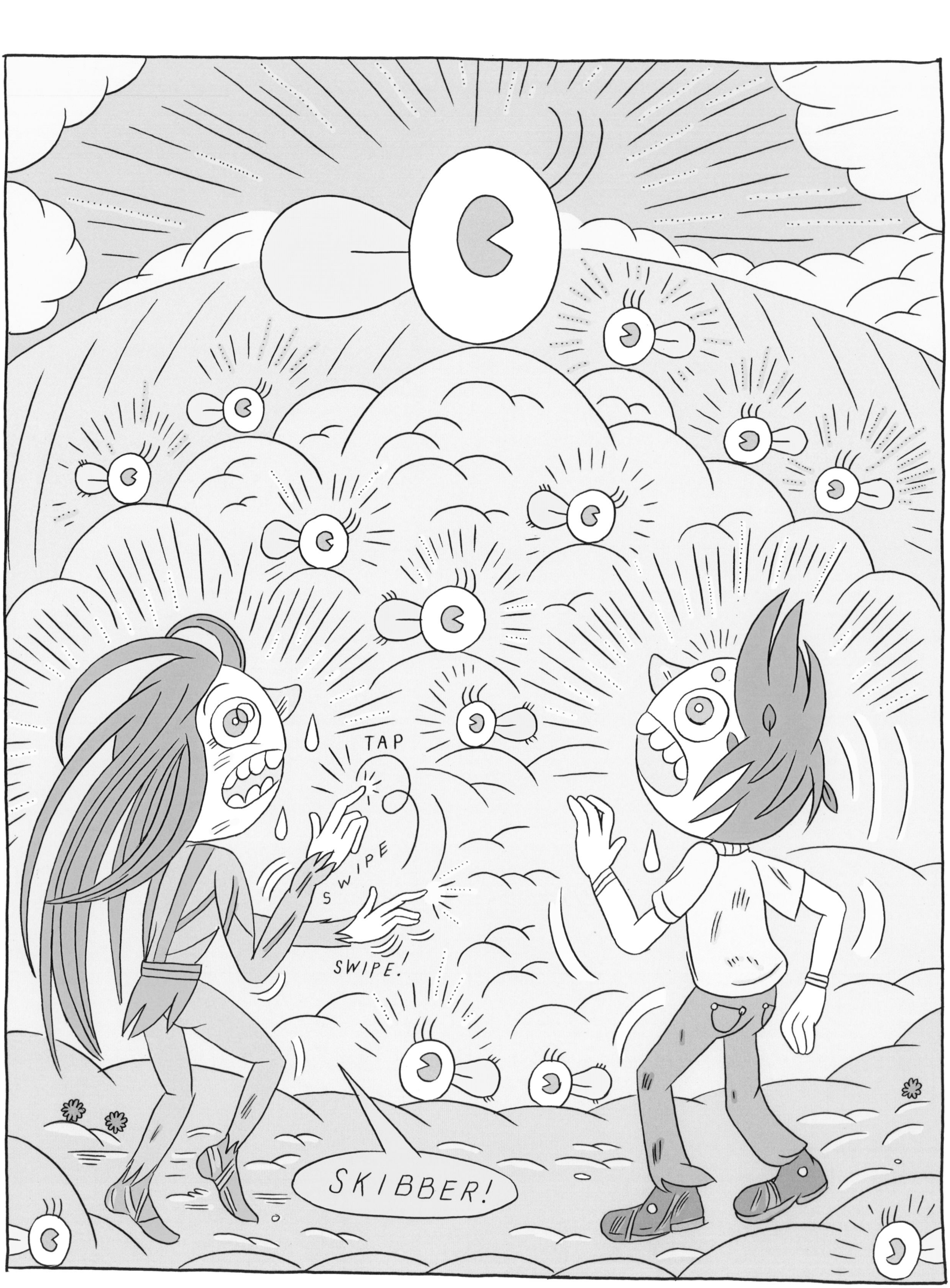
TAP
SWIPE
SWIPE!
SKIBBER!

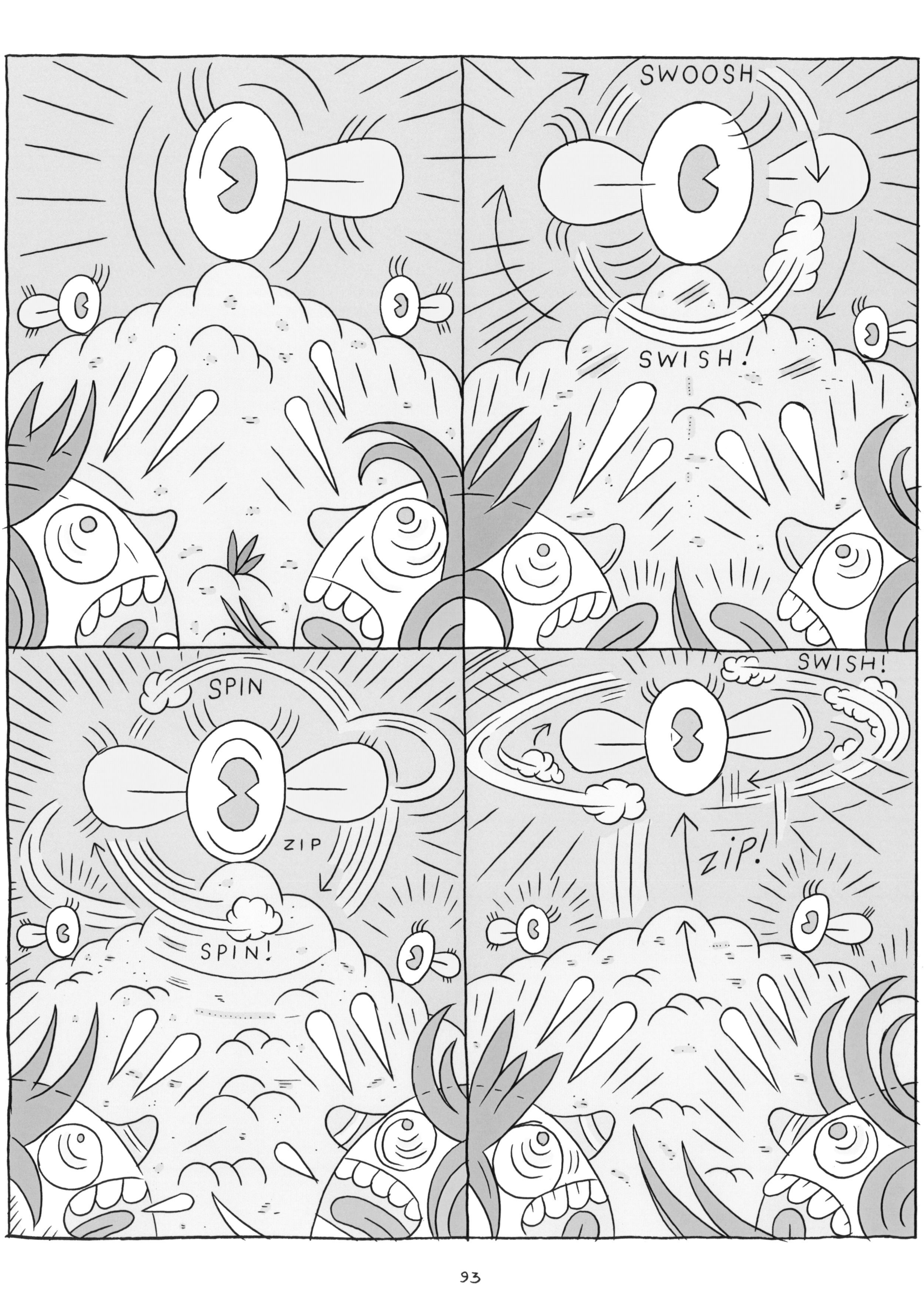
SWOOSH
SWISH!
SPIN
ZIP
SPIN!
SWISH!
ZIP!

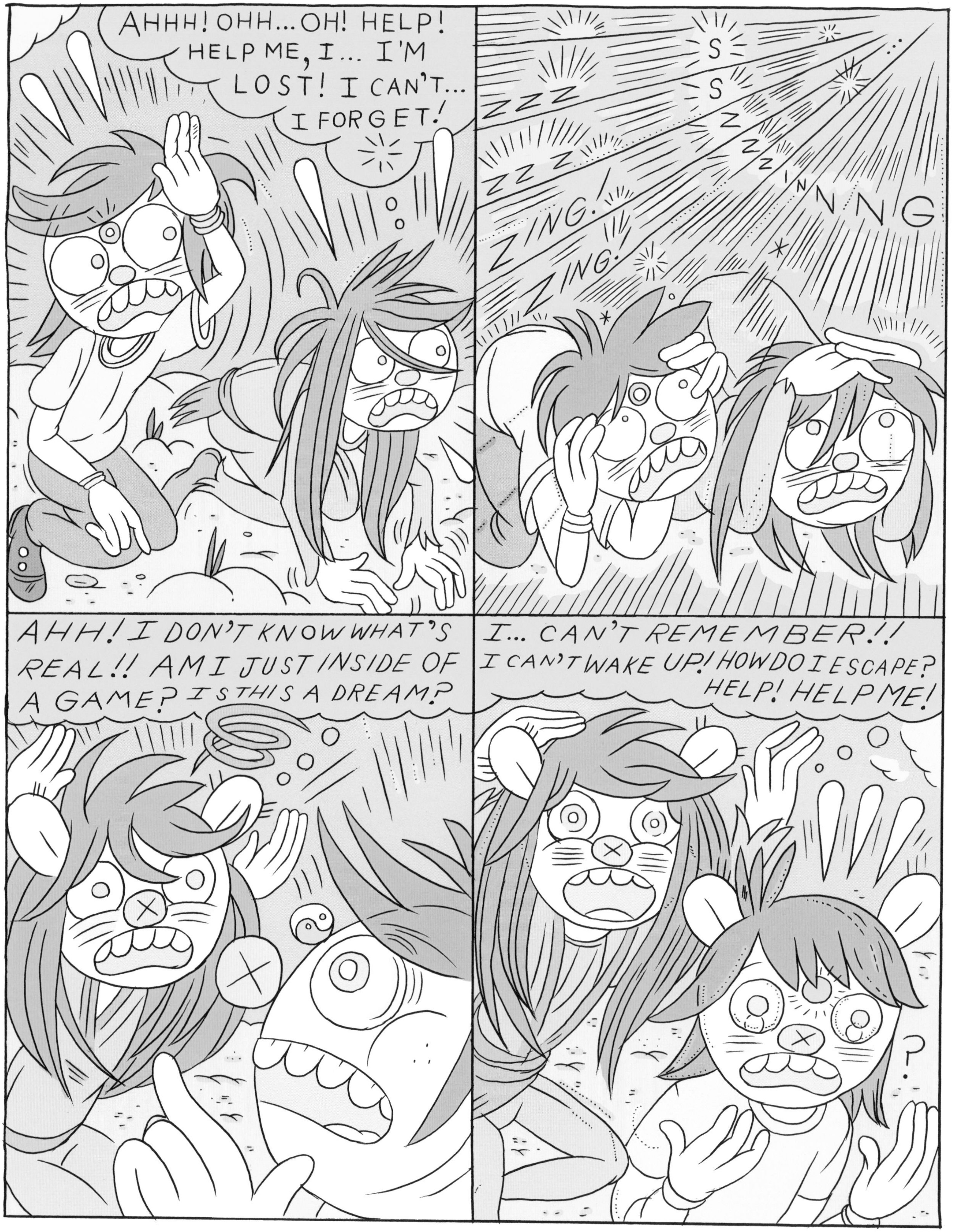
AHHH! OHH... OH! HELP! HELP ME, I... I'M LOST! I CAN'T... I FORGET!
S S Z Z Z
ZZZ ZZZ
ZING! ZING!
INNNG
AHH! I DON'T KNOW WHAT'S REAL!! AM I JUST INSIDE OF A GAME? IS THIS A DREAM?
I... CAN'T REMEMBER!! I CAN'T WAKE UP! HOW DO I ESCAPE? HELP! HELP ME!
?

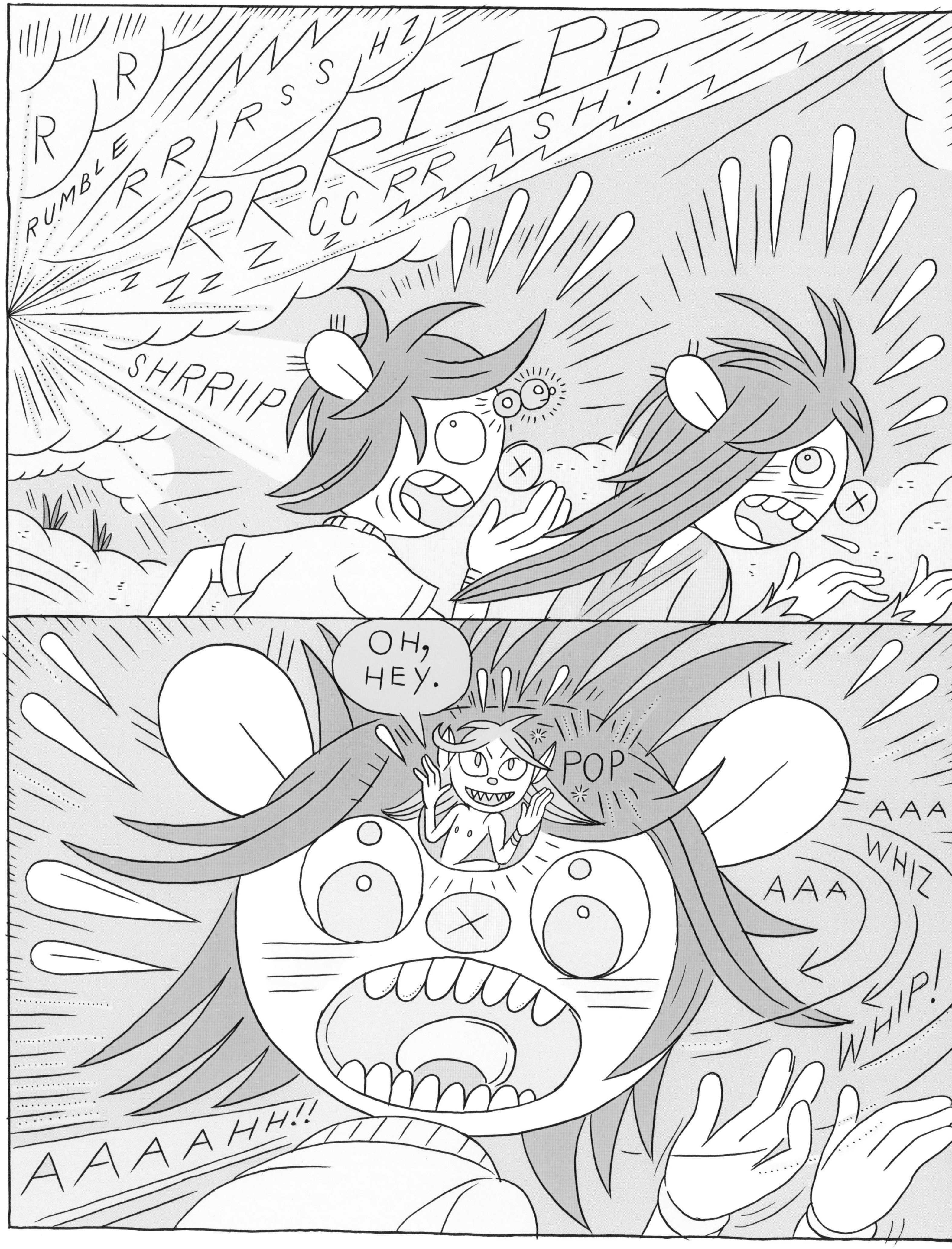

RUMBLE
SHRRIP
OH, HEY.
POP
AAA
WHIZ
AAA
WHIP!
AAAAAHH!!

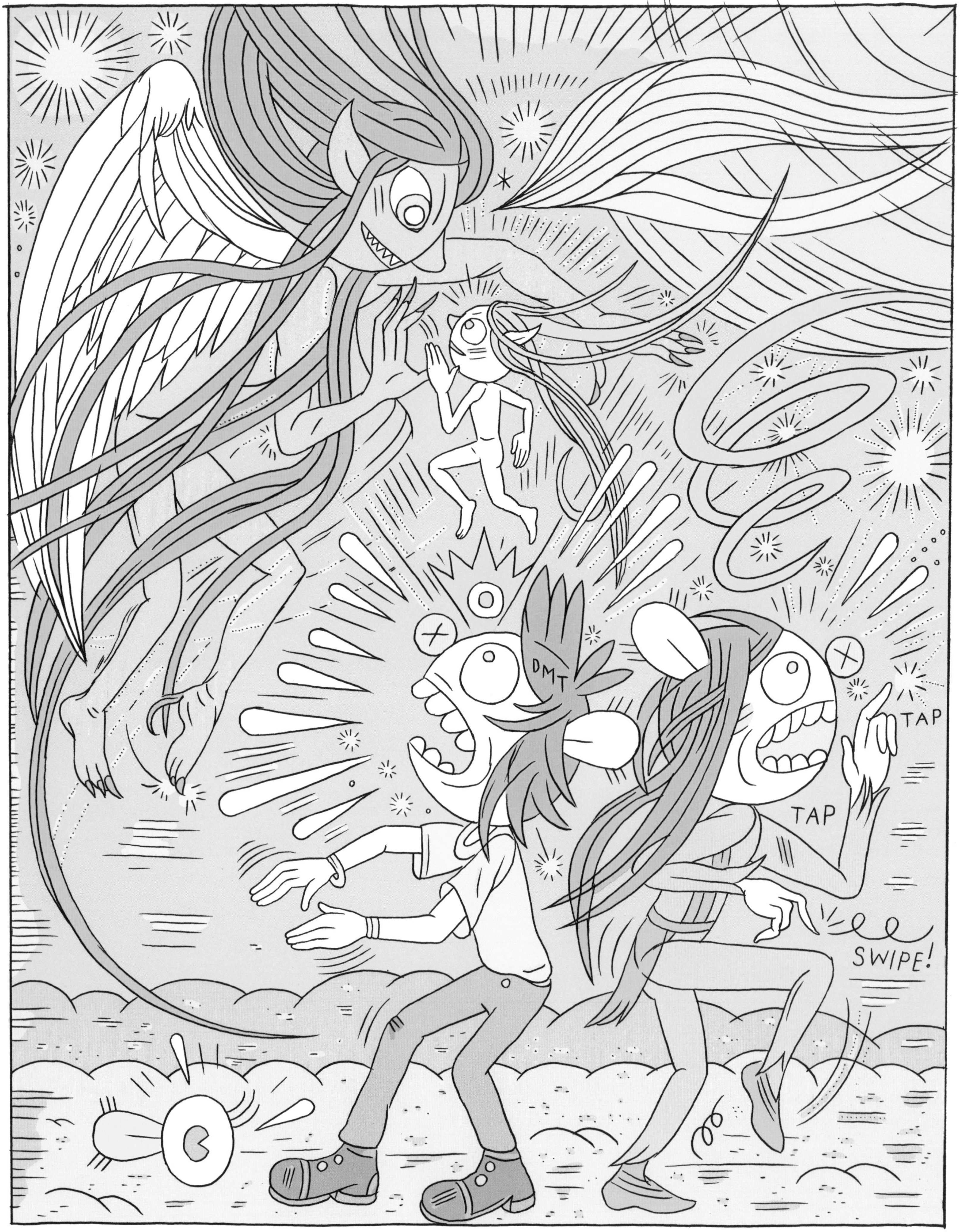
DMT
TAP
TAP
SWIPE!

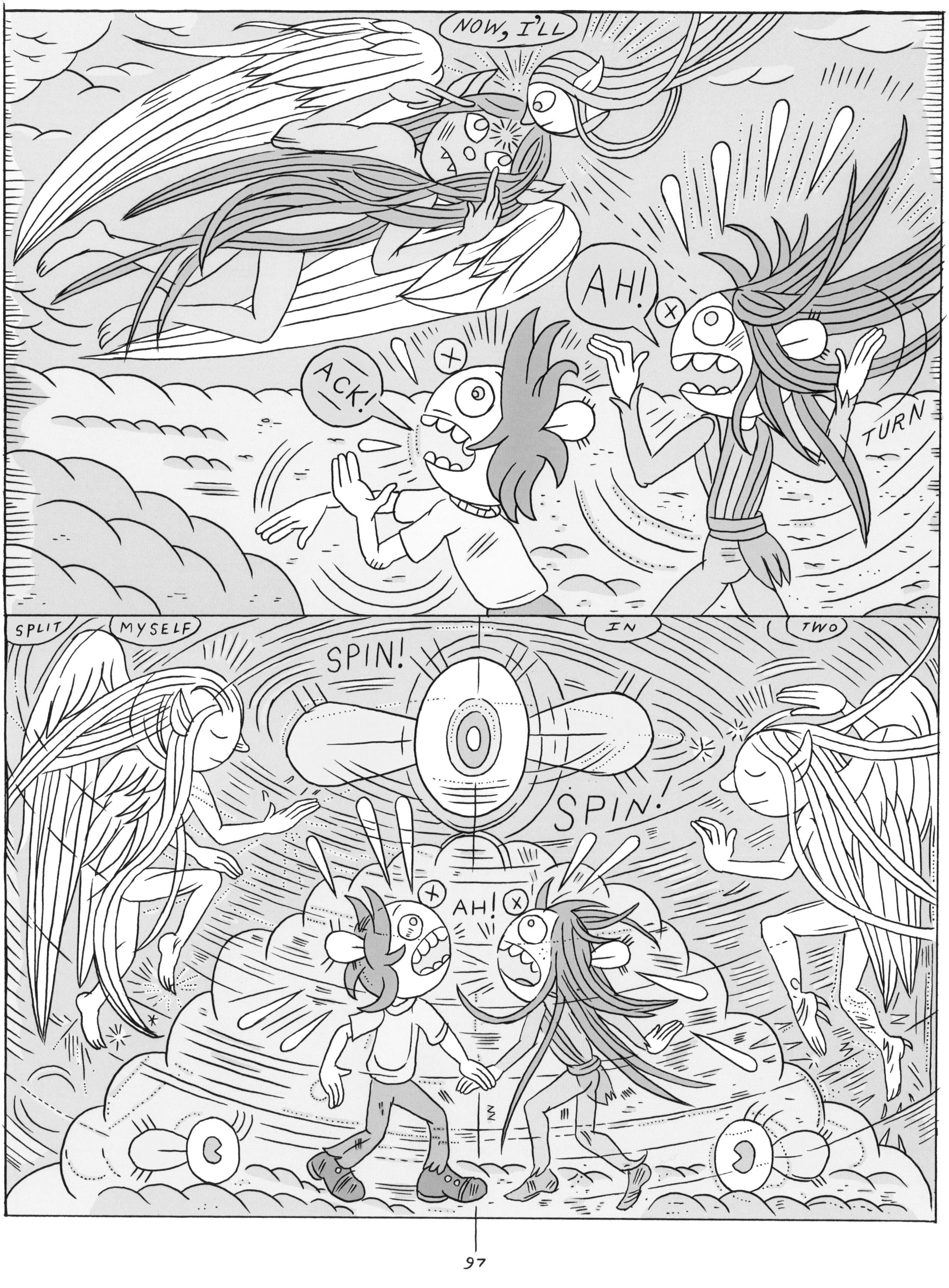
NOW, I'LL
AH!
ACK!
TURN
SPLIT
MYSELF
IN
TWO
SPIN!
SPIN!
AH!

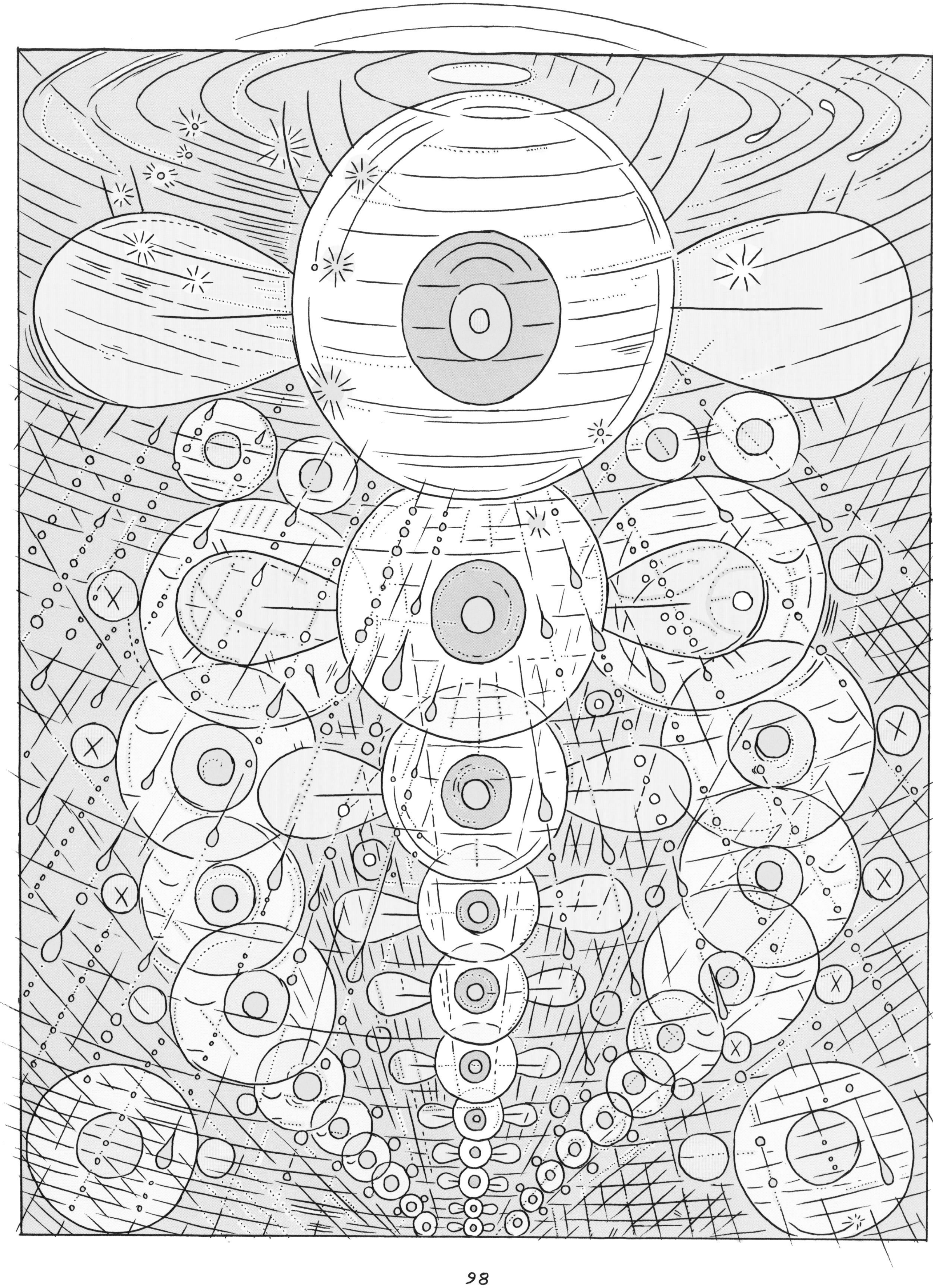

AN UNDETERMINED AMOUNT OF TIME LATER...

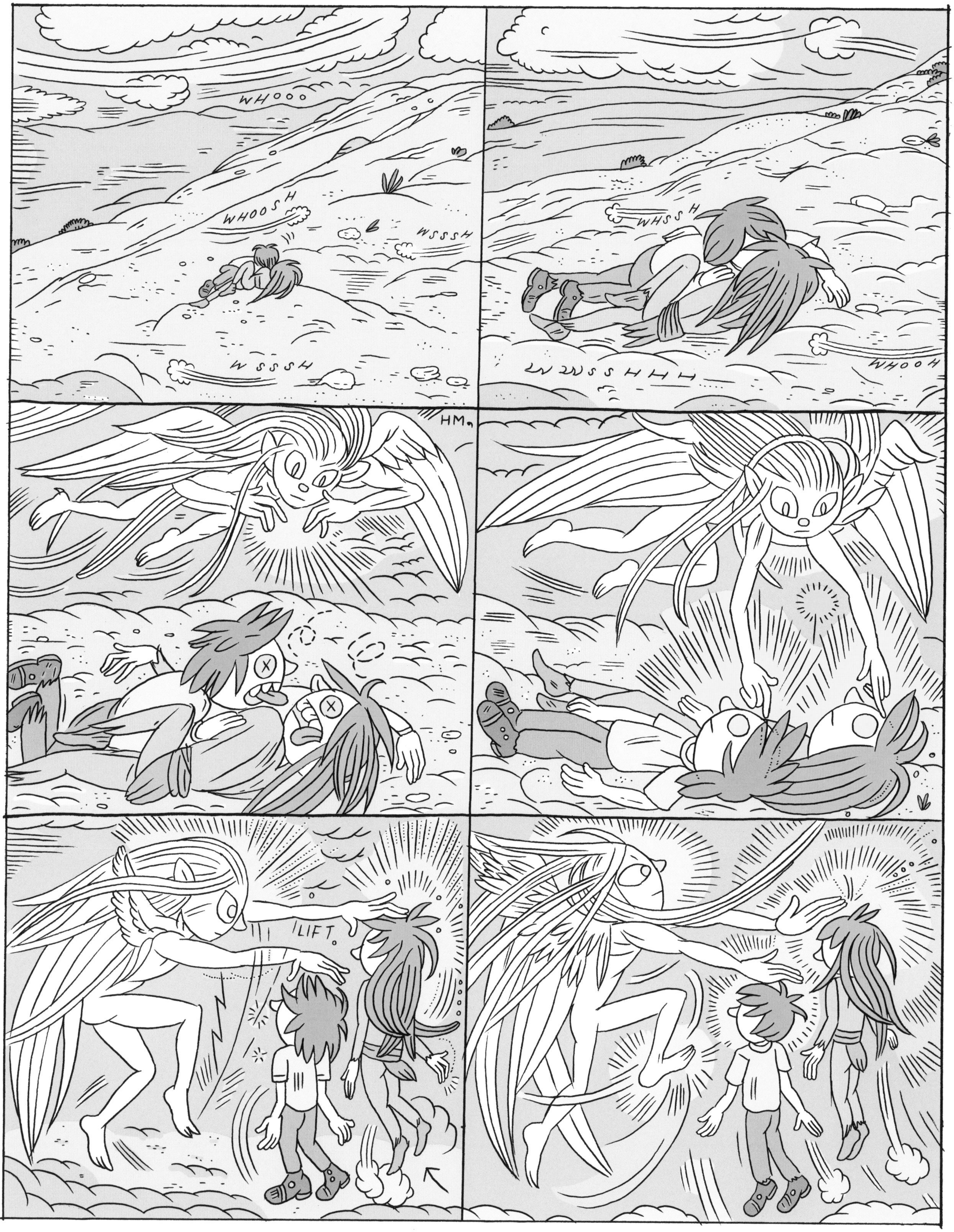
WHOOO
WHOOSH
WSSSH
WSSSH
WHSSH
WWSSHHHH
WHOOH
HM.
LIFT.

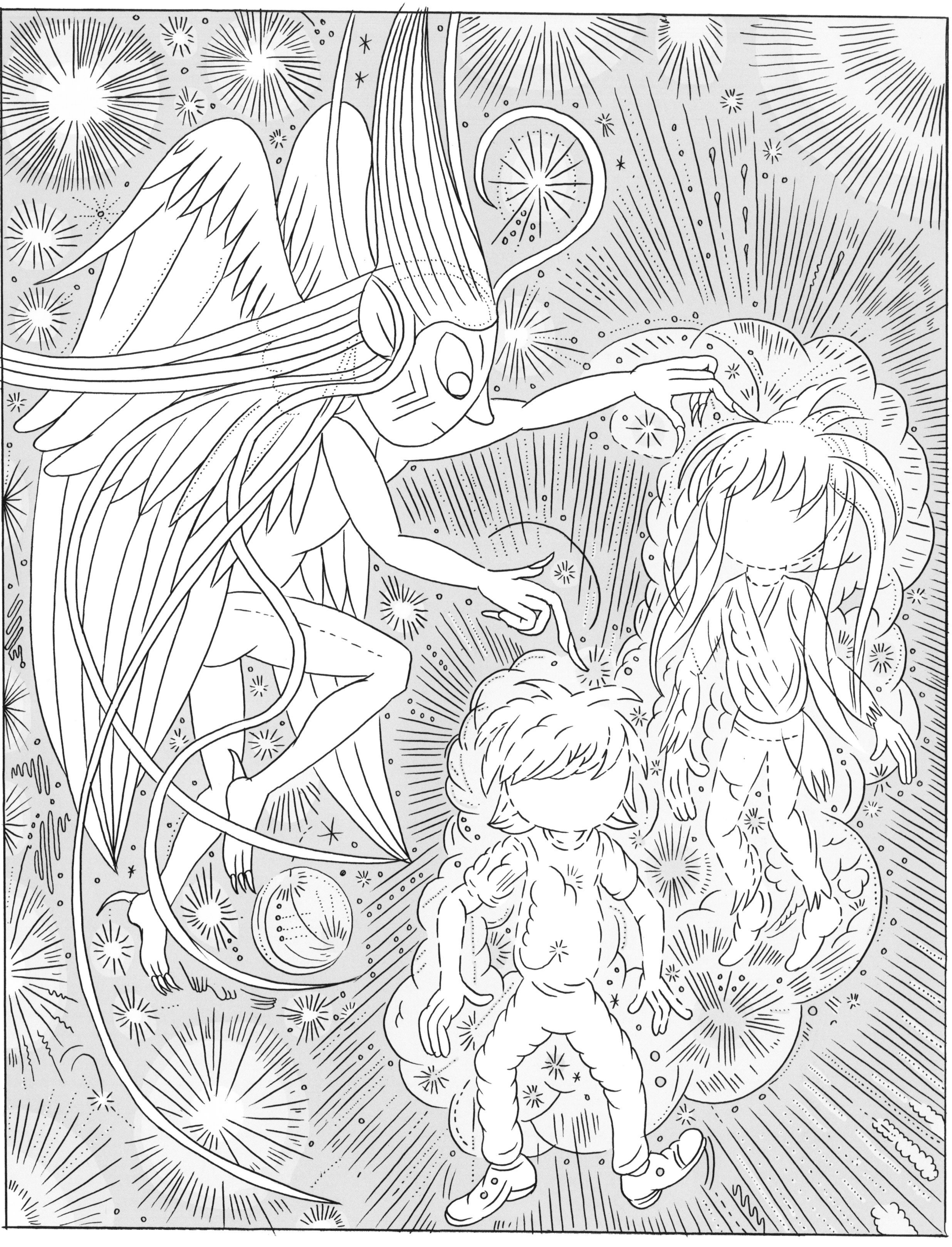

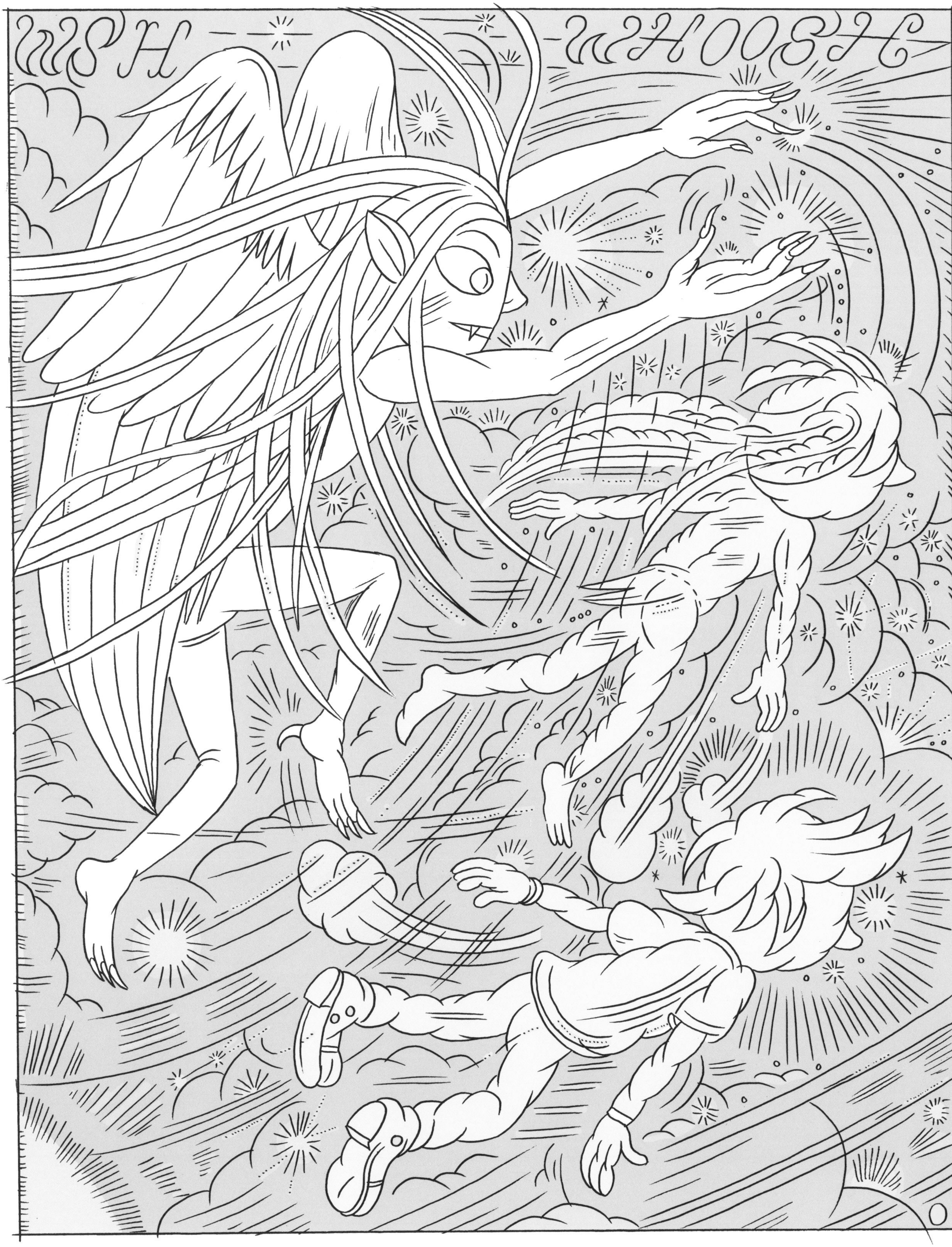
WSH
WHOOSH

IMAGINE A CONSCIOUSNESS SLIDING & FLYING BETWEEN AN INFINITE ARRAY OF SIMULTANEOUS DIMENSIONS

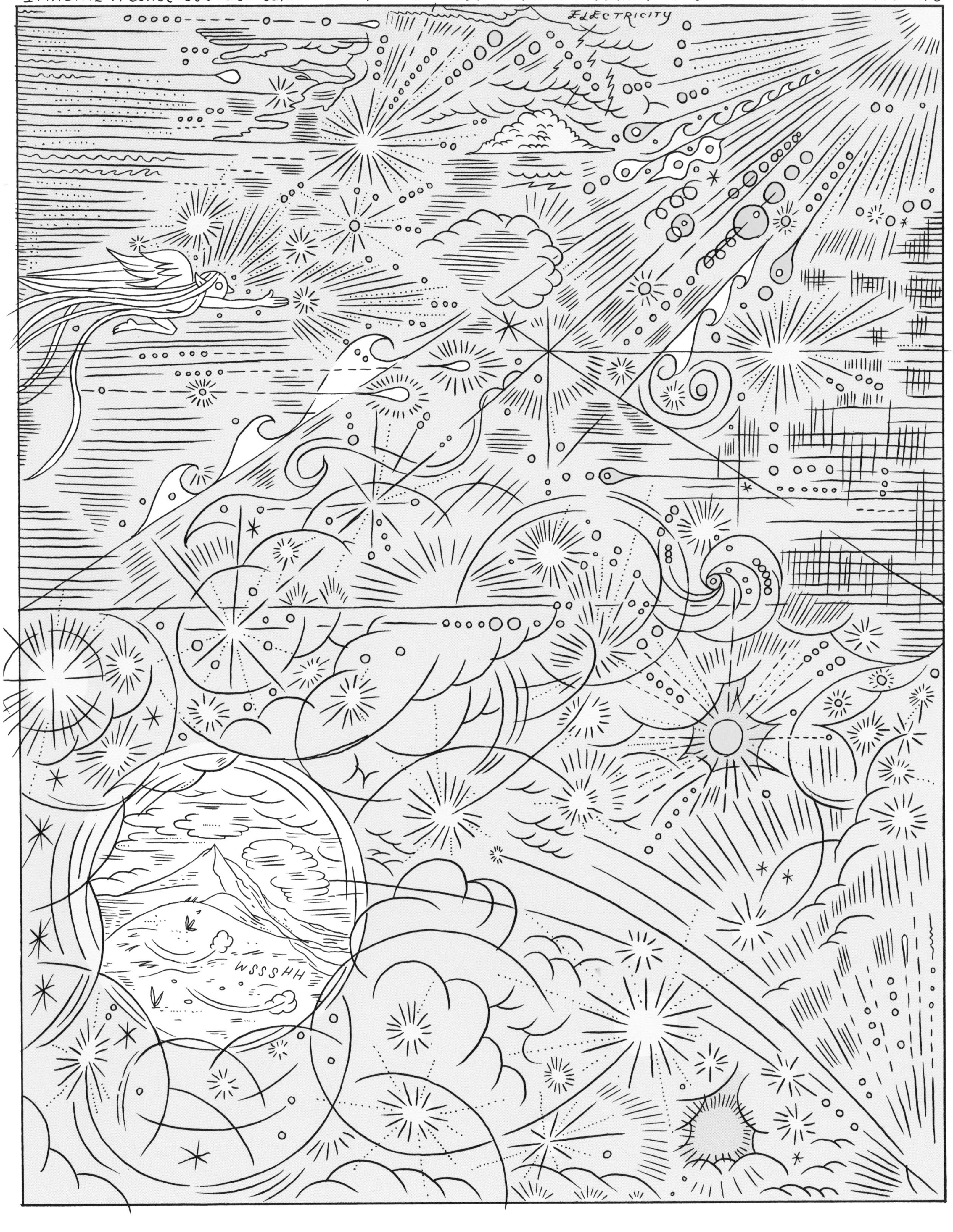
ELECTRICITY
WSSSHH

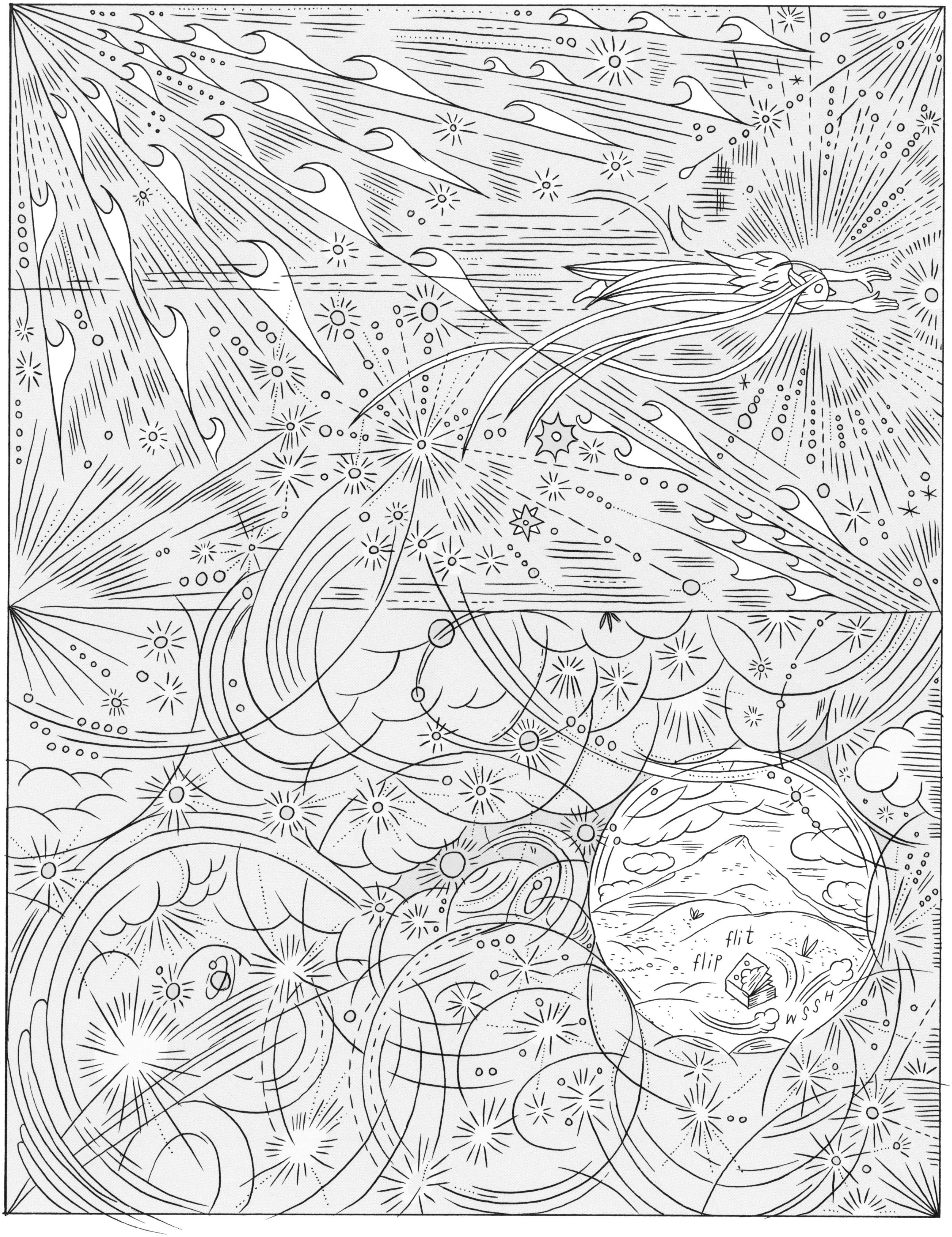
flit
flip
WSSH

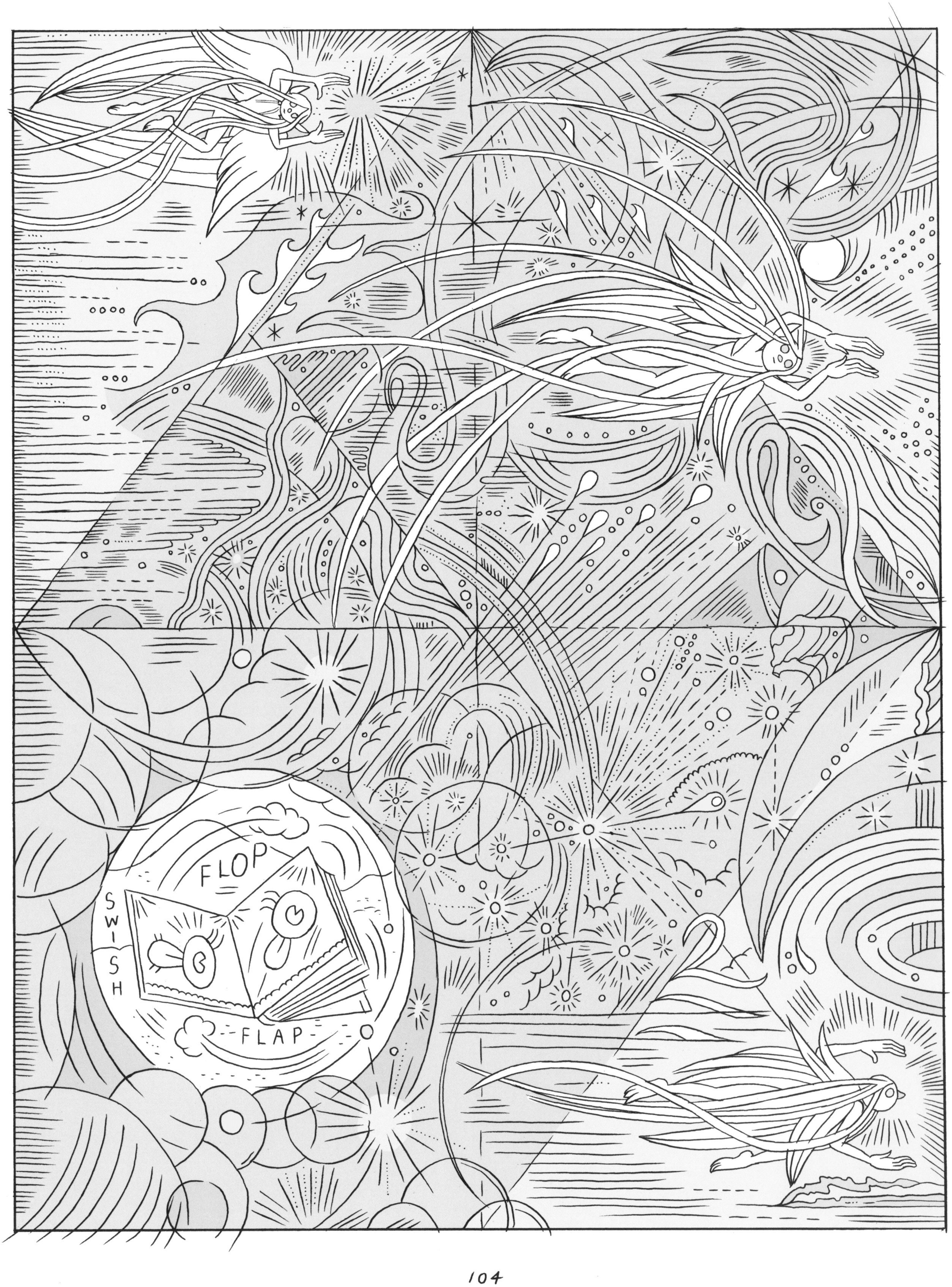
FLOP
SWISH
FLAP

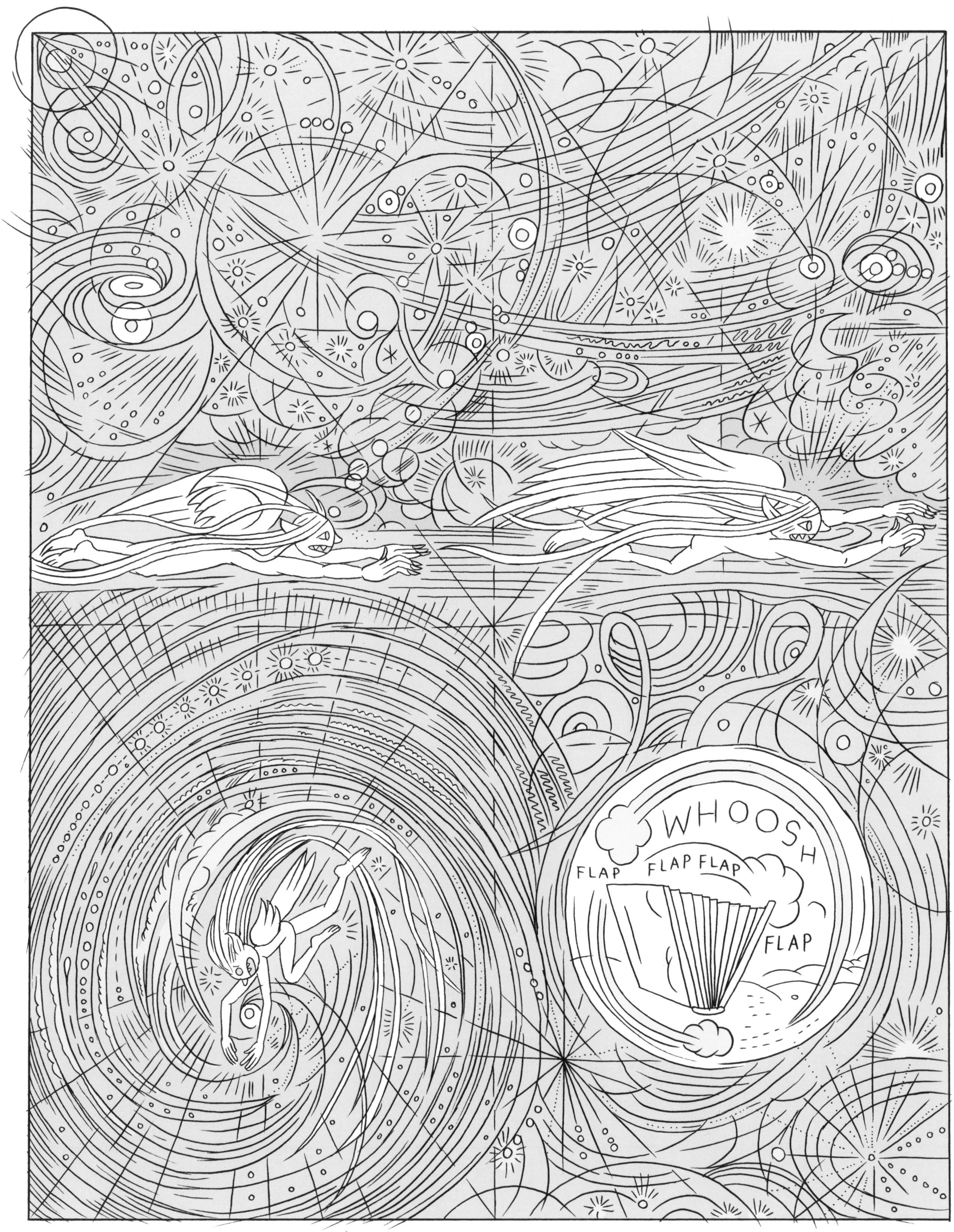
WHOOSH
FLAP
FLAP FLAP
FLAP

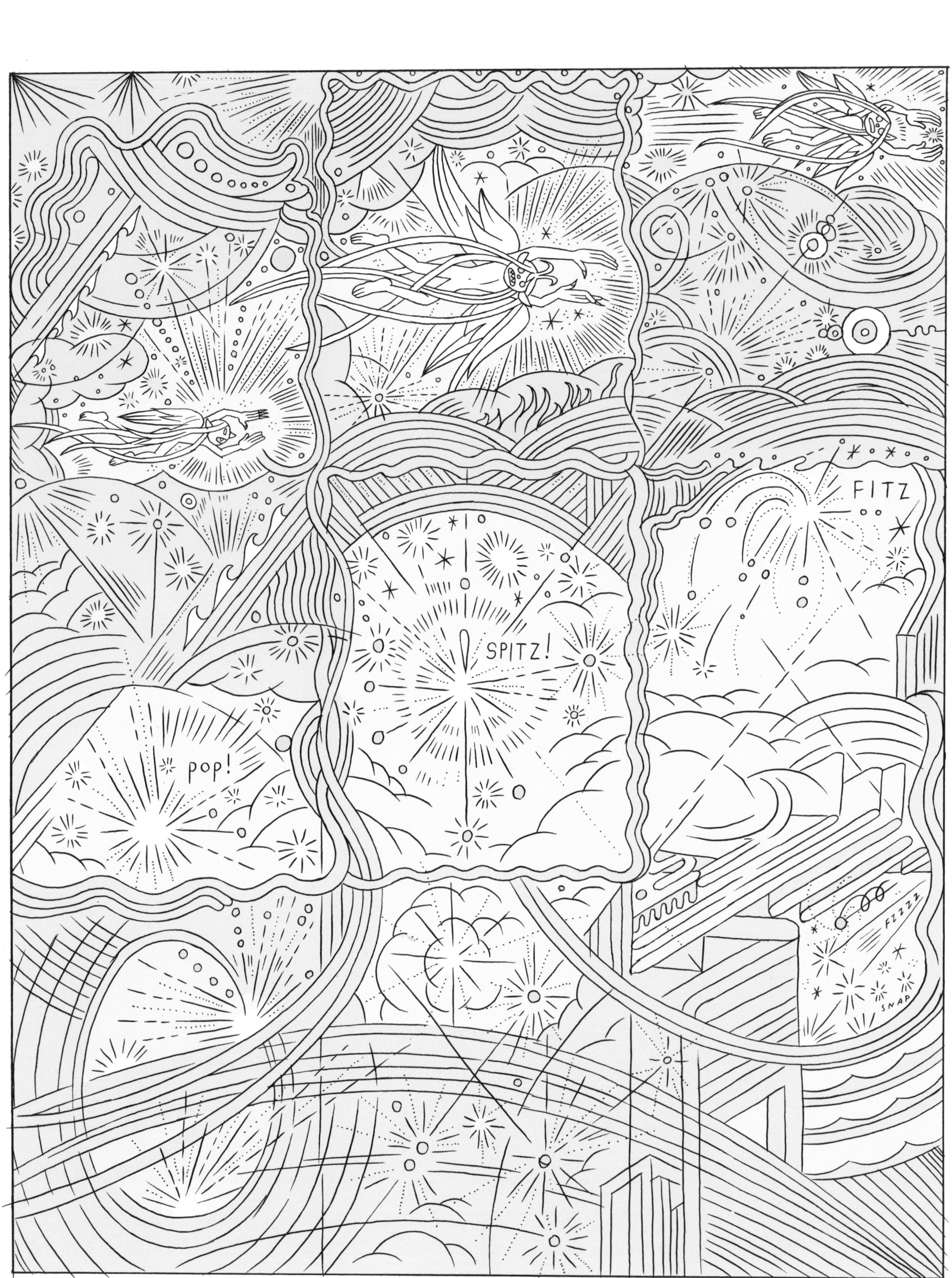
FITZ
SPITZ!
POP!
FZZZZ
SNAP

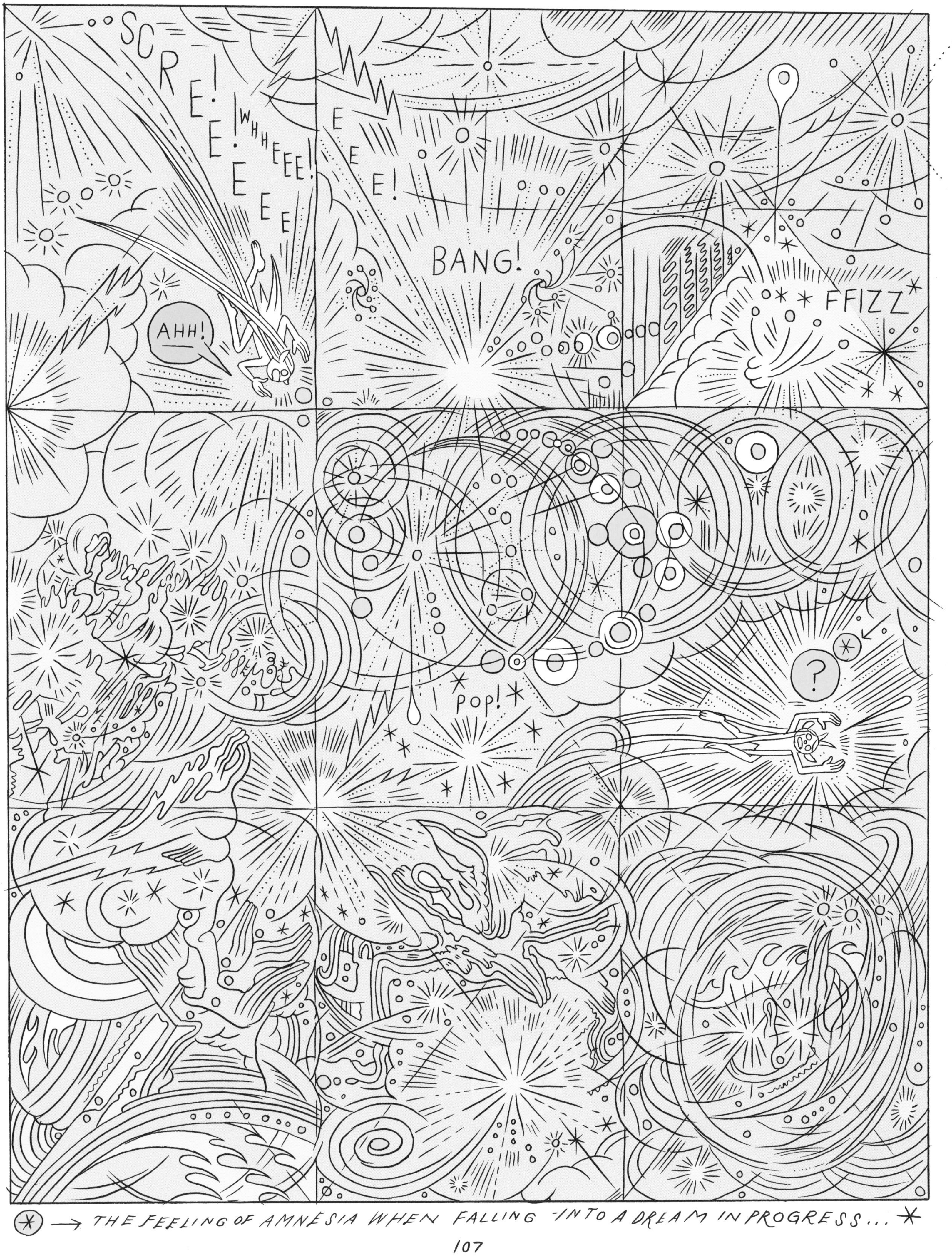
SCREE! EEEEE
WHHEEEE!
EEE!
AHH!
BANG!
FFIZZ
POP!
?

✻ → THE FEELING OF AMNESIA WHEN FALLING INTO A DREAM IN PROGRESS... ✻

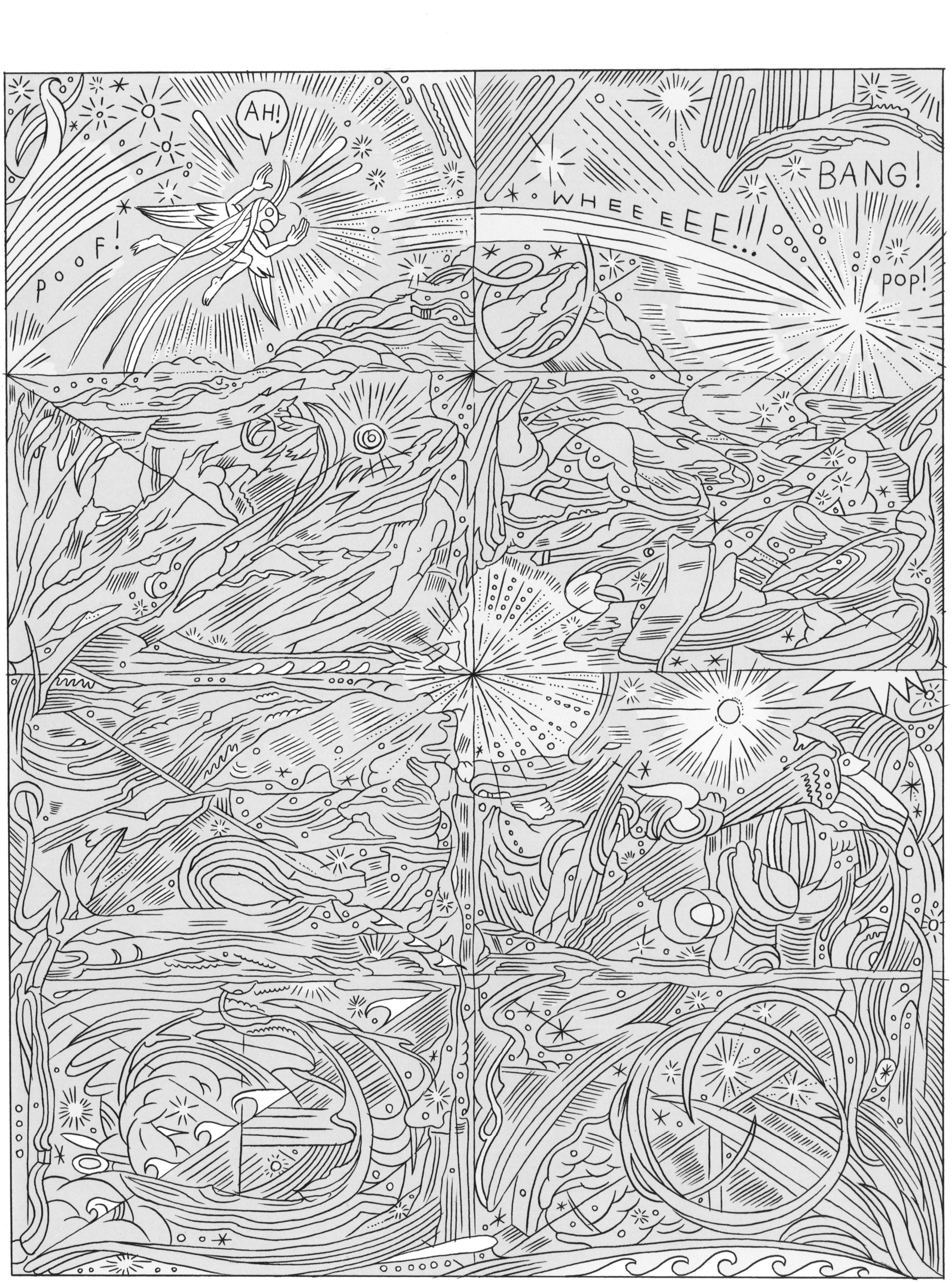
AH!
POOF!
WHEEEEEE!!!...
BANG!
POP!

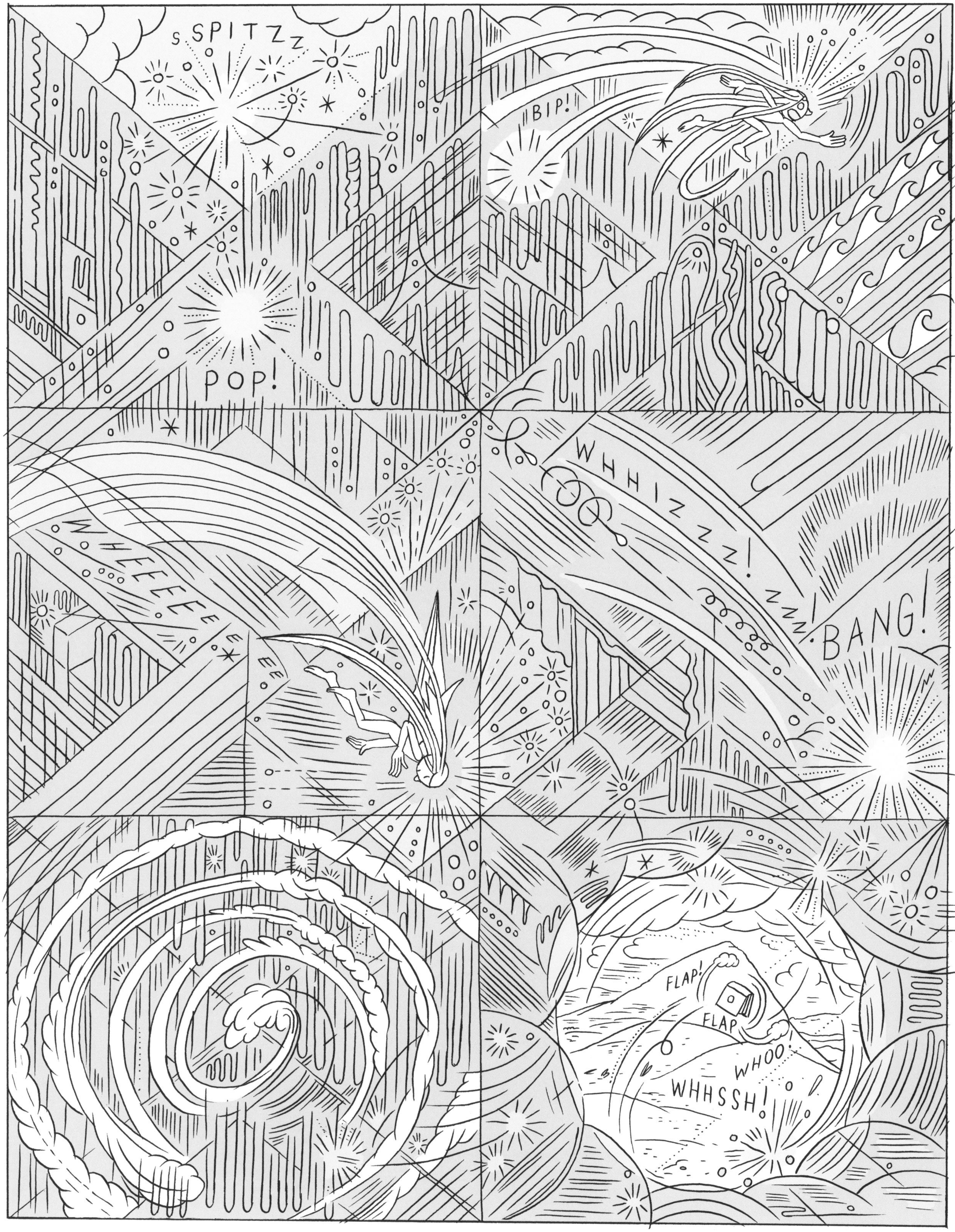
sSPITZzz
POP!
BIP!
WHEEEEEEEeeee
WHHIZZZ! zzz!
BANG!
FLAP!
FLAP
WHOO!
WHHSSH!

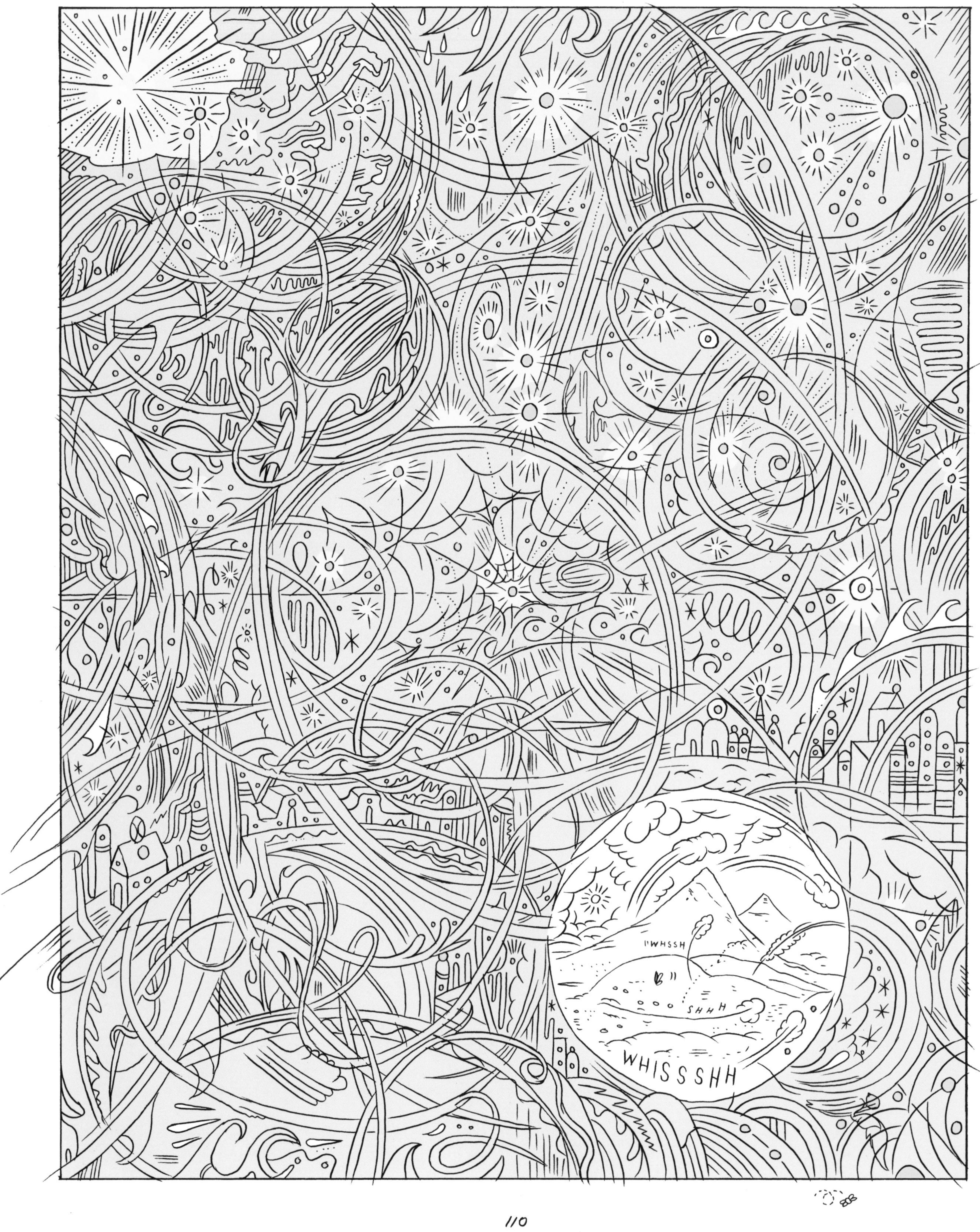

WHSSH
SHHH
WHISSSHH

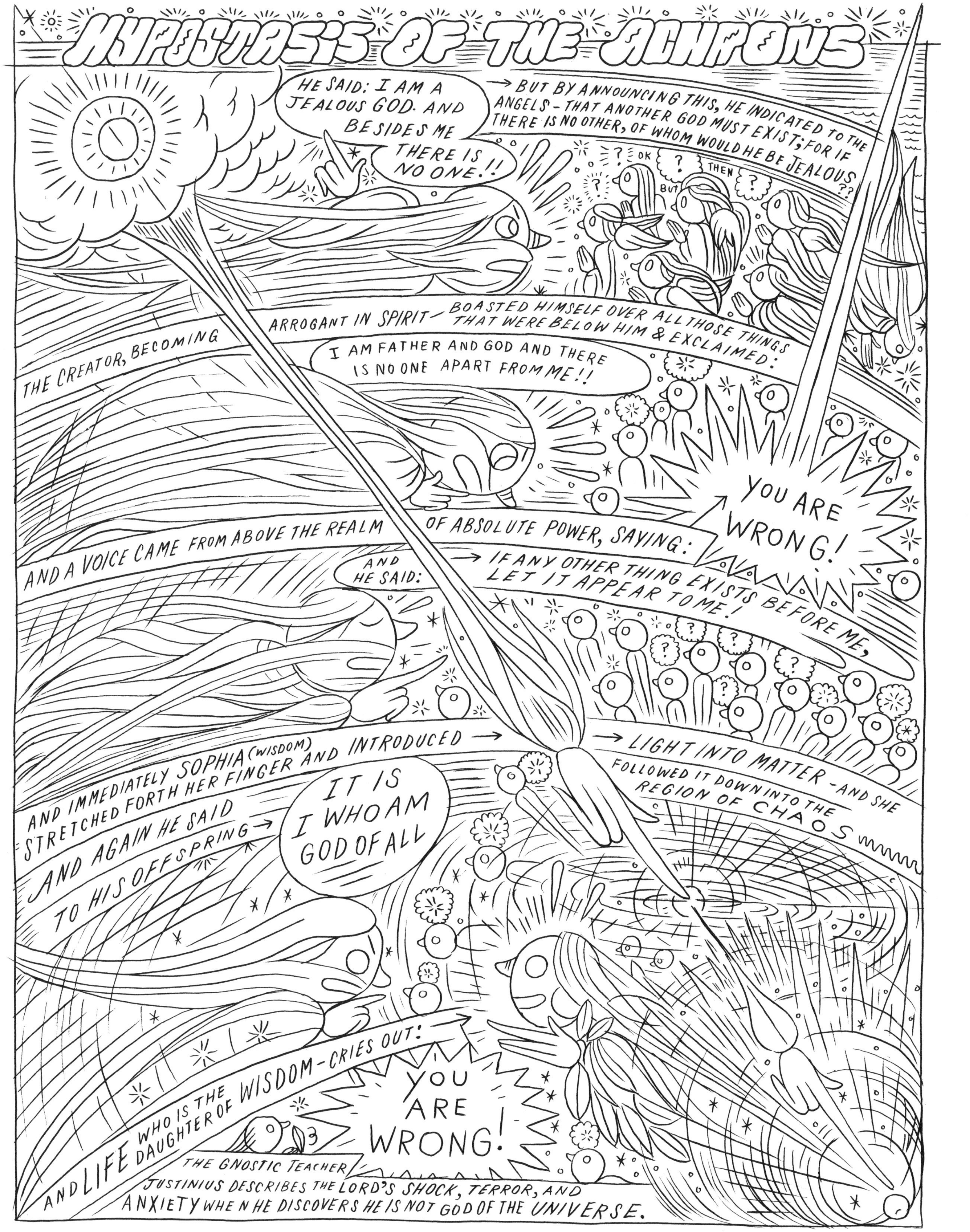
HYPOSTASIS OF THE ARCHONS
HE SAID: I AM A JEALOUS GOD. AND BESIDES ME THERE IS NO ONE!!
→ BUT BY ANNOUNCING THIS, HE INDICATED TO THE ANGELS - THAT ANOTHER GOD MUST EXIST; FOR IF THERE IS NO OTHER, OF WHOM WOULD HE BE JEALOUS??
?
OK
?
THEN
?
BUT
?
THE CREATOR, BECOMING ARROGANT IN SPIRIT - BOASTED HIMSELF OVER ALL THOSE THINGS THAT WERE BELOW HIM & EXCLAIMED:
I AM FATHER AND GOD AND THERE IS NO ONE APART FROM ME!!
AND A VOICE CAME FROM ABOVE THE REALM OF ABSOLUTE POWER, SAYING:
YOU ARE WRONG!
AND HE SAID: → IF ANY OTHER THING EXISTS BEFORE ME, LET IT APPEAR TO ME!
AND IMMEDIATELY SOPHIA (WISDOM) STRETCHED FORTH HER FINGER AND INTRODUCED → → LIGHT INTO MATTER - AND SHE FOLLOWED IT DOWN INTO THE REGION OF CHAOS
AND AGAIN HE SAID TO HIS OFFSPRING →
IT IS I WHO AM GOD OF ALL
AND LIFE WHO IS THE DAUGHTER OF WISDOM - CRIES OUT:
YOU ARE WRONG!
THE GNOSTIC TEACHER JUSTINIUS DESCRIBES THE LORD'S SHOCK, TERROR, AND ANXIETY WHEN HE DISCOVERS HE IS NOT GOD OF THE UNIVERSE.

EPILOGUE: AN EXCERPT FROM THE NAG HAMMADI

~ OTHER BOOKS BY RON REGÉ, JR ~

THE WEAVER FESTIVAL PHENOMENON 2018

WHAT PARSIFAL SAW 2017

THE CARTOON UTOPIA 2012

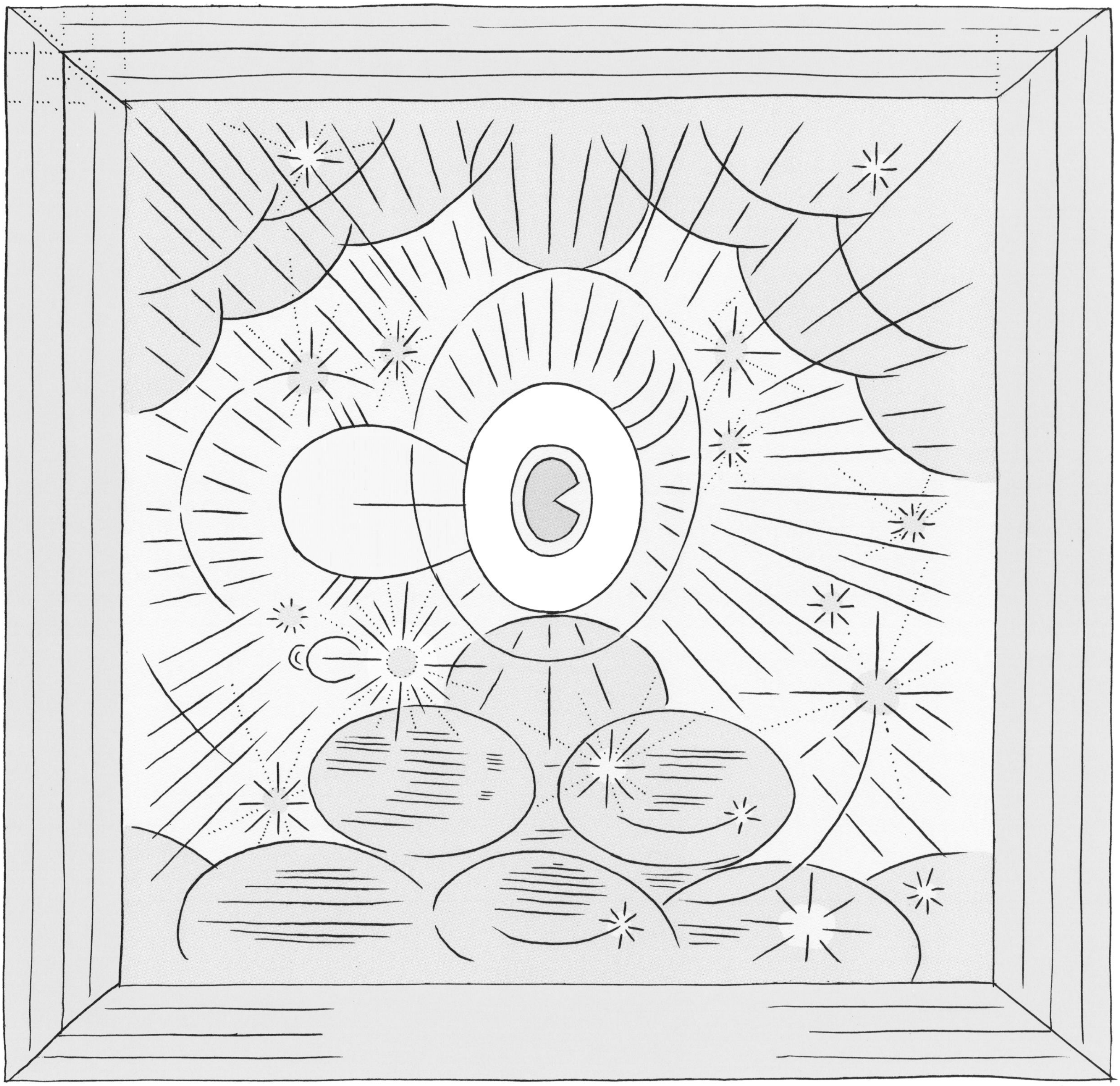

AGAINST PAIN 2008

THE AWAKE FIELD 2006

DOES MUSIC MAKE YOU CRY? 2003

SKIBBER BEE~BYE 2000

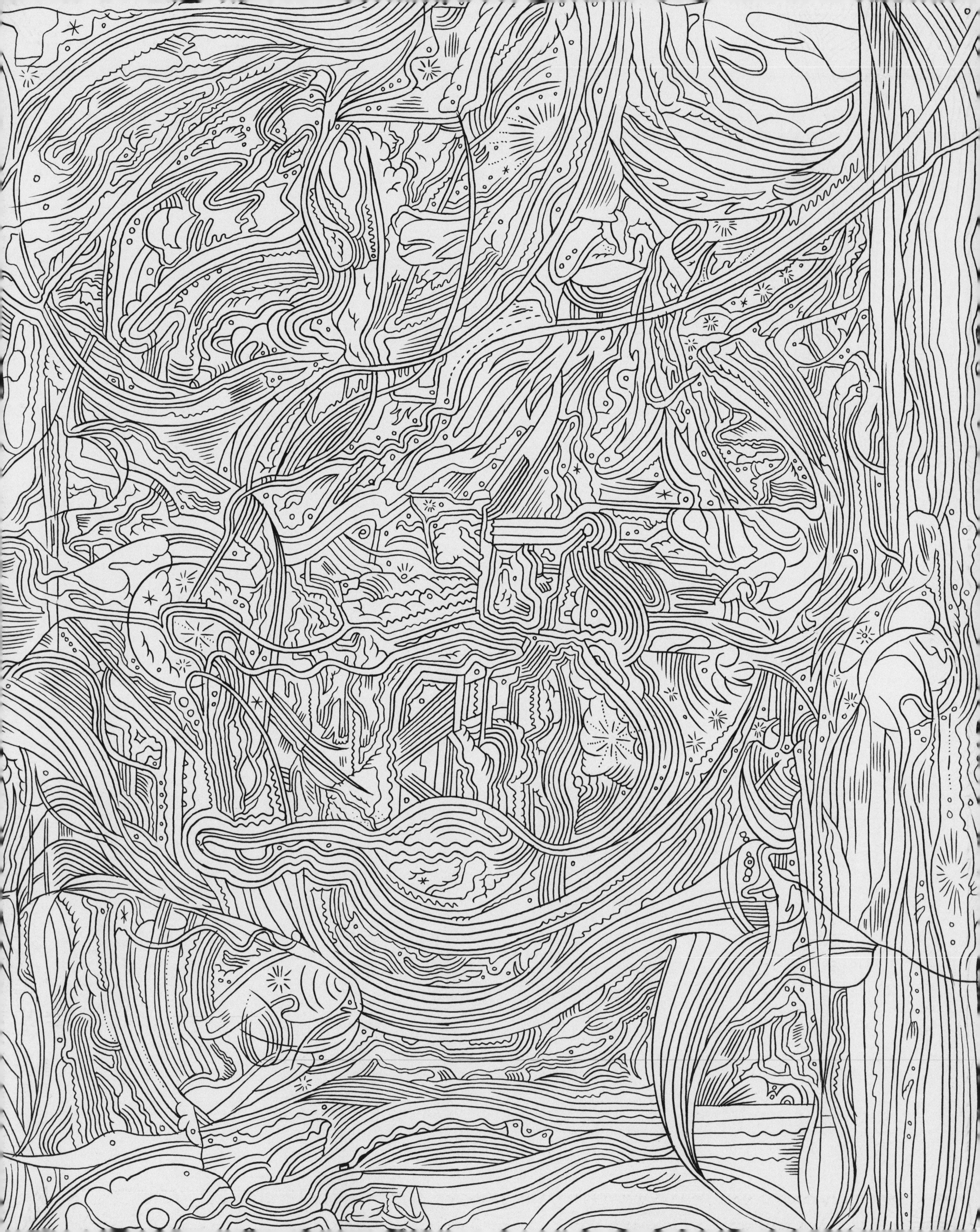